T A R O T
CONSTELLATIONS

BOOKS BY MARY K. GREER

TAROT FOR YOUR SELF:
A Workbook for Personal Transformation

TAROT CONSTELLATIONS:
Patterns of Personal Destiny

Forthcoming:

TAROT MIRRORS:
Reflections of Personal Meaning

PATTERNS OF PERSONAL DESTINY

BY
MARY K. GREER

NEWCASTLE PUBLISHING CO., INC.
NORTH HOLLYWOOD, CALIFORNIA
1987

Edited by Ed Buryn and Douglas Menville
Cover/Book Design by Riley K. Smith

FIRST EDITION

A NEWCASTLE BOOK

First printing, October 1987

10 9 8 7 6 5 4 3

Printed in the United States of America

*To my mother, Rita Alice West Greer,
and my father, John Cox Greer—
who raised me to believe in myself.*

ACKNOWLEDGEMENTS

Angeles Arrien has again (as with several processes in my first book) given me permission to present her basic ideas and to explore them in my own way. I want to acknowledge her great gift for innovation and insight, and her generosity of spirit in allowing others to present her work. Angie is truly a master teacher (Hierophant Personality and Soul) who opens doors and provides students with ideas they can then improvise on for themselves. She has been like a Muse, inspiring me (and many others) with haunting themes that I feel compelled to expand and explore further in my own way.

I have also used techniques and concepts from many other people, and from countless books. I've tried wherever possible to acknowledge these in the text. Occasionally a single word or sentence bore a seed out of which a whole flowering concept emerged for me. Unfortunately, through the years I can't always remember the specific sources. Also, I often found the same ideas in many different sources; these I consider general information and therefore I don't specify a source. If you feel I've missed a reference that needs acknowledgement, please write to me (c/o Newcastle Publishing Co.) and I will rectify the situation in subsequent editions, if appropriate.

I specifically want to thank fellow taroists Angeles Arrien, Christine Payne-Towler (who opened me to the significance of the French School), Tina Rosa, Rachel Pollack, Elissa Heyman, Vicki Noble, Jonathan Tenney, Alaina Zachary, Jim Wanless, Gary Ross, Tracey Hoover, Ffiona Morgan, Twainhart Hill, Dee Schwartz, José Tamez, and again, my students, who continue to teach me my most important lessons.

Thanks also to my friends and colleagues at Newcastle who read the manuscript and helped greatly with both suggestions and encouragement; to Riley Smith, book-designer extraordinaire, Tina Tessina, and to my publisher, Al Saunders, for his steadfast support.

I also gratefully acknowledge the multidimensional contributions of my partner, Ed Buryn, whose editorial and professional services were exceeded only by his love and unrelenting domestic efforts as househusband and all-around guardian angel. And I thank our daughter Casi for her impatience, reminding me with hugs when it was time to stop work and play.

CONTENTS

LIST OF MAJOR ILLUSTRATIONS

Note: All cards used as margin illustrations, unless otherwise indicated, are
from the Rider Waite-Smith deck.

LIST OF CHARTS

CHART 1
SUMMARY OF
CARD NAMES
CHART

THE BASIC CARD DIVISIONS

Major Arcana (Cards) = Trump Cards	= Triumphs	= Keys		22
Minor Arcana (Cards) { Number Cards = Pip Cards		4 Suits		40
Court Cards = People Cards				16

Total = 78

THE LIFETIME CARDS

	Birth Cards		Name Cards		
Major Arcana (Cards)	Personality Card Soul Card Hidden Factor Card = Shadow Card = Teacher Card Year Card(s)	Personality-Soul Pattern = Pattern of Personal Destiny	Desires & Inner Motivation Card Outer Persona Card		Life Potential Card (Name + Birth)
			Theme Note Card Rhythm Card Melody Card Hidden Factor Name Card(s)	Destiny Cards (all have same Root Number)	
			First-Name Card Middle-Name Card Last-Name Card	Theme Chord	
Minor Arcana (Cards)	Lessons & Opportunities Cards				

INTRODUCTION

The process of writing this book, *Tarot Constellations*, has been much different from that of my first book. Originally I thought I would simply write down all the things I've discovered about the various tarot cards associated with your birth-date which describe your soul purpose and life lessons. But nothing is ever as easy as it seems. I kept looking for what I called the "soul" of the book, something that would take it beyond its mere descriptive qualities. Then, through a series of "coincidences," I discovered an entirely new aspect of the tarot. In exploring and writing about this, the mansucript became so long that my publisher asked me to rework it and divide it into two books.

To do this, I went back to my original concept and finally found the soul that had been waiting patiently for me to see it: *Patterns of Personal Destiny*, the subtitle of this book. (The second book became *Tarot Mirrors: Reflections of Personal Meaning*, to be published soon after this book.)

Both *Tarot Constellations* and *Tarot Mirrors* are linked through the image of The Star card. As The Star corresponds to Aquarius, I feel that the information in these books can help us as individuals to make the transition into what is called the Age of Aquarius, wherein we begin to understand our planetary place among the stars. While these new books stand alone and can be read independently of each other, they are both related to my first book (*Tarot for Your Self: A Workbook for Personal Transformation*) in that the emphasis is on achieving personal growth and insight through self-teaching techniques. You are your own teacher. All rules given here are made to be broken. Question everything I say and accept nothing until it brings you results you can perceive. As you go through this book, clarify for yourself your intentions in working with the tarot: What do you want to learn from it?

HOW TO USE THIS BOOK

This book is intended to be read with a tarot deck and a pencil at hand. Since the major arcana are emphasized, for the majority of the techniques you can use any deck whose 22 trump cards appeal to you. (If you do not own a deck, see Appendix B for a discussion of the various "schools" of tarot, with recommended decks.) Although this is less of a workbook than my first book, you will not gain full benefit from it if you neglect to do the exercises included here. In addition, since your written responses will sometimes require more blank space than is (or can be) provided here, I strongly urge you to start and keep a personal Tarot Notebook as well. For overall convenience, try a spiral-bound notebook the same size as this book (8½" × 11"), preferably with holes so you can later insert the pages in a standard three-ring binder. You can also include photocopies of the charts in this book, as well as your own charts, notations, sketches and doodles, images cut from magazines, etc. You can arrange your notes according to the relevant tarot cards, while having another section for collecting your own tarot readings.

Although the book is designed so you can work alone (I did for many years before I found anyone else as interested in tarot as I was), you will probably progress much faster if you work with other people. Find a tarot partner, or form a tarot study group. Get together once a week and do one segment from the book, beginning with the exercises in Chapter One. As you continue to work your way through this book, continue using the exercises from Chapter One each week. These first exercises help immeasurably to make the material your own and build up respect and appreciation for the wisdom of each member of your group! I will be with you in spirit, so if at any time you do not understand an instruction, simply pause to hear me say, "What do you *want* to do?" or, "What feels right to you?" Then do it.

TAROT AND YOUR DESTINY

You were born on a day whose energy harmonized with something you chose to develop in this particular lifetime. This energy is described, in terms of your culture and its historical timing, by your birthdate. You were also named in such a way that you were further linked to your family, culture, and heritage—those things chosen to provide you with the experiences you would need to succeed at your purpose. Your destiny is to actualize these potentials to the best of your ability. This is the basic premise of this book.

The tarot cards, in the numerical sequencing common at this time, provide a visual tool for ascertaining both the potentials and pitfalls that you have set for yourself through your birthdate and name. They provide a method of looking at and even communicating with that energy, so that you can know when and how you are actually living it in the world.

The tarot cards associated with your birthdate and name form your individual mandala; they are the pattern of your personal destiny. Although your destiny is also mapped in your astrological natal chart, or can be calculated by traditional forms of numerology, none of these other perspectives allows you to work with the power of the picture, each one of which expresses a thousand words and tells a thousand times a thousand stories. Only tarot introduces you to personal power figures with whom you can dialogue and ask for guidance in achieving your personal destiny.

The tarot deck has 78 cards, normally divided into three groups:

> The 22 Major Arcana or Trump or Key Cards
> The 40 Number or Pip Cards
> The 16 Court or People Cards

The Number Cards and the Court Cards when combined are called the minor arcana; they are both divided into four suits representing the four elements:

Wands (Rods)	= Fire	Cups	= Water
Swords	= Air	Pentacles (Disks)	= Earth

But in this book the cards will also be divided in a new way: into "constellations." Nine groups of cards constellate, or cluster, around nine basic principles. These nine groups are made up of the major arcana cards plus the minor arcana Number Cards that correspond through their numbers. The People Cards are dealt with separately.

The nine basic principles are:

> *The Principle of Will and Focused Consciousness*
> *The Principle of Balanced Judgment through Intuitive Awareness*
> *The Principle of Love and Creative Imagination*
> *The Principle of Life Force and Realization of Power*
> *The Principle of Teaching and Learning*
> *The Principle of Relatedness and Choice*
> *The Principle of Mastery through Change*
> *The Principle of Courage and Self-Esteem*
> *The Principle of Introspection and Personal Integrity*

THE PURPOSE OF THIS BOOK

The purpose of this book is to open communication between your everyday conscious self and your inner subconscious self that is aware of your personal destiny.

From the viewpoint of achieving your spiritual purpose, a sense of meaning is necessary. Why does your experience come into your life? And what do you need to learn from it? When you begin asking these questions you find that the answers come. It is as if an inner part of yourself has been waiting for you to ask.

Through a symbol system such as the tarot, practitioners believe it is possible to discover an inner meaning to the words, images, and events that we experience in our lives. Carl Jung coined the term "synchronicity" to indicate the simultaneous occurrence of meaningfully, but not causally, connected events. Everything is linked with everything else, like a giant living web in which any vibration is organically felt in all parts simultaneously. By knowing this and watching closely, you can begin to connect outer action with inner meaning, harmonizing with your soul purpose.

THE CONSTELLATIONS

Symbolic tools such as the tarot take you beneath the surface of events and mirror the "constellations" that are affecting many areas of your life.

And what are these constellations? According to the definition in the *American Heritage Dictionary*, constellations are "groupings of objects, properties, or individuals," especially ones that are "structurally or systematically related." I find that most events and concerns that are current at any particular time are "constellated," or clustered, around a specific core issue in your life. This means that you can look at the cards in any one reading to see how they mirror several things in your life, not just your original question. The more issues that fit the description, the more you are involved in a core issue (or dilemma) in your life that will continue to project itself and its meaning onto outer events. A tarot spread with its positions will break the essential constellation down into several constituting properties. Like a constellation in the sky, which is a grouping of stars defining the lines of a figure and representing a story, a spread pictures you and tells a story about you. Thus, spreads are constellations picturing the events that have likewise constellated, or come together, to form your inner story.

These constellations are made up of cards (stars) of major and minor intensity that resonate to the same theme, and each card within a constellation gives a different perspective on the theme. The Tarot Constellations are thus the Patterns of Personal Destiny.

THE CONSTELLATIONS DISCOVERED

I was first introduced to the concept of the Tarot Constellations by Angeles Arrien. She currently teaches tarot (using the Crowley-Harris Egyptian Thoth deck) and cross-cultural symbolism and healing practices at several graduate schools in the San Francisco area. Over the last nine years I have taken many inspiring and mind-expanding classes from her. When I repeated her beginning tarot class two years ago, she presented the cards within the entirely new framework of the "constellations."

Since I am interested in the creative process, I asked her how she had come to see the cards from this perspective. She was playing with the cards one evening, she told me, and had laid out on the floor both the major and minor arcana cards in groupings based on the numbers: all the One's together and all the Two's, etc. She also placed with each of the groups all other cards that added up to the nine basic (prime) numbers. For instance, 17 = 1 + 7 = 8, and so the 17th card, The Star, was placed with the Eight's, and so on.

She was arranging the groups so that they made pictures or patterns, when the phone rang. It was Joseph Campbell, author of many books on mythology and symbols, with whom she was leading a workshop at the Esalen Institute. He was excited by a realization he had recently had of how constellations are not just in the heavens and the stars, but that such pattern groupings occur everywhere in our lives. Angie says she stood there, as he spoke to her on the phone, looking around the room at the cards grouped together on the floor and saw—the Tarot Constellations.

USING THE TAROT CONSTELLATIONS IN A READING

Imagine that you have come to me for a tarot consultation. I always begin (even before knowing your question) with the Tarot Constellation determined by your birth date: your Personality, Soul, Hidden Factor and Year Cards. These are all explained in detail in this book. From the information contained in your Personality and Soul Cards, I gain some idea how to communicate with you in a reading

—it may modify how I interpret a card and lets me know how you can best hear what the cards are saying. During the process of describing to you your basic characteristics and life issues, my intuitive self tunes into your "wavelength."

You will probably find that this basic information sounds like you. It also affirms that there is a reason for acting the way you do. If you are a Chariot Personality and Soul, for instance, it is natural for you to protect your inner feelings. You are not just hiding behind a mask of bravado, or a role in your life, but those are the sanctuaries within which you are developing your abilities. Nevertheless, those sanctuaries must eventually be torn down when you have learned what you needed from them. As a Chariot, if your life is currently in upheaval, we will look to see if you are breaking through an old and restricting identity that has been holding you back.

Thus even before an actual reading has commenced, you have some insight as to not only "what" but "why" something is occurring in your life. This is especially pertinent if you ask the question, "Why is this always happening to me?" Repetitive occurrences can often be traced to the lessons inherent in your Personality, Soul, and Hidden Factor Cards—those cards that answer the question, "What have I come here to learn?" The minor arcana Number Cards of the same constellation show the kinds of life situations in which you are most likely to find these lessons. Often, after only a few minutes of my describing the characteristics of your particular constellation pattern, you will begin to see for yourself, in the images on the cards, their relevance to your life.

Then I calculate your Year Cards for the last several years and for the next three to five years. From the description I give of these cards, you begin to see a developmental pattern forming—for instance, how the choice of one year is acted on in the next, or how you move from an inner or more reflective state to a social or more aggressive energy. You can see how this allows you to experience complementary lessons in succeeding years. For instance, in a Chariot Year you attempt to maintain control over opposing instincts and drives, but in the Strength Year that follows you learn to come to terms with your instincts so that you can act in harmony with that power from within. Such an opportunity will not last forever—you have only a limited time to directly face your inner "beast" and discover what you truly "lust" after. Then you will move on to your next lesson, carrying with you what you learned this time around. Thus you begin to see each year as exciting opportunity for growth. The lessons of the current year usually directly affect the situation that you've come to the consultation for.

This process generally takes one-third or more of the time I allot to a consultation. By the time I ask you the specific issue you want clarified, you may have had your most pressing questions answered. Your immediate concerns are now in perspective, so that you see them as part of a larger life pattern. This is the purpose of the Tarot Constellations. This is one way in which they can be used. The remainder of this book explains the concepts in detail, and describes other ways to put them to use.

Chapter One shows that just as the constellations in the sky are used to find our way on the earth, so too the Tarot Constellations can help us find our way through life. You will learn an exercise to help you triumph daily, and also the only thing you really need to know to read a tarot card.

Chapter Two shows you how to find your Personality and Soul Cards and introduces the Hidden Factor Card. *Chapter Three* describes the Tarot Constellations and their basic principles and teaches you how to use them personally. In *Chapters Four* through *Twelve*, each of the nine constellations is described in depth with examples from the lives of famous people.

Chapters Thirteen and *Fourteen* explore the potentials of your Year Card and the importance of the High Priestess Year to humanity as we enter the second millennium. *Chapter Fifteen* tells you how to find your Name Cards, and then how to read your Name Spread, whose influence lasts a lifetime. In *Chapter Sixteen* the traditional Court Cards are redefined, with a new spread to help you recognize their significance in your readings.

THE 8–11 CONTROVERSY

In writing this book, I've had to deal with a basic dilemma concerning the numbers assigned to the Strength and Justice cards of the major arcana. Traditionally, in what I call the "French School" decks (see Appendix B), epitomized by the classic Marseilles-style deck dating from around 1700, Justice is number 8 and Strength is number 11. However, many variations in the sequence exist historically, where the numbers were primarily used for counting points in card games.[1]

In 1910, occult scholar Arthur Edward Waite made tarot history by publishing a new deck with artwork by his student Pamela Colman Smith, wherein he reversed the sequence of the two cards, making Justice number 11 and Strength number 8.

Both numbering systems are used today, which requires each new tarot author or deck designer to make their own 8–11 choice. Since I have chosen to use numerological systems in this and my previous book, this number assignment is fundamentally important. Personally I hold an allegiance to Waite's numbering, in part because my first and only deck for many years was the Waite-Smith deck. My observation is that whichever numbering system you learn first becomes mentally imprinted and then difficult to dislodge. Perhaps, as Gareth Knight suggests in his book, *The Treasure House of Images*, all orders limit the tarot's possibilities.

In Appendix A, I discuss in detail the historical, functional, and personal aspects of this "8–11 controversy," and why both systems can be "right." Meanwhile, in this book I use the Waite-Smith numbering system: *Strength is number 8 and Justice is number 11*. However, I believe that the French School (and perhaps other systems) have validity. Feel free to adapt and make adjustments where appropriate. I will make suggestions for this where I can.

NOTES

1. See: Stuart Kaplan, *The Encyclopedia of Tarot*, Vols. 1 and 2 (New York: U. S. Games Systems, 1986), or Michael Dummet, *The Game of Tarot from Ferrara to Salt Lake City* (London: Gerald Duckworth and Co., 1980).

CHAPTER ONE

MAPS OF MEANING

You are about to embark on an adventure with this book as your guide. The *Tarot Constellations* will be the map of your journey and reveal the significance of sights and happenings along the way. The "constellations" of tarot can indicate where crossed roads will take you, although which road to take you must always choose for yourself. This book describes a landscape in which your own emotions and imaginings are the ever-changing terrain through which you move. The country is your potential self. Your ability to explore it depends on your commitment to the adventure. The ideas and exercises in this book are like travelers' aids that deepen the experience and provide insight into the wonders enroute. You hold in your hands a map of the territory of your self, designed to give you a new sense of where you've come from, where you're going, and how to get there in a variety of interesting ways. It will help you to reach "scenic overlooks," to pause for refreshment at a spiritual oasis, to chance upon uncharted islands of the soul, and to glimpse the wheels of destiny behind the veils of personality. Most importantly, it gives you the ability to discover just where you are right now. So if you are ready . . . let's go.

This is a magical journey, illuminated by what I call the Tarot Constellations. The universe that we gaze at in the night sky above us was first mapped into meaningful constellations by the ancient Chaldeans, "the sky gazers," six centuries before Christ. Today we "perceive" 88 constellations and have named them for mythical beings, animals, and objects. Similarly, the tarot deck is another map of consciousness evolved by the ancients and transmitted to us, in which we chart the journey of our Self. A semi-mythical philosopher by the name of Hermes Trismegistus described the relationship between the inner and outer universe like this: "That which is above is like that which is below and that which is below is like that which is above, to achieve the wonders of the one thing." Called the Hermetic Axiom, it is central to all alchemical and metaphysical philosophy and the key to an understanding of the use of symbols such as the tarot.

Consider, however, that the astronomical and astrological constellations are not actually connected star systems; they are imagined collections of points of light, some originating relatively near us and some far more distant, that appear related only from our personal viewing platform, which we call Earth. Because of our own inner need for personal meaning, humans throughout history have projected our own consciousness upon the night sky in the form of complex patterns and pictures. Nevertheless, the meaning we find in them is completely valid: when we gaze at the stars, we see ourselves clearly. As author Joseph Chilton Pearce has aptly said: "Man's mind mirrors a universe that mirrors man's mind."[1]

ARCHETYPES AND THE TAROT

The tarot cards hold great personal significance for us because they symbolize our inherent and eternal human characteristics, which psychologist Carl Jung labelled "archetypes." These archetypes, visualized and projected upon decks of two-dimensional painted cards, speak to us at the deepest levels, like the stars, telling us secrets veiled behind our everyday personalities.

The events in your life develop around myriad patterns or themes, in a way similar to the themes of ancient myths. Once you begin to perceive such patterns, you realize that your life is not meaningless but has great mythic and spiritual significance. M. Esther Harding, a Jungian psychoanalist, says:

> The fact that the path unfolds in this way, step by step, leading the individual on, often by quite unexpected turns, towards the goal of wholeness, must mean that there are in the psyche patterns or rules of development analogous to the patterns operative in the physiological realm—such as . . . lead to the growth and development of the embryo. Surely we should not be surprised to find in the psychic life such a priori patterns.[2]

She goes on to say that men and women, by finding such wholeness within, and in freeing themselves from the conflicts and division in their own lives, will "be doing something constructive towards the solution of the very problems that are devastating mankind."[3] A world free of conflict and division can only exist if it is inhabited by people who have first freed themselves from conflict and division.

In the concepts of Jungian psychology, which I want to explore a little further, the term ''constellated'' refers to a particular archetype possessed of great power and activated by an excess of energy. This constellated archetype can dominate your psyche unless you understand its energy and integrate it into your personality. Otherwise its qualities will be projected onto other people whom you deem more powerful and capable. You will then feel either inadequate and inferior or egotistical and bombastic in that area. Yet the values inherent in that archetype are accessible to you, and you will gradually assimilate them.

Although at any point in your life an archetype may constellate in your psyche, at birth you are born into a particular constellation. This is actively demonstrated through your astrological chart calculated for the exact minute of your birth. Yet another level of this ''birth-mark'' is the archetype whose energy is constellated on the date of your birth, symbolized by the tarot card corresponding to the numerological sum of your birthdate. When you are named, another energy is constellated, which it is your task to assimilate. This apparently ''chance'' occurrence becomes more understandable if you accept that your greater Self *chose* your particular birth circumstances so that you could develop particular characteristics, face specific kinds of challenges, and focus on fulfilling a Self-determined goal. Your name given at birth, with its cultural, family, and generational significances, indicates the social constellations you selected to work with. If you change your name, you choose to express new archetypes that continue to reflect the energies constellated within. Often when you release an archetype into consciousness, it cannot fit back into its old container, so a new one—a new constellated formation, a new name—must be made for it.

Each year of your life is also defined by a particular confluence of energy, represented by an archetype whose passing influence gives you the opportunity to understand and integrate its values and lessons into your Self. If that energy already exists in your name or in the date of your birth, it becomes activated and more accessible than usual. You must deal with it directly and constructively, or its powerful effects can be destructive rather than beneficial.

You could say that the cards determined by your birth name and birthdate represent the major tensions with which you will struggle all your life. Author Marie-Louis Von Franz calls these constellated archetypes ''a mass of dynamic energy,'' and ''a factor of psychological probability.'' According to Von Franz, the constellating of an archetype actually creates an inner pattern or structure in the psyche. Oracular techniques, she says, are attempts to get at these basic structures so that the psychological probabilities can be read. To quote her: ''Divination oracles are an attempt to contact the dynamic load of an archetypal constellation and to give a reading pattern of what it is.''[4]

Although she is referring to the spontaneous appearance of an archetype in the psyche (she does not refer to its origins), I believe that the central archetypal constellations in a person's life—with which they must cope through an entire lifetime—are the forms of their chosen purpose, and are expressed in their birthdate and their name given at birth. These personal data deeply represent what one is destined to "realize," meaning "to make real," as well as "to comprehend the meaning of."

Another way of looking at the Self, choosing its own destiny, is the image of the child or fool in the act of playing a game of chance: gambling. Although fanciful, this image occurs in nearly all mythologies. When dice are rolled (to use one of the oldest forms of gambling), the "luck of the throw" determines the move. Fate supposedly rules that moment. But, according to Jung's theory of synchronicity in which everything that happens at any given moment in time is meaningfully related, fate then becomes a synchronistic phenomenon.[5] Thus, synchronistic events—which seem to be unique, sporadic, and unpredictable—happen within a larger firmament that we are rarely, if ever, able to see. Therefore these coincident events are a mirror of the constellation, with each event illuminating a small portion of the greater field—the archetype that is seeking expression. I see this in the image of The Fool, who throws fate—and himself—to the wind; and yet the wind came from somewhere and is going somewhere. The Fool simply steps into and goes with the existing current, which he cannot see. He trusts his pattern of destiny, and eventually he may come to recognize its modes and perimeters.

But, you may ask, how can a *number* tell me what my central archetypal constellation is? Scientifically speaking, we live in a time-space continuum based on mathematical "relativity." We measure both time and space in numbers. Again, according to Von Franz:

> Number gives information about the time-bound ensemble of events. In each moment there is another ensemble, and number gives information as to the qualitative structure of the time-bound clusters of events. . . . I think we have to see that number is an archetypal representation or idea which contains a quantitative and a qualitative aspect.[6]

Von Franz quotes Richard Wilhelm, a translator of the *I-Ching*, who explains that the Chinese felt the future could be predicted by knowing how a tree contracted into a seed. "Thus if we know the kernel point of a situation [such as one's life], we can predict its consequences." I interpret "consequences" here to indicate *what one's life stands for*. Von Franz continues: "Now what that means in psychological language is that if we know the deepest underlying archetypal constellation of our present situation, then we can, to a certain extent, know how things will go."[7] In this book, I attempt to give you some of the tools for discovering this "kernel" constellation.

THE NATURE OF BELIEFS

The tarot cards act as mirrors enabling you to look at your experiences with some objectivity. The tarot images reflect our beliefs about life and literally depict the hereditary and societal belief structures that we have been born into, specifically in our "Western" culture. They show great affinity with Hermetic philosophy, Kabbalah, astrology, numerology, Jungian psychology, mythic and symbolic psychologies, alchemy, and other esoteric metaphysical systems.

Each of these describes a particular framework of reality, much as scientific systems describe the kind of structure that exists within atoms and molecules. If there is a dance of Shakti and Shiva (deities of the Hindu pantheon), the tracings would resemble a web. And as Shakti and Shiva express the basic duality of female and male, their framework would be described in a sort of binary code arrangement: on/off, order/chaos, conscious mind/inner mind, black/white, energy/matter, masculine/feminine, the blinking in and out of manifestation.

Each individual contributes to the mass beliefs that together form our society. As long as we act in accord with a belief, whether we think it's a good one or not, we perpetuate it. Most of the time we are not even aware that our actions are based on beliefs. We just "do what comes naturally." Why question our every move, we ask ourselves? Just be "natural." But what is natural? Is it natural to blindly follow a set of beliefs and ideas inculcated in us, first by our parents and teachers, then later by employers, politicians, and television? That is what most people do. They call it natural, but it has nothing to do with nature. It is habitual and reactive rather than active; it leads to a sense of powerlessness because we are caught in the crossfire of conflicting beliefs from each of our many teachers.

Beliefs are helpful as well as harmful, and most of our beliefs are only helpful in the appropriate context. The problem is that they tend to become generalized as rules of conduct, and the reasons for them are forgotten. For instance, some people are taught never to put a hat on a bed or chair. They nag everyone around them, and nasty disagreements can be started from finding a hat on the bed. Few people question where this idea came from. ("It's just good manners.") Actually, this idea has a very practical source. Many communities even today have problems with head lice. They can spread very quickly from a hat to a bed, then to someone else's body hair. If you don't live in a lousy environment you need not be concerned about a hat on the bed. It is a rule of conduct cut off from its origin. Bad effects may follow but they are imposed or created out of the fear, not directly as a natural consequence. Other beliefs are much more insidious: "If you go out in the rain you will catch pneumonia." Or "blondes have more fun"—tell that to Whoopi Goldberg.

When people believe and expect that psychic things happen in their lives, they look for and notice them. If you find benefit in developing your psychic sense, why not believe in it? If you don't want war but believe it to be inevitable, you will act with an expectation of hostility and violence. One of the first things for you to do is to become aware of your emotions and beliefs!

One of the basic tenets of all metaphysical systems of thought is that we create our own reality in accord with our beliefs. These beliefs form the actual structure of that reality and hold it together. But in some sense these beliefs are purely arbitrary. This is why, for instance, you can believe in precognitive dreams and experience them often, while another person who does not believe this will find "proof" in each case that it was prior knowledge or coincidence. A skeptic will not experience anything counter to his beliefs until a related belief changes, allowing him to perceive another reality; that is, crack open his universe.

This is why you can read a book that you read years ago, but now discover that it says something else than before. How could you have misread it in the first place? Because you don't notice things that don't fit into your belief system. Beliefs direct your perceptions, as well as your emotional responses.

I try to use the terms "I think . . ." or "I believe . . ." very consciously to point out a personal belief of mine that you may or may not hold. But even if I don't use these words, you should know that they are implied *at all times* in this book. If you do not hold a similar belief, you may not find significance in what I say, or you may ascribe a completely different meaning to it. At the least, I am urging you to question the ideas I express, while remaining aware that there is an infinite variety of beliefs. Nevertheless, I urge you to maintain a "willing suspension of disbelief" to the extent that you approach the ideas and exercises in this book with an attitude of fun and nonchalance. You must be willing to come play with me, to try out the suggestions here to see if they can teach you something new; then, by all means, develop your own rules for the game.

THE TRIUMPH EXERCISE

Much of this book necessarily consists of my telling you about the traits and characteristics of the cards and constellations. While these may be helpful, they are also limiting, and may even get you onto the wrong track, or keep you from examining your own individual potentials. Just as no book that tells you the meaning of dream symbols will ever adequately or accurately explain your own dreams, so too, my interpretations are not adequate to the task of exploring your own possibilities. Meanings can be found in hundreds of books, but the following exercise shows how to discover them for yourself while actually in the midst of a reading (and even if you have never seen a tarot deck before in your life!). I use this procedure myself in my own professional consultations at those times when I look at a card in a spread and realize my mind is blank; panic washes over me and I think, I can't remember a thing about this card! What will I say? Yes, it happens to everyone. I then take myself firmly in hand and go through the exact steps I've outlined for you.

In my classes this is what I ask every student to do when they say to me, "I don't know what this card means." or, "What significance could it have here in this reading?" This exercise is truly empowering!

I call it "The Triumph Exercise" because it uses only the major arcana cards (although the principles apply to all cards). Early in the history of playing cards they were called the trump suit because they outranked the other cards. The term is believed to come from their development as pictorial representations of carts in the triumphal processions of Renaissance Europe. Each cart contained persons and symbols portraying an allegorical story of the triumph of a virtue or universal principle (such as Love, Prudence, Time, Death, etc.).[8] Applying this to the tarot cards as used today, the major arcana as "trump cards" represent the ways we can "triumph" in a situation.[9] A contemporary definition of trump given by the *American Heritage Dictionary* is: "a key resource to be used at the opportune moment." Major arcana cards are also often referred to as "keys." These terms indicate that the information you receive from these cards can be used to prevail successfully in any given situation.

Use only the 22 major arcana at this time, but this technique can be used with all 78 cards, if there are pictures on them.

Right now, at the moment you are reading this, think of a major arcana card. (If you are not at all familiar with the cards, separate the 22 major cards from the rest of the deck, mix them thoroughly face down, spread them in a fan, and select one at random.)

The card I have drawn is: *Strength*. Write it down here in your book or in your Tarot Notebook right now. (Always read this book with a tarot deck and pen or pencil in hand.)

The card you drew has something to tell you. All you have to do is ask it "what?" The card is mirroring you at this moment. There are 22 possibilities, each a different mirror into which you can look.

THE MAGICIAN.

Describe the card. Be liberal with adjectives and descriptive phrases. What is going on? Write quickly and without thinking about what you are going to say before writing. Surprise yourself. *(For example: A magician is in a garden full of flowers in full bloom. He is standing before a table on which are spread symbols of all the elements: his tools, perhaps. He has a rod in his raised right hand and is pointing his left hand toward the earth.)* You will probably describe this card differently each time you see it, noticing things that you were unaware of previously, while ignoring others. *She is full of patience and compassion - it shows in her face - no frustration there at all. The lion feels her love and responds - unifying its strength with hers. There is peace, calm, unity - the two are one in purpose. Her rose belt is freshly alive - renewal - her gown is purity. There is no concern for failure - none exists.*

If you haven't done so already, describe how the figures feel in the situation you've described. What is their attitude or mood? What does the situation feel like? *(For example: He is concentrating as if manifesting something or channeling some power with complete confidence. It seems like he wants to demonstrate how to do something.)*

Make at least one fictitious fantasy statement about the card, beginning with the phrase "What if . . ." Do it off the top of your head right now, without thinking about it, and in a spirit of fun. *(What if the Magician were a storyteller, improvising a tale for his supper, in which he must use each item on the table.)*

What if she were to ride the 'lion like a horse?

Next, repeat the basic elements of what you wrote in the statements above, but now use the first-person, present-tense "I am . . ." form. You become the figure in the card and assume the characteristics you described. Also, take the words "What if" off your fantasy and transform it into part of the same declarative sentence. *(I am a magician in a garden of flowers in full bloom. I am standing before a table on which are spread symbols of all the elements: my tools. I have a rod in my raised right hand and am pointing my left hand toward the earth, channeling power with complete confidence and concentration. I am totally focused on demonstrating how to do something. I am a storyteller, improvising a tale for my supper, in which I use each item on the table.)* Notice that I have eliminated unnecessary words like "perhaps" and "seems" to make stronger statements, and have linked ideas together.

Now transform your statements into the first-person present tense:

Immediately you will see that some statements are very appropriate to your life right now. Underline these.

Turn each of your phrases into a question. Depending on the phrases you used, ask yourself, for instance, "What am I concentrating on in my life now?" From the above example, you might ask, *"What elements or tools am I using?"* and *"What is the story I am improvising and how can it feed (or reward) me?"* You can even go back to the images on the card and ask, *"How could I use each item on the table in my improvisation?"*

THE EMPRESS.

JUSTICE .

Examine all the images you used as symbols of events, beliefs, and choices in your life; that is, of the reality you are creating. *Additional examples of this are: "The Empress: A woman, big with child, sits in a very rich field,"* becomes *"I am a woman big with child sitting in a very rich field."* Then ask yourself, *"What kind of child or creation am I pregnant with?"* and, *"What sort of riches surround me?"* Or, for the Justice card: *"She appears to be in a courtroom or in some rigid setting. She is trying to be stern and just and looks like she will take nothing less than her due . . ."* becomes *"I appear to be in a rigid setting or place of judgment. I am trying to be stern and just and I will take nothing less than what is due me."* What is rigid about my setting or in my environment? What is being judged? Where in my life am I trying to be stern and just? What do I feel is due me?"*

Now list several questions of your own, based on your description of your card.

Answer your questions as honestly as you can, focusing on your current life situation.

Since each card is a way you can "triumph," you must now consider the card you drew as an opportunity for growth, or a challenge to meet, while also portraying the qualities required to do so.

How can you triumph? What are the highest qualities you see in the card? What characteristics does it suggest that you value or that you would like to develop? Write down at least five qualities you see. Do this quickly, without thinking about it first.

Streagth
love
unity
Success
patience

In this exercise, it is important to avoid negative statements; instead, transform them into their opposite, beneficial qualities. For example, if you wrote that you can triumph through being "not afraid," what positive qualities are implied? Courage? Acceptance of your fear? Determination? Compassion?

Transform any negative statement from your list above into its triumphal qualities.

Now put these qualities into the "I am . . ." form, affirming that you have those qualities in yourself.

I have strength
I have love
I have unity
I have success
I have patience

To further amplify the meaning that this one card can hold for you, and to confirm its relevance, return to this page tomorrow and write in the space below a quick review of what happened in the 24 hours since beginning this exercise. Note especially how thoughts, assumptions, and events might relate to your card, or how you used its qualities in your activities.

Card _____*Strength*_____   Date (1st review) __12/28/95__
Observations or synchronicities: Date (2nd review)_____

Review the same card one more time in seven to ten days to see if you can add further perspective. Use a pen of another color the second time, so you can differentiate your comments.

This exercise is deceptively simple. It is a basic interpretation technique that can be used in any reading. After doing it several times, following the instructions above, it will feel natural and proceed easily as an automatic process seen "wholistically" in your "mind's eye." Done in depth, it can provide you with as much information as you receive from an average multi-card reading and will be *more relevant to the issue than any meanings you will find in a book*. You may never have to look up a meaning again! You will gradually define the cards according to your personalized criteria and in terms of actual situations, truly making the cards your own. This is the essence of personalizing the cards; of making them speak to you; of discovering tarot for yourself.

YOUR DAILY TRIUMPH EXERCISE

Drawing one "triumph" a day is like looking at yourself in your mirror. It gives you the chance to see what assumptions and beliefs will be activated that day. The card also suggests how you can triumphantly meet the challenges that appear. While you may later choose to use a different daily spread, or not to have a daily tarot practice at all, *do not skip this exercise now* as being too elementary or unnecessary. Each of the steps in this one-card exercise represents a technique important to later work. In using the tarot for yourself, you need a feedback mechanism. Symbols are personal. You will discover quickly from this seemingly simple exercise what the cards represent in your own life, and you will begin to see how your beliefs are attached to each other in clusters or constellations.

Keep your tarot deck in a special container on your dresser or on a personal altar. Every morning (or at the time you've chosen), take the 22 major arcana, shuffle the previous day's card back into the stack, and then select a new card for that day. You can do this as part of a centering ritual or meditation, at the end of an exercise session, or draw your card simply and quickly with no fanfare. Doing it at the same time every day (usually early morning or in the evening) is highly recommended. Leave your "daily triumph" card in view so that you are reminded of it throughout the day and its imagery can begin to sink into your consciousness.

If in shuffling the deck you drop a card, use it as your card for the day. If you drop two cards, then use both and blend their meanings, or watch to see if they represent conflicting ideas. Allow the experience of the moment to speak to you, and welcome the unexpected as a significant message from your inner self. And remember that although I am giving you some guidelines, they are not rules to be followed blindly.

Rather than trying to formulate different questions each day, I always ask the same question: "What do I need to look at today?" Or you could ask, "What is my greatest challenge today?" In this way, the symbolism of the card will point to the major challenge and learning opportunity at hand.

Each day, write the name of your card on *Your Daily Triumph Chart*; use the one in this book (or make your own as follows: Fold a regular piece of blank paper in half three times [from the bottom up]. Unfold it and you will have eight horizontal spaces. Draw lines along the folds with your pen, then write the headings in the first space, leaving the seven days of the week for each of the other spaces). To facilitate review of Your Daily Triumphs and to serve as an ongoing psychic record, keep your charts in your Tarot Notebook.

Working with Your Card

At the bare minimum, write down which card you drew and the date. I also urge you to write down anything else that seems appropriate.

In the daily chart, you may not have time to write about the card in depth. But in just two to five minutes you can note several important things under the indicated heading:

1) DATE: Give day of week as well as the month, day, and year. You can also note the Moon phase or significant astrological aspects. If you should miss a day, yet want a continuous record for each day of the week, then draw a card when you think of it, while stating the intention that this card is for the preceding day. Indicate that you've done so on your chart.

2) CARD: Write down which card you received. If you use more than one tarot deck, make sure you indicate which deck you used that day.

3) EMOTION: The cards bring up memories and emotions automatically. As you turn over your card-for-the-day, note your emotional reaction upon seeing it: Do you feel disappointed or relieved? Welcoming or apprehensive? Glad or angry? Acknowledge these first feelings to yourself and write them down on your chart next to "Emotion." Only a word or two is necessary.

4) IMAGE: Stay with that initial emotion for a moment, allowing images and memories triggered by that emotion to emerge from your memory. Briefly describe them next to "Image."

5) BELIEFS: Your responses are usually based on beliefs about yourself and your world, beliefs that are often reflected in the image. Write down any that you recognized next to "Beliefs." *(For instance, once when I drew The Sun, I found myself thinking happily, You must have done something right! Once with The Hanged Man, I suddenly caught an image of my daughter, her hands snarled in something, saying with frustration, "I can't do this.")* Watch for how that belief comes up during the day; notice whether it is a helpful belief or whether it limits your possibilities.

6) WHAT HAPPENED: Complete this section on the following day, with a thumbnail sketch of what you did and who you saw. When you review the events of the preceding day, the card you drew will demonstrate a challenge you had to face and a basic attitude or belief you needed to become aware of.

7) HOW TO TRIUMPH: On this final line write down briefly the highest (most beneficial, joyous, and growth-producing) qualities you see in the card. By taking that attitude toward whatever happens, you can triumph.

Noticing Trends in Your Daily Triumph Exercise

Notice whether certain cards come up when a particular person is prominent on that day, or when you are involved in certain kinds of work, or with specific issues.

What cards come up on days that seem the most stressful? What cards come up on especially happy days?

At the end of the week go back through the cards you've drawn. Cards that appeared several times are issues still pending, or problems whose root cause has not yet been dealt with. Notice when such a card stops appearing regularly. What happened on the last day of its appearance? Notice when a new or long unseen card appears; does it herald a change or new circumstance?

Notice whether your daily card appears among your Birth Cards and your Name Cards, as discussed in Chapters Two and Fifteen. Watch the cycles, patterns, and synchronicities that appear. They are confirmations of the significance and importance of certain symbols.

If you work with your dreams: Before going to sleep, look through the deck and select a card that mirrors an issue that you want to dream about. Setting your intention in this way (called "incubation") tells your inner self what to focus on in the dream state. After writing down your dreams in the morning, draw one major arcana card as an indicator of your primary dream message.

READING THE CARDS: SUMMARY

In summary, I want to emphasize that the basic processes given for the one-card reading (summarized in Chart 3), are central to reading *all* cards in *any* spread. Eventually the process becomes so automatic that it happens quickly and naturally.

CHART 2
YOUR DAILY TRIUMPH CHART

DATE	CARD	COMMENTS
		Emotion: Image: Beliefs: What happened: How to triumph:
		Emotion: Image: Beliefs: What happened: How to triumph:
		Emotion: Image: Beliefs: What happened: How to triumph:
		Emotion: Image: Beliefs: What happened: How to triumph:
		Emotion: Image: Beliefs: What happened: How to triumph:
		Emotion: Image: Beliefs: What happened: How to triumph:
		Emotion: Image: Beliefs: What happened: How to triumph:

Whenever you are unsure what a card "means," use this technique with the confidence that you will discover the significance in the process. Trust that the things you notice *at that moment* and the adjectives you use, as well as the memories and images that arise, will be appropriate.

In reading for others use this same technique by rephrasing the description as "you are" statements, or by guiding the querent through the steps below.

CHART 3
TO READ
A TAROT CARD

> 1) Simply describe the card! Be liberal with adjectives and descriptive phrases. What is going on? How do the figures feel in the situation you've described? What is the atmosphere?
>
> 2) Being careful to use the exact phrases from the previous step, repeat what you've just said, but in the declarative "I am . . ." form.
>
> 3) Turn the statements into open-ended questions and answer them. *For example: "How are you being devilish?"*
>
> 4) Examine the images as symbols of events, beliefs, and choices in your life. In what ways are they beneficial or limiting?
>
> 5) How can you triumph? What qualities does the card have that you value or that you would like to develop?

On Making Judgments

For the purposes of reading the cards, there is no such thing as right and wrong. When reading for yourself, but especially when reading for others, look at the querent's thoughts and actions as pictured in the cards to see whether they are helpful, that is, promoting growth and well-being, or limiting and counterproductive. Practically speaking, such judgments can only be made by the person for whom the reading is being done. As a reader, you must ask the querent (or yourself if reading for yourself) how to judge these situations. Since you cannot force moral opinions on another, your job is to help the person acknowledge their own—to see what they value (and thus want to promote in their life), and what they find counterproductive (and thus want to eliminate). The ways to do these things are always symbolized by the cards in the reading, but again, it is ultimately up to the querent to choose, and not for the reader to try to impose.

NOTES

1. Joseph Chilton Pearce, *Exploring the Crack in the Cosmic Egg* (New York: Pocket Books, 1975), p. 19.

2. M. Esther Harding, *Psychic Energy: Its Source and Its Transformation*, Bollingen Series X, (Princeton, N.J.: Princeton University Press, 1973), p. 307.

3. Ibid., p. 308.

4. Marie-Louise Von Franz, *On Divination and Synchronicity: The Psychology of Meaningful Chance* (Toronto: Inner City Books, 1980), p. 57.

5. Ibid., p. 58.

6. Ibid., p. 72.

7. Ibid., p. 94.

8. Gertrude Moakley, *The Tarot Cards Painted by Bonifacio Bembo* (New York: The New York Public Library, 1966), pp. 43–53.

9. I originally learned this concept from Angeles Arrien.

CHAPTER TWO

YOUR BIRTH CARDS

LIFETIME CARDS

One of the most helpful concepts I've found in working with the tarot is what Angeles Arrien calls the "Lifetime Cards." She originally developed these about fifteen years ago as the Personality, Soul, and Year Cards. I have used her concept extensively for nine years as a major part of my tarot work and introduced them in my book, *Tarot for Your Self*. This book, *Tarot Constellations*, explores the Lifetime Cards more extensively, expanding the concept to include the Hidden Factor/Teacher Card, described in this chapter, and the Name Cards, described in Chapter Fifteen. In general, the Lifetime Cards refer in this book to a set of cards that are determined by: 1) the date of your birth (called Birth Cards); and 2) the name given to you at birth (called Name Cards). These cards apply to you throughout your entire lifetime. (For clarification of the card names used in this book, refer to the *Summary of Card Names Chart* at the front of the book.)

FATE AND DESTINY

In recent years a revival of the concepts of fate and destiny has spurred much discussion and argumentation. There is also much gratuitous use of the term "responsibility." For example, one version says that you are "responsible" for everything that happens to you, just as if you directly went out and caused it. This sort of "responsibility" has caused much psychic pain to people who are victims of violence, parents of deformed and severly handicapped children, and people who contract debilitating or life-threatening illnesses. Are we fated to have these things happen, or did we cause them? Are we fated to be born Vietnamese, South African, Afghan, Nicaraguan, or White-Anglo-Saxon-Protestant American—or did we *cause* it, and now must pay the price?

I certainly don't have *the* answers, but the observation of our basic Lifetime Cards can give us some idea of how this might work.

The cards determined by your birthdate (and by your birth name) are based on what could be considered an arbitrary system. We use the Gregorian, or New Style, Calendar, which was not adopted in England and the United States (then the American colonies) until 1752. There are literally hundreds of different calendars in use in the world today, such as the Chinese, Hindu, Hebrew, Roman Catholic ecclesiastical, and Moslem calendars. These not only have different month names but different new years, and compensate for the solar year's "extra" one-fourth day per year in a wide variety of ways, usually by the

*Every year we gain an extra 5 hours, 48 minutes, and 46 seconds, for which every four years we make an adjustment of a leap day in our calendar.

device of a leap year.* The oldest continuous calendar seems to be the lunar calendar of the Chinese—in use since 2397 B.C.! Our own version was originally taken from an Egyptian calendar modified by the Romans and ''rectified'' by Pope Gregory XIII in 1582.

So, you might ask, how could such an arbitrary system have any validity for us? Have you ever tried thinking in another time system? There are many people whose language does not have words for ''past,'' ''present,'' or ''future''; they think, for instance, in terms of what ''has manifested'' and what ''is being manifested.'' Yet that definition is not quite right either, because we have no words for what they experience.

We are tied to our own perception of time, inculcated from childhood. Ask any five-year-old when their birthday is, and they will probably know the date and perhaps even how long until their birthday. Our definitions of time literally structure how we perceive it, and we are not really free to rid ourselves of this learned understanding. By being Americans or ''Westerners,'' we are ''fated'' to relate to time in the way we do, and to ''know'' that February (or *Febrero*) follows January (or *Enero*). It is part of our cultural conditioning, and just as our chromosomes give us a certain ''fate'' in our genetic conditioning—Caucasian, Negroid, Asiatic; curly red hair and green eyes, or kinky black hair and brown eyes, etc.—so we are fated to experience time through our cultural heritage and the calendar and clocks to which it adheres. This is nothing we have individually ''caused,'' nor are we in any practical way ''responsible'' *for* it. We *are* responsible for what we are going to do *with* it.

Many spiritual teachers point out that before birth your soul chooses the kind of life you need to experience in order to complete your physical-plane education, and that sometimes your soul will choose a short life of pain and suffering in order to develop much more quickly or to help with the growth and learning of the whole planet. Who are we to say? I like to believe that at some level my greater Self sees a larger plan, but in the meantime I can only work with what I've got. To this way of thinking, the life you are ''fated'' with can be described psychically by your name and birthdate, just as it can be mapped physically by your chromosomes. Your birth name and birthdate are lifetime keys to your inner psychic self *as you perceive yourself through your culture, language, and ethnic heritage.*

By understanding the significance of your Lifetime Cards, including your various Birth Cards and Name Cards, you can take responsibility for what you choose to make of your destiny: this is free will.

YOUR PERSONALITY AND SOUL CARDS

In any tarot reading, I always first determine a querent's PERSONALITY CARD and SOUL CARD, based on their birthdate. With just this information, we are able to see what a person most needs to learn in their life, and what lessons will bring them to an understanding of this urge.

Using your birthdate, let's numerologically calculate your Personality, Soul and Hidden Factor Cards.*

First, to find your Personality-Soul combination (destiny pattern), add together your month, day, and year of birth like this:

For example:

December 16, 1901 =	12
Margaret Mead	16
	<u>1901</u>
	1929

Then, add each digit in the resulting number: 1 + 9 + 2 + 9 = 21. *Keep any number from 1 to 22.* The resulting number is your Personality Number, which in this case is 21 and corresponds to the twenty-first major arcana card, The World (21). *Your Personality Card indicates personality characteristics that you develop easily and lessons that you learn early in your life as they seem to resonate with your essential nature.*

You then add together 2 + 1 = 3 to find your Soul Number. Anthropologist Margaret Mead's Soul Number (3) corresponds to the third major arcana card, The Empress (3). *Your Soul Card shows your soul purpose: those qualities in yourself that you must express and use in order to feel fulfilled in whatever you do.*

In some cases, the number will add up to more than 22. Since there are only 22 major arcana cards, reduce the number to 22 or less.

For example:

July 26, 1943 =	7		
Mick Jagger	26		
	<u>1943</u>		
	1976		
	1 + 9 + 7 + 6 = 23		2 + 3 = 5

In the case of rock singer Mick Jagger, the fifth card, The Hierophant (5), is both his Personality and Soul Card. Anyone with the same number for both cards is specifically working on their soul purpose in this lifetime. It makes the person more focused and directed.

There is one case in which more than two cards can appear. If your first number is 19, you will have three cards.

For example:

January 15, 1929 =	1		
Martin Luther King, Jr.	15		
	<u>1929</u>		
	1945	=	19
		1 + 9 =	10
		1 + 0 =	1

*If you have *Tarot for Your Self*, you already know how to determine your Personality and Soul Cards. However, in this book I will expand on the significance of these cards and further in this chapter introduce the Hidden Factor Card, which is also derived from your birthdate. Therefore, I suggest you read through this section.

THE WORLD.

Waite-Smith

THE EMPRESS.

Neuzeit

Hanson-Roberts

It is only when your birthdate totals 19, like that of Martin Luther King, Jr., above, that you will have such a triple sequence. In some ways all three cards defy categories, but for your use here you can consider The Sun (19) as your Personality Card, The Magician (1) as your Soul Card, and The Wheel of Fortune (10) as your Teacher Card (more about the Teacher Card later). People with this sequence must learn to communicate their individual creative expression. Their personal identity and sense of self will be inextricably combined with their life and soul purpose. Their ability to relate to others will depend on a harmony of vision and sense of shared purpose.

Native American

If your birthdate adds up to 22, you combine great impulsiveness and great mastery, a fine line to balance. The number 22 represents 0 (The Fool), since there are 22 cards in the major arcana, and 22 in numerology is a Master Number signifying great wisdom or great folly. It reduces to 4 (The Emperor). I stated in *Tarot for Your Self* that the Emperor is the Personality Card and the Fool is the Soul Card, but through experience I have found that it is not so easy to pin these people down. For convenience I'll now call The Fool the Personality Card and The Emperor the Soul Card—simply because it makes later calculations and tables easier. Don't expect Emperor-Fools, like Woody Allen, below, to sit still for anyone's system, though.

For example:

December 1, 1935 =	12		
Woody Allen	1		
	1935		
	1948	=	22 (Fool)
		2 + 2 =	4 (Emperor)

CHART 4
**YOUR PERSONALITY
AND SOUL CARD
CHART**

Determine your own Personality and Soul Cards as follows:

Add: The month you were born: _____08_____
      The day you were born: _____06_____
      The year you were born: _____1956_____
                    Equals: _____1970_____

Add each digit: __1__ + __9__ + __7__ + __0__   = ____17____
If you have a double-digit answer, add again: __1__ + __7__   = ____8____

My Personality Number is __17__ (the higher of the two numbers if 22 or less).
The major arcana card corresponding to this number is __The Star__:
                                        PERSONALITY CARD

My Soul Number is __8__ (the single-digit number in your final reduction).
The major arcana card corresponding to this number is __Strength__:
                                        SOUL CARD

(Note: If you are a 19–10–1 you also have The Wheel as your Teacher Card.)

THE HIDDEN FACTOR CARD

In addition to the numbers obtained directly through addition and reduction, there is frequently another number-and-card concept indirectly connected with your birthdate, which I call your HIDDEN FACTOR. The following *Constellations Chart* will help you determine this number. A Tarot Constellation consists of all the cards with the *same prime number* (1 through 9), as well as all the other major arcana cards whose numbers reduce to that prime number. Their energies constellate, or come together, based on similar principles; that is, on vibrational essences of like quality.

The chart aligns all the major arcana numbers above the "Root (or prime) Numbers" to which they reduce. For example, in the 19–10–1 column, each of those numbers reduces to the Root Number 1. Each of the nine groups or constellations thus formed also includes all the minor arcana cards of the same Root Number.

CHART 5
**CONSTELLATIONS
CHART**

19	20	21	22						
10	11	12	13	14	15	16	17	18	MAJOR ARCANA
1	2	3	4	5	6	7	8	9	
10's, 1's	2's	3's	4's	5's	6's	7's	8's	9's	MINOR ARCANA
1	2	3	4	5	6	7	8	9	ROOT NUMBERS

Let's go back to the first birthdate used as an example, that of Margaret Mead: her Personality Card is The World (21) and her Soul Card is The Empress (3). By combining these numbers, we are able to refer to her as a "21–3." Now look at the *Constellations Chart* and notice that there is one other major arcana number listed in her constellation, namely 12. Since she did not get a 12 in the calculations, it is a hidden aspect of her birth vibrational essence. This, then, is her Hidden Factor Card: The Hanged Man (12). It is the number that did not appear when we did the calculations, but which is also in her constellation. All the Three's of the minor arcana also belong to her constellation.

To make this clearer, let's try another birthdate, that of anarchist and feminist Emma Goldman.

June 27, 1869 =	6	
Emma Goldman	27	
	<u>1869</u>	
	1902	= 12 (Hanged Man)
	1 + 2 =	3 (Empress)

Her Personality Card is The Hanged Man (12) and her Soul Card is The Empress (3); she is a 12–3. Therefore, her Hidden Factor Card is The World (21), since 21 is the only number in her constellation not directly used in the birthdate reduction. The Three's of the minor arcana also belong to her constellation.

Mick Jagger, with The Hierophant (5) as both his Personality and Soul Card, has Temperance (14) as his Hidden Factor Card. The Five's in the minor arcana are part of his constellation.

Variations

There are three situations in which the hidden factor determination differs from the above:

1) The first variation occurs in the constellations 5 through 9, involving the Personality-Soul Patterns 14–5 through 18–9.

For example:

June 1, 1926 =	6	
Marilyn Monroe	1	
	<u>1926</u>	
	1933	= 16 (Tower)
	1 + 6 =	7 (Chariot)

Marilyn Monroe is therefore a 16–7, with The Tower (16) as Personality Card and The Chariot (7) as Soul Card. There is no number not accounted for in her constellation and therefore no Hidden Factor Card. Thus this combination (and that of the 14–5's, 15–6's, 17–8's, and 18–9's) includes the hidden factor in itself. The cards Temperance (14) through The Moon (18) are called the "night-time cards." They follow the Death Card (13), precede the dawning of The Sun (19), and are all depicted at night. Thus, in the Waite-Smith deck Temperance (14) depicts sunset, The Devil (15) is in darkness, and The Tower (16), The Star (17), and The Moon (18) are definitely images of the night. These cards inherently possess a "dark" or ignored, unrecognized side. I want to caution you, though, not to think of the dark side as bad, evil, or valueless; after all, in our journey through the dark (without the distractions of the light), we come to feel who we really are.

2) The 19–10–1's are the second variation. Because The Wheel of Fortune (10) was involved in the computation, it is not "hidden." I call it the Teacher Card because it does not manifest the "shadow" quality normally associated with the Hidden Factor Card.

3) Lastly, people who are a Single 1, 2, 3, or 4 (that is, having Personality-Soul Patterns of 1–1, 2–2, 3–3, or 4–4) have *two* Hidden Factor Cards, as shown by the chart. For instance, a Single 4 (4–4) has The Fool (22) and Death (13) as Hidden Factor Cards. People with single-card combinations have been rare until recently. In fact, there have been no Single 1's at all since January 1, 998 A.D. The single numbers of 2, 3, and 4 have been appearing primarily for people born since December 31, 1957, and are becoming much more frequent since the 1970's.

THE HIDDEN FACTOR CARD AS SHADOW CARD

Your Hidden Factor Card indicates aspects of yourself that you fear, reject, or don't see, and thus it can also be called the SHADOW CARD. The "shadow," a term used and defined by Carl Jung, refers to unknown or little-known parts of the personality. They are aspects of ourselves that we deny, and thus can't see directly. However, we remain sensitive to these qualities and therefore tend to see them in others via the psychological mechanism of "projection."

These shadow qualities are dualistic, having a "dark" side and a "bright" side. What is called the "dark shadow" refers to those qualities we mistrust and dislike, the little "sins." They contain tremendous psychic power that we can use if we contact them without fear. The "bright shadow" refers to the qualities that we admire (appearance, creativity, assertiveness) and actually have the potential to be manifesting, but again, we cannot see them in ourselves. Often these inner impulses pop out at inappropriate times and in unexpected ways, because they are not under the control of our conscious functioning.

The Shadow Card functions in much the same way that Saturn does in one's astrological chart. Saturn is the outermost personal planet and, as such, establishes the limits beyond which we cannot go without expanding into transpersonal and metaphysical experience. The card thus represents a doorway into that transpersonal and metaphysical realm, the inner planes. Most of us, though, experience this card as a mirror in which we see fears and fascinations. In it we are confronted with our limitations, our obsessions, our anxieties—the sources of stress. Often the hidden factor points out "invisible beliefs": those that lie out of sight behind other beliefs, such as the belief that "you are responsible for your lover's happiness," which for some people lies invisibly behind the belief that "if your lover isn't happy, it's your fault and you must do something to fix it."

THE HIDDEN FACTOR CARD AS TEACHER CARD

I've found that the Hidden Factor Card acts as your Shadow Card most strongly during your younger years. The planet Saturn takes 28 to 30 years to complete a circuit of the zodiac; that is, to return to where it was in the sky when you were born. This approximate 29-year cycle of Saturn is known as your "Saturn Return." As I mentioned before, Saturn—which represents many of the qualities of your shadow and which has much the same significance as the hidden factor—has to face itself every 29 years. By the time they are 30, most people find that they have learned their greatest lessons from their shadow issues. Carl Jung declared that the shadow is your greatest teacher, and that only by getting to know your shadow can you achieve individuation.

Therefore, with people over 30, I tend to call their Hidden Factor Card their TEACHER CARD, because they are ready to work actively and consciously with its principles. I'm not saying that you can't do this before your Saturn Return—many people become aware of their hidden factor issues much earlier and experience their Saturn Return as a time of liberation and joy. Most people at least intermittently confront their fears, inner restrictions, and limitations. All of these can relate to the Teacher Card. If you have a "nighttime card" (a Personality Card between 14 and 18), then that card will include in its characteristics some of the hidden factor qualities.

If you are a 19–10–1, you have no Hidden Factor Card; instead, you have the Wheel of Fortune (10) as your Teacher Card. In this pattern, the shadow qualities are not emphasized; instead, you consciously feel that life brings you the experiences you need to achieve your purpose. At worst, lacking the determination developed from dealing with your shadow, you tend to drift through life, never challenged to use your abundant talents.

Your hidden factor always challenges you to go beyond your usual experiences. Often it becomes your goal; it represents what you strive to understand and develop in yourself and in the world around you.

The following *Hidden Factor Chart* lists all 22 Personality-Soul Patterns and their associated Hidden Factor Cards. Mark your own by underlining or circling it.

Personality-Soul (Destiny) Patterns	Hidden Factor (Shadow/Teacher) Card(s)
1–1	10 & 19
10–1	19
19–10–1	10 (Teacher Card only)
2–2	11 & 20
11–2	20
20–2	11
3–3	12 & 21
12–3	21
21–3	12
4–4	13 & 22
13–4	22
22–4	13
5–5	14
14–5	*
6–6	15
15–6	*
7–7	16
16–7	*
8–8	17
17–8	*
9–9	18
18–9	*

CHART 6
HIDDEN
FACTOR
CHART

*Personality Cards 14 through 18, as "nighttime cards," include the hidden factor concept within themselves and therefore have no separate Hidden Factor Card.

LESSONS AND OPPORTUNITIES CARDS

*Additional cards with personal significance based on your birthdate are described in *Tarot for Your Self*.

Based on your birthdate, you also have cards from the minor arcana with the same number as your Soul Card.* Therefore, if your Soul Card is The Hierophant (5), for example, you also have all the Five's in the minor arcana as your LESSONS AND OPPORTUNITIES CARDS. These cards simply define the kinds of situations in which you are most likely to encounter your blocks and challenges, as well as your personal gifts and opportunities. Through the experiences indicated by these cards, you learn the *lessons* necessary to develop your personality and the *opportunities* most likely to express your soul purpose.

If you are an Emperor-Fool (22–4), for instance, all the Four's of each suit in the minor arcana are your Lessons and Opportunities Cards. The exception is the Sun/Wheel-of-Fortune/Magician (19–10–1), in which you have both the Ace's and the Ten's of each suit.

The salient characteristics of your Personality, Soul, and Hidden Factor Cards, as well as your Lessons and Opportunities Cards, are presented in the next ten chapters. I want to stress that these characteristics are general tendencies. Each individual finds their own unique way to express the possibilities that fate deals them. I urge you to meditate upon and dialogue with the figures on your cards (and to observe when these cards appear as your Year Cards, as described in Chapter Thirteen). Determine their personal significance to you, using my sketches of the territory only as a starting point for your own contemplation and insight.

THE TAROT CONSTELLATIONS

CHAPTER THREE

THE TAROT CONSTELLATIONS

In the preceding chapter you learned how to find your Personality, Soul, and Hidden Factor Cards, and that they all are in the same constellation. This chapter provides a detailed overview of the constellations and also shows several ways to use the information given in the individual constellation chapters. These next nine chapters (Chapters Four through Twelve) describe what your cards mean in each of the nine constellations and illustrate them, using a variety of decks.

THE CONSTELLATIONS: WHAT THEY ARE

Your Personality Card is a major signpost along your life's journey, while your Soul Card reveals the goal or purpose of your being. These cards can be paired together in 22 combinations that I call the Patterns of Personal Destiny (or destiny patterns), constellated around nine basic principles of the journey. These patterns and their associated constellations are the heart-matter of this book. Also constellated around the nine principles are the associated minor arcana cards, which provide further landmarks on the map of your spiritual travels. If you are unfamiliar with the four suits of the minor arcana, there is a description of their primary traits later in this chapter.

The Nine Constellations										
The Magician	The High Priestess	The Empress	The Emperor	The Hierophant	The Lovers	The Chariot	Strength	The Hermit		
19	20	21	22						MAJOR ARCANA CARDS	
10	11	12	13	14	15	16	17	18		
1	2	3	4	5	6	7	8	9		
10, Ace	2	3	4	5	6	7	8	9	Wands	MINOR
10, Ace	2	3	4	5	6	7	8	9	Cups	ARCANA
10, Ace	2	3	4	5	6	7	8	9	Swords	CARDS
10, Ace	2	3	4	5	6	7	8	9	Pentacles	

CHART 7
TAROT
CONSTELLATIONS
CHART

The Tarot Consellations are groupings of the major arcana trumps plus the minor arcana pip cards, numerologically arranged to express the nine major principles or archetypes underlying our metaphysical makeup. The basic archetypes, though in themselves impossible to pinpoint, are actually the unconscious trends that cause certain motifs to appear in all human cultures. The Soul Card of the Tarot Constellations gives us nine representations of the most common and essential motifs of the Self:

CHART 8
SOUL CARD
MOTIFS CHART

1	Magician	Outer, Conscious Sense of Self
2	High Priestess	Inner, All-Knowing Self, Virgin
3	Empress	Fertile, Creative Mother
4	Emperor	Ordered, Structured Father
5	Hierophant	Teacher, Bearer of the "Word"
6	Lovers	The Twins—Dual Self
7	Chariot	Hero, Warrior
8	Strength	Enchantress, Animal Nature/Helper
9	Hermit	Old Wise One, Journey into the Underworld

Each of these nine basic motifs is further amplified by the other cards in its constellation. The constellations that are especially yours, because they correspond with your Birth Cards and your Name Cards (the latter will be explained later in the book), tell you the archetypes constellated for you at your birth. These then are particular energies and principles that you will express, explore, and develop in your life, as well as the challenges you will have to meet to understand them. They point to your purpose in being here, and to particular qualities you can manifest in this lifetime.

THE CONSTELLATIONS AND THEIR PRINCIPLES

This section contains a summary of the constellations and their principles. This information provides a way of perceiving the tarot that I hope will be used and expanded upon by tarot practitioners to come.

1) *THE CONSTELLATION OF THE MAGICIAN* (19-10-1):
   Includes Personality-Soul Patterns 1-1, 10-1, and 19-10-1.

   The Principle of Will and Focused Consciousness.

   The *Ace's* indicate the opportunity to begin new things, and reveal your four basic skills.

   The *Ten's* demonstrate the developed skills with which to meet challenges and the results of taking the principles to their extremes.

2) *THE CONSTELLATION OF THE HIGH PRIESTESS* (20-11-2):
   Includes Personality-Soul Patterns 2-2, 11-2, and 20-2.

   The Principle of Balanced Judgment through Intuitive Awareness.

   The *Two's* represent the four ways in which judgments are made.

THE PATTERNS		ASSOCIATED WITH			
No.	Personality-Soul Cards	Hidden Factor (Teacher) Card(s)	Minor Arcana Cards	Constellation of	
1 2 3	1–1 10–1 19–10–1	10 & 19 19 10 (Teacher)	10's and 1's	The Magician (19–10–1)	1
4 5 6	2–2 11–2 20–2	11 & 20 20 11	2's	The High Priestess (20–11–2)	2
7 8 9	3–3 12–3 21–3	12 & 21 21 12	3's	The Empress (21–12–3)	3
10 11 12	4–4 13–4 22–4	13 & 22 22 13	4's	The Emperor (22–13–4)	4
13 14	5–5 14–5	14 *	5's	The Hierophant (14–5)	5
15 16	6–6 15–6	15 *	6's	The Lovers (15–6)	6
17 18	7–7 16–7	16 *	7's	The Chariot (16–7)	7
19 20	8–8 17–8	17 *	8's	Strength (17–8)	8
21 22	9–9 18–9	18 *	9's	The Hermit (18–9)	9

*"Personality Cards 14 through 18 have no hidden factor.

**CHART 9
PATTERNS OF
PERSONAL DESTINY
CHART**

3) *THE CONSTELLATION OF THE EMPRESS* (21–12–3):
   Includes Personality-Soul Patterns 3–3, 12–3, and 21–3.

The Principle of Love and Creative Imagination.

The *Three's* indicate the opportunities and challenges to creatively demonstrate love.

4) *THE CONSTELLATION OF THE EMPEROR* (22–13–4):
   Includes Personality-Soul Patterns 4–4, 13–4, and 22–4.

The Principle of Life Force and the Realization of Power.

The *Four's* indicate the opportunities to consolidate and complete something in preparation for renewal.

5) *THE CONSTELLATION OF THE HIEROPHANT* (14–5):
   Includes Personality-Soul Patterns 5–5 and 14–5.

The Principle of Teaching and Learning.

The *Five's* indicate the challenges faced when learning through experience.

6) *THE CONSTELLATION OF THE LOVERS* (15–6):
Includes Personality-Soul Patterns 6–6 and 15–6.

The Principle of Relatedness and Choice.

The *Six's* indicate the challenges of maintaining and sustaining relationships and of taking responsibility for your choices.

7) *THE CONSTELLATION OF THE CHARIOT* (16–7):
Includes Personality-Soul Patterns 7–7 and 16–7.

The Principle of Mastery through Change.

The *Seven's* test whether mastery and control can be sustained through change.

8) *THE CONSTELLATION OF STRENGTH* (17–8):
Includes Personality-Soul Patterns 8–8 and 17–8.

The Principle of Courage and Self-Esteem.

The *Eight's* indicate the gifts and challenges in developing the self-confidence to follow a vision.

9) *THE CONSTELLATION OF THE HERMIT* (18–9):
Includes Personality-Soul Patterns 9–9 and 18–9.

The Principle of Introspection and Personal Integrity.

The *Nine's* indicate the challenges to be faced by looking within and discovering your own wisdom.

USING THE CONSTELLATIONS

The information on the constellations in the next nine chapters can be used in various ways:

1) For looking up your own or a querent's Personality, Soul, and Hidden Factor Cards. Refer back to the Introduction ("Using the Tarot Constellations in a Reading") for a description of using these cards as a preliminary part of a complete tarot reading.

2) Use the constellation descriptions for interpretating individual cards in any reading. This emphasizes the principles you are accessing, as well as the lessons and challenges presented. Use the descriptions to focus your reading on the potentials available and the purpose of the experience. They tell you what energies are presently active.

3) Use the descriptions for understanding your Daily Triumph Card (see Chapter One) as the energy of the day.

4) When a reading hinges upon a card that stands out as especially important, or if three or more cards from one constellation appear in a reading, consider

how the basic principle of that constellation applies. Then examine all the cards of that constellation to find ways to work with that energy in your life.

5) Notice that the next nine chapters are preceded by illustrations of the constellation patterns, using a variety of decks. Use your own deck, placing your cards in the same pattern to help you see the relationships that make up the pattern as a whole. Then move the cards around until you find a pattern that works for you.

6) Determine the Personality-Soul Patterns of your family and friends. Write their names and birthdates in the margins by the corresponding destiny pattern, or in your Tarot Notebook. Connections will begin to become apparent within your family and among the people you choose to be around.

7) Read about the famous people in your constellation. (Refer to a good biographical dictionary or encyclopedia during a library visit.) Look for any interesting similarities and coincidences. Remember that the cards won't describe what the subjects did so much as *why they did it.* For writers and philosophers, this is often reflected by the key issues in their books. See what quotations they are remembered for. Ask yourself if the themes in their lives apply to yours. Note that a particular destiny pattern can contain quite different "types," as the themes are expressed across a spectrum of sometimes opposing behaviors.

8) Take the cards in your constellation and spread them on the floor or table. Move them around in various ways until you find a pattern that seems to make sense to you. Ask yourself the following questions:

> How are the cards similar and how are they different?
> How do the minor arcana express the qualities of the major arcana of the same constellation?
> How do these minor arcana express beneficial and inspiring characteristics, and how do they express limiting and problematic ones?
> What do the corresponding major arcana recommend you do about the challenges presented in the minor arcana?
> What are the kinds of situations, as described by the minor arcana, that will teach you to actualize the potentials inherent in the major arcana? In what ways are the minors the tests and resources of the majors?

9) Dialogue with the figures in your Personality, Soul, and Hidden Factor Cards; find out what they have to say to you directly. This is such an important technique that it needs to be developed on its own.

DIALOGUING WITH THE CARDS

With this technique, you learn to personally interact in writing with a figure or symbol found on your Personality, Soul, or Hidden Factor Card(s). These are parts of yourself that don't usually have an opportunity to speak. To do this, select who or what seems most receptive to a conversation (objects can talk in this magical realm). Address him, her or it directly with a good opening question. *For instance: "Lion, what are you staring at?"* Then allow yourself to

speak for the lion with *the first thing that comes to mind*. It is important to be spontaneous, and not to censor or hesitate when responding. If you feel a little silly doing this, then imagine the silliest thing the lion would say. This helps to break the ice and get the conversation going. Yes, you *are* making up the responses, but that's exactly what it's all about.

Don't think about handwriting, spelling, grammar, or anything else that might get in the way of the actual conversation. Continue "conversing" in your Tarot Notebook for at least 12 to 15 minutes. Once you are used to the process you can write as long as you like, although I still think the commitment of a timed writing is helpful. Many people find their handwriting changes the longer they go on, becoming looser and more childlike. This simply indicates you are by-passing the normal "controls" set on your thinking mind and freeing up your "inner knowing" to be simply and directly expressed.

You will also come to what I call "thresholds." A threshold is a point at which you feel you have written enough and it's not really necessary to go on. You may suddenly feel tired and distracted. You have reached a barrier beyond which your thoughts do not usually go. If you truly want to know yourself, *now* is the time to act on your intention. Simply acknowledge to yourself, "I am at a threshold." Then make the intention to go on, saying to yourself, "I choose to go on, to find what is on the other side." Your inner self has probably been waiting a long time to hear that! Usually you'll find that what seemed like a brick wall is now an open gate. Anyway, you should find it easy, if not exhilarating, to go on. Go through no more than one or two thresholds the first few times. You can work your way up to move through more thresholds later. If you need assistance, ask a special tarot guide like the Temperance Angel (on card 14) or the Star Woman (on card 17) to help you find the way through.

Some questions you might want to ask in your dialogues are:

> What is the significance of particular symbols in the card? (Eventually, with this process, you can make a personal symbol directory with your own insights into each of the tarot symbols.)
> How can you use any particular symbol in your own life?
> What do you need to learn from this card?
> Why are you so attracted or repelled by the card?
> How can you best face the problem or challenge indicated by the card?
> What are the triumphal qualities of the card that you can use?
> Why did you choose to dialogue with that particular figure or symbol and what does it have to teach you?

Don't be surprised if the figure begins asking you questions! How you answer these questions is especially significant. Any resistance to this change of affairs means you are at a threshold.

SPECIFIC CARD QUESTIONS

You can always ask the general, all-purpose question, "What do I have to learn from you?" However, each card has particular characteristics and issues that you may want to ask about. Here is a list of some other questions you can ask the individual cards.

THE MAGICIAN: What is my own personal magic? How do I focus and direct it? Who is my magical self? How can I use the four elements in my life? How can I communicate in four ways?

THE HIGH PRIESTESS: My inner wisdom: how do I become aware of your knowledge? What questions must I ask in order to know myself? How do I go within? What are my dreams or intuition trying to tell me?

THE EMPRESS: What am I giving birth to? How do I grow in beauty? What is rich and lush in my life? My physical environment: what surrounds me? What wants to creatively express itself through me?

THE EMPEROR: Where does my power lie? How can I establish my own authority? What must I conquer within myself? In what direction have I chosen to focus my energies?

THE HIEROPHANT: What do I need to learn from my problems? On what values do I base my decisions? What do I have to teach? What beliefs must I question? How do I learn?

THE LOVERS: How do I open myself and communicate my love? What choice do I have to make? How can I accept others for whom and what they are? What do I want and need from relationships?

THE CHARIOT: What energies must I harness in order to move toward my goal? Where am I going? How can I control my instincts and keep myself centered?

STRENGTH: Beast: who are you? Where does my strength lie? Where can I use it? How can I balance power with love, and lovingly express my power? How do I link myself to my desires?

THE HERMIT: What am I searching for? Where should I look? How do I persevere on my own path? What do I need to complete? What have I mastered that I can teach others?

WHEEL OF FORTUNE: What is changing and how can I best handle those changes? How can I alter my perspective? How do I reach my center and leave the ups and downs to the perimeter?

JUSTICE: What needs to be reconciled or adjusted? Where is justice needed? On what basis can I judge or evaluate? How can I be true to myself?

THE HANGED MAN: What is hanging me up or leaving me suspended? What must I see from a different perspective? What do I need to surrender to? Where must I be humble?

DEATH: What must I sever in order to grow anew? How can I release any unnecessary patterns? What will letting go relieve me of? Where do I go from here?

TEMPERANCE: What is my art? What things must I combine? How can I revive my interests and renew my spirit? How can I tap energy and resources for healing?

THE DEVIL: What ambitions do I aspire to? What do I hate or fear? To what does emotion bind me? How do I free myself from these bonds? What knowledge will liberate my thinking?

THE TOWER: How can I express my angers and aggressions? What must I do to break through constrictions? What personal barriers have I built up? What in my life needs liberating?

THE STAR: How can I experience my spirit more deeply? What does hope offer me? How do I make my dreams come true? What makes me truly free?

THE MOON: How do I learn from my dreams? How can I draw on my hidden resources? Where has my evolution brought me? What must I digest from my past in order to move on?

THE SUN: Where can I find my happiness? How can I experience joy and love? What do I reveal when I open myself without restriction?

JUDGEMENT: What does my purpose ask of me? How will I recognize my calling? What can I do to be part of a new aeon and recognize my kinship with others? What needs to be resurrected in my life?

THE WORLD: What do I have the potential to manifest? How can I express freedom within structure? How can I dance on my limitations? What is the whole of which I am a part?

THE FOOL: Where is my soul taking me? What is the wisdom in my folly? How am I being foolish? What must I trust to? How can I live more spontaneously and joyfully?

THE SUITS OF THE MINOR ARCANA

The following chapters on the constellations contain meanings for the suit cards of the minor arcana, which can be applied to any reading. If you are unfamiliar with the four suits, the following discussion will introduce them to you, or serve as a review.

The four suits of the minor arcana are based on the four elements: Wands are Fire, Cups are Water, Swords are Air, and Pentacles are Earth.* You contain these four suits and elements within you in a combination that is constantly in flux, never in perfect balance. When you read these tarot cards, they tell you what is happening on these four levels, or within these four aspects of yourself.

In reading, you should always determine which suit predominates and whether any suit is not represented. Usually a missing suit indicates an area that is functioning efficiently on its own, with no necessity to examine it at the time. If the missing element seems central to your question, you need to ask yourself why it didn't appear. The predominating suit indicates where your energy is focused. If mostly problematic cards are involved (which is likely with Swords,

*Although the assignment of elements to suits can vary, these are the most common correlations for decks that use pictures on the minor arcana (as opposed to numerical designs). See Appendix B for a further discussion of different decks.

for instance), they point to impediments that need to be overcome—something
to move through in order to access the highest potentials shown in the reading.

Symbol	Suit & Element	Meaning of the Suits
	WANDS Fire	Self-growth. Spirit. Inspiration. Energy. Creativity. Initiation. Enthusiasm. Desire. Passion. Perception. Action. Movement. Optimism.
	CUPS Water	Feelings and Emotions. Unconscious. Imagination. Intuition. Being psychic. Dreams. Visualization. Inner processes. Relationships. Receptivity. Reflection.
	SWORDS Air	Thoughts. Struggles. Conflict. Decisions. Wit and cunning. Analysis. Discussion. Communication. Mental processes. Acuity. Criticism. Pessimism.
	PENTACLES Earth	Results. Actualization. Sensation. Security. Grounding. Centeredness. Manifestation. Skills. Craftmanship. Rewards for accomplishment. Fruits of labor. Tradition. The Physical and Material.

CHART 10
**MINOR ARCANA
SUITS CHART**

FROM THE THOTH TAROT

The emphasis in this constellation is on the return to the center. No matter how far-ranging or diverse one gets, the Magician energy always reinforces unity. The individual becomes the channel through which consciousness is aware of itself, change is perceived, and the solar cycle is personified.

CHAPTER FOUR

THE CONSTELLATION OF
THE MAGICIAN: 19–10–1

THE SUN (19)   THE WHEEL OF FORTUNE (10)   THE MAGICIAN (1)

ACE & 10 OF WANDS   ACE & 10 OF CUPS
ACE & 10 OF SWORDS   ACE & 10 OF PENTACLES

THE PRINCIPLE OF WILL AND FOCUSED CONSCIOUSNESS

THE MAGICIAN	WHEEL OF FORTUNE	SUN
Mercury	*Jupiter*	*Sun*
Unity of Self	Unity in Diversity	Unity in Spirit
The Individual	The Individual in Society	All as One

Keywords: Communication. Self Consciousness. Individualization. Self-Expression. Initiative. At-one-ment. Originality.

If you are a 10–1, read the following sections in this chapter:
    THE MAGICIAN (1) AS SOUL CARD
    THE WHEEL OF FORTUNE (10) AS PERSONALITY OR
        TEACHER CARD
    THE SUN (19) AS HIDDEN FACTOR
    FAMOUS 10–1's
    THE MINOR ARCANA ACE'S AND TEN'S

If you are a 19–10–1, read:
    THE MAGICIAN (1) AS SOUL CARD
    THE SUN (19) AS PERSONALITY CARD
    THE WHEEL OF FORTUNE (10) AS PERSONALITY OR
        TEACHER CARD
    FAMOUS 19–10–1's
    THE MINOR ARCANA ACE'S AND TEN'S

THE MAGICIAN (1) AS SOUL CARD

(This applies if you are a 19–10–1 or a 10–1.)

Unity of Self, the Individual

THE MAGICIAN represents focused consciousness and will. As a card relating to Mercury, it indicates that you are a communicator and a skilled craftsperson.

THE MAGICIAN.

The symbols of the four suits on the table indicate your ability to work with all four elements as your tools.

As a Magician, you work creatively using your hands as well as your mind. You are capable of great mental focus and are self-initiating in your activities. Logical analysis comes easily to you, and you use this ability to manipulate anything under the sun.

It is probably hard for you to work for other people because you want to concentrate on your own ideas. You channel all your energies into your tasks. This helps you believe in and communicate your ideas, but your tendency toward egocentricity doesn't always leave room for others, unless they are willing to follow you. You are an individualist. You are not very patient and expect instant gratification.

To develop your highest abilities, you need to realize that you can be a channel for a higher consciousness. If you open up to Spirit and let the divine Will move through you, you may join the company of 19–10–1's who are outstanding healers, teachers, leaders, innovators, inventors, and communicators of all kinds.

You have an innovative mind and think quickly "on your feet." Correspondingly, you are also easily sidetracked by new ideas; it may help to have a co-worker who completes the task at hand. You tend to identify with your work and your creations, experiencing them as an integral part of yourself, and are thus sensitive to criticism of your projects.

You have the magical ability to transform and change yourself and to transform mundane, ordinary events into magical ones. You understand your place as the consciousness that gives meaning to synchronicities, as the actor without whom no action can take place.

At your worst, you can become a con man, or fast-talking trickster with the ability to convince others that they can get something for nothing. You play games and create illusions to achieve your personal ends. You are then something different to every person you come in contact with, appearing to be just what that person wants to believe you are. You are at your best with an audience who appreciates you, a model of fascination and charm.

Magicians are also liable to what is called the "Peter Pan" complex—not wanting to grow up and accept adult responsibilities. Although you easily retain a sense of fun and play, your urge for self-gratification is characteristic. You mean what you say at the moment, but don't want to be held to anything later. If you are a woman and repress this happy-go-lucky side of yourself, you may project it onto your men, whose refusal to grow up reflects your own wishes.

The Magician acts only as a Soul Card, and therefore you will never experience it as a Personality, Hidden Factor, or Year Card. The number 1 has not appeared by itself since January 1, 998 A.D., and won't reappear until December 31, 9957 A.D., when dates will again begin to add up to 10,000—if our calendar lasts that long.

WHEEL OF FORTUNE (10) AS PERSONALITY OR TEACHER CARD

(This applies as a Personality Card if you are a 10-1, and a Teacher Card if you are a 19-10-1. It has not been possible to have The Wheel of Fortune as a Hidden Factor Card since 998 A.D.)

WHEEL of FORTUNE.

Unity in Diversity, the Individual in Society

The WHEEL OF FORTUNE represents change, movement, and expansion of ideas. It is a card of luck, both good and ill. As the wheel turns, new opportunities appear and old projects reach a new turn of the spiral. The wheel bordered by the four figures in the corners stands for a sacred circle protected by divine entities.

Jupiter is most often associated with this card and thus expands the thinking of the Magician to a new level, adding a philosophical perspective. You have a sense of choice that comes from being able to see the sum of the whole—an overview. Your beliefs and hopes either sustain you or plunge you into despair (although probably not for long). Your ideas are favored to reach the public through publishing or other forms of communication, as indicated by the books held by the corner figures.

The Wheel of Fortune brings the potential for rewards from the creative projects that the Magician initiates. If you have a Wheel personality you learn through change. You gamble and take risks for the challenges they present you. You experience the effect of your work in the world and often see it come back to you at a later time, transformed and implemented in ways you may not have imagined. Thus, you may have to face the results of the occasional thoughtlessness of your Magician soul.

On the problematic side, you can easily drift along without exerting yourself, being lucky and quick-witted enough to keep on your feet and moving. Sometimes ambition is negated as new and interesting situations arise with intriguing avenues to explore. It seems that if you just wait long enough everything you need will come to you. You then lack persistence and are impatient with details; therefore you leave many projects by the wayside. This drifting and dilettante attitude could keep you from achieving your highest potential.

Above all, though, The Wheel of Fortune shows flexibility and the ability to grasp opportunities when they happen. You are easy-going, magnanimous, and forgiving. You ride the low points with as much ease as the crests, knowing that such extremes are temporary, and you will endure.

The Sphinx stands guard at the gateway to further development, asking if you are willing to be spun on the wheel of fate, thus to arise again with greater understanding.

THE SUN (19) AS HIDDEN FACTOR

(This applies if you are a 10–1.)

As a 10–1 Personality-Soul Pattern, THE SUN ironically is your Shadow Card. However, your particular shadow is what Carl Jung calls a "bright shadow." You probably have some difficulty acknowledging your good qualities and accomplishments. Look around you: Is there someone you wish you could be like? You may not sufficiently value your own worth, feeling "outshone" by others.

In your youth you might find it difficult to be open with others. You are essentially a loner and feel more comfortable working by yourself on your own projects. You don't let others get too close, finding it hard to put your trust in someone else, since with the instability of life they could be here today and gone tomorrow. Later, with The Sun as your Teacher Card, you will slowly open yourself to discover the joys of friendship. One of your greatest lessons is to learn trust—to trust yourself to do well, and to trust others with your deepest feelings. When you lack trust you experience doubt in your projects, yourself, and the value of your friendships. With the shape-changing qualities of The Magician as your Soul Card, your identity is elusive, changing to meet every new circumstance. The Sun challenges you to recognize yourself as the creator of your own reality.

FAMOUS 10–1'S

I only have one 10–1 in my entire list of famous people, but he is a most interesting one. Philosopher René Descartes based his "proof" of God on the fact that we doubt, and if we doubt, we think, and therefore must be fashioned after a thinking being: "I think, therefore I am." But to Descartes mind and matter were totally separate substances—one above (Spirit), the other below (the physical world). There are many 10–1's being born now (since December 31, 1965), as we move into the turn of the second millennium. As these are still too young for fame, we can only surmise and observe.

René Descartes (French philosopher) 3/31/1596

THE SUN (19) AS PERSONALITY CARD

(This applies if you are a 19–10–1.)

Unity in Spirit, All as One

THE SUN represents wholeness, achievement, and the revelation that comes when the full light of the sun shines and there is nothing to hide. Walt Whitman, a 19–10–1, wrote: "Give me the splendid silent sun, with all his beams full-dazzling!" With a Sun personality you are basically optimistic and cheerful. Like the sunflowers, you are always looking for the light side of things. The wall in the card indicates awareness of your limitations. You are learning to acknowledge your achievements, and if you have been successful on the inner path of the Wheel, then you realize you can fully reveal yourself and your motivations to others.

Like a child, you take innocent delight in the small things in life and have found that you can ride your instincts, since without hidden motivations they will lead you true. You radiate your belief that others can also accomplish their dreams, and therefore you are an inspiration to them. Your trust brings out their best.

Most tarot decks picture two children dancing under the light of the sun. This emphasizes that you love to share your experience with others. Thus this is the card of co-creativity. You need someone else to share your ideas and to work and play with. As the sun is always paired in myth and story with the moon, so too you feel the need to pair, to have a complement. With The Magician as your soul essence, you identify so strongly with your work that it is hard to be in a relationship with someone who is not also interested in what you do. It's a "love me, love my work" kind of situation. You cannot separate yourself from your projects and ideas, so it helps to have a partner who is just as involved and interested as you, or at least who is willing to listen. Because you are a leader and idea person, your "other half" should be a supporter and finalizer. You like to be in the limelight. You'll have a great partnership if your partner takes on the sustaining tasks; otherwise there could be too much competition.

If you have a job in which you cannot be creative or cannot work independently, you will never consider it your "work," but just a job. You will therefore need another outlet through which you can "shine."

FAMOUS 19–10–1'S

As you can see from the list, 19–10–1's are leaders and inventors. They initiate new movements and have many "firsts" to their credit. They often become figureheads for their followers and spokespeople for any cause they identify with.

Sir Isaac Newton (English scientist) 1/4/1643
George Washington (First U.S. President) 2/22/1732
Napoleon I (Emperor of France) 8/15/1769
Benjamin Disraeli (Prime Minister of England) 12/21/1804
Karl Marx (German social philosopher) 5/5/1818
Herman Melville (Writer) 8/1/1819
Walt Whitman (Poet) 5/31/1819
Susan B. Anthony (Reformer and feminist) 2/15/1820
Florence Nightingale (Founder, modern nursing) 5/12/1820
Leo Tolstoy (Russian novelist) 9/9/1828
Konstantin Stanislavski (Theatrical actor/director) 1/18/1863
Carl Jung (Swiss psychiatrist) 7/26/1876
George Gurdjieff (Metaphysician) 1/13/1877
Ernest Hemingway (Novelist) 7/21/1899
Werner Heisenberg (German physicist) 12/5/1901
Walt Disney (Animator and film producer) 12/5/1901
Simone De Beauvoir (French existentialist author) 1/9/1908
Lyndon B. Johnson (U.S. President) 8/29/1908

Jacques Cousteau (Marine scientist) 6/11/1910
L. Ron Hubbard (Founder of Scientology) 3/13/1911
Arthur C. Clarke (Science-Fiction writer) 12/16/1917
Billy Graham (Evangelist) 11/7/1918
Rev. Sun Myung Moon (Religious leader) 1/6/1920
Betty Friedan (Feminist) 2/4/1921
Nancy Davis Reagan (Wife of U.S. President) 7/6/1923
Frank Borman (Astronaut) 3/14/1928
Martin Luther King, Jr. (Civil-rights leader) 1/15/1929
Colin Wilson (English writer) 6/26/1931
Dalai Lama (Religious leader) 12/18/1933
Ralph Nader (Consumer-rights spokesperson) 2/27/1934
Carl Sagan (Science spokesperson) 11/9/1934
Judy Collins (Singer) 5/1/1939
Jean Houston ("Consciousness" writer/lecturer) 5/10/1939
Ringo Starr (Beatle) 7/7/1940
Janis Joplin (Singer) 1/19/1943
O. J. Simpson (Football athlete) 7/9/1947

THE MINOR ARCANA ACE'S

The ACE'S (or One's) indicate the levels of consciousness at which you operate. They are also your four basic skills and the four areas into which you can focus your energies. In order to truly focus your consciousness and energy, you must choose a direction. The Ace's represent that beginning point, the seed ideas, the recognition of opportunity offered you by the hand of Spirit pictured on each card. They also represent a progression that is necessary for any new project to get off the ground. At any point, if one of the Ace energies is weak, the project may fail and have to begin anew.

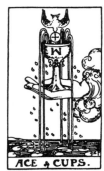

The ACE OF WANDS represents inspired consciousness. With it, you can grasp opportunity firmly. Like a lighted brand or brilliant idea, it blazes forth with energy and the light of enthusiasm. You warm to the task. You have the spirit to begin and want your ideas to grow and prosper. This Ace gives you the first impulse and the passionate will to begin.

The ACE OF CUPS represents love consciousness. With it, you open yourself to your feelings and acknowledge your resistances. You must be receptive to all the hopes and doubts that arise when you pursue any goal. Do you feel an inner connectedness with this project and a willingness to nurture it along? If not, it will lack meaning and be discarded once your initial enthusiasm wears off. The abundance pouring over the edge of the cup represents your ardor for your idea, which gives it the sustenance it needs to grow. With this Ace, your emotional acceptance is required for any project to develop and flourish.

The ACE OF SWORDS represents reasoning (focused) consciousness. With it, you can analyze what needs to be done, using logic and discrimination to take the necessary steps. You judge the pros and cons of various methods and research and synthesize the information you need. The sword symbolizes cutting through unnecessary details and keeping focused on the point. With this Ace, you first dare to develop the idea systematically.

The ACE OF PENTACLES represents crystallizing consciousness. It provides you with the stability and skills to get results. You stubbornly keep at it because you want to see the final form, to experience the fruits of your labor. The hand holds the product of your efforts, which is actually the seed of a new project. With this Ace, you silently visualize your hoped-for results and decide how to use them in a new way.

THE MINOR ARCANA TEN'S

The TEN'S are the end of any cycle and the beginning of the next cycle. They remind us that all One's (Ace's) are really the result of a previous process. It is in contemplating the Ten's that we get the image of the Ouroboros—the snake with its tail in its mouth—and realize that life is a continuous process. So like The Wheel of Fortune, Ten's mark a transition and bring change. Usually the change is helped or hindered by the kind of conditions shown on each of the suit cards. Ten's represent the result of all we have completed through the Nine's. They also represent the logical result of following through with the energies of each suit.

For those people in the Constellation of the Magician, Ten's are gifts or challenges to your communication and individuation process.

The TEN OF WANDS indicates that your creativity is blocked when you take on too many responsibilities. Dynamic change will seem impossible if you are burdened by too great a load or too many activities. You don't have time for yourself when you take on other people's cares and projects. Your vision can be blocked by immediate concerns and day-to-day drudgery.

On the other hand, the Ten of Wands shows the importance of developing a sense of responsibility. When you fulfill your obligations and agreements, you develop the maturity essential to all social relationships; you develop faith in yourself and your ability to accomplish your goals.

The TEN OF CUPS indicates that you have the gift of bringing light and good cheer to those around you. Your family and relations are important to you, and without them you don't feel whole. You need other people with whom to communicate your inspirations and ideas, and their reactions matter to you. Even though individuality is your main characteristic, you need a highly social environment in which to express it. This is what prosperity means to you.

As a challenge, the Ten of Cups can indicate "pie-in-the-sky" fantasies and unrealistic dreams. The rainbow represents the promise, but the actuality has to be worked for. Still, your dreams of social harmony and global coexistence, or more personal hopes for a happy family, must first be clearly envisioned before they can be realized.

The TEN OF SWORDS indicates that you feel most blocked when you think your friends are against you. The image is that of being stabbed in the back. This can be deadly to your sense of self-worth.

One of your greatest challenges is to know when to give up—when to turn away from ungrateful friends or abandon a futile project. It is like a nightmare in which "something" is chasing you but you can't run; as with a severed spinal cord, you are paralyzed and can't move. You may need to quit trying, to stop fighting a losing battle. Once you surrender you'll find that a change occurs; there's a release and you can run, or you discover that the monster isn't so bad after all. It's the "down-so-low-the-only-way-is-up" card. The black clouds are lifting and a new day is beginning.

As a gift, the Ten of Swords indicates that you are able to examine things from every angle and are very thorough in trying to pin down all aspects of a situation. You stretch yourself in your search for knowledge, and with diligence you will develop wisdom.

The TEN OF PENTACLES indicates that you can use the wealth of your resources and talents to build lasting structures in the world. You are challenged to make this a better place to live in and to leave something solid and tangible behind you. You are also challenged to support with your gifts those traditions that are meaningful to you. Like the Ten of Cups, this card indicates that you gain valuable support from your friends, relations, and heritage. Most people with The Wheel of Fortune as one of their Lifetime Cards are never penniless, as this picture affirms.

The magical signs on the robe of the old man, the wand leaning against the arch, and the cabalistic (Tree of Life) placement of the ten pentacles are indicators that this is, in reality, a card of magic. The old man is The Magician, now an ancient wizard after having gone through the experiences of life. Although you leave to those who come after what knowledge you can, in your wisdom you realize that each new child must repeat the journey.

FROM THE MORGAN-GREER TAROT

In this constellation, the hoped-for result of balanced judgment is Truth; its method is Intuition. All the cards in this group exhibit some sort of bipolar or paired image. The pictures demonstrate how such pairs can relate to each other—whether they parallel, oppose, intertwine, cross, blend, or are juggled. They mirror and repeat each other and thus create rhythm.

CHAPTER FIVE

THE CONSTELLATION OF THE HIGH PRIESTESS: 20–11–2

JUDGEMENT (20)   JUSTICE (11)   THE HIGH PRIESTESS (2)

2 OF WANDS   2 OF CUPS   2 OF SWORDS   2 OF PENTACLES

THE PRINCIPLE OF BALANCED JUDGMENT THROUGH INTUITIVE AWARENESS

THE HIGH PRIESTESS   JUSTICE/ADJUSTMENT   JUDGEMENT/AEON
Moon   *Libra*   *Pluto*
Personal Knowledge   Social Wisdom   Cosmic Understanding
Inner Truth   Social/Public Truth   Spiritual Truth

Keywords: Intuition. Self-Sufficiency. Self-Trust. Independence. Duality. Self and Other. Choice. Analysis. Struggle. Division. Reflection. Counterpoise or Contraposition. Equilibrium. Adjustment.

If you are a Single 2 (2–2), read:

>   THE HIGH PRIESTESS (2) AS PERSONALITY OR SOUL CARD
>   JUSTICE (11) AS HIDDEN FACTOR
>   JUDGEMENT (20) AS HIDDEN FACTOR
>   FAMOUS SINGLE 2'S
>   THE MINOR ARCANA TWO'S

If you are an 11–2, read:

>   THE HIGH PRIESTESS (2) AS PERSONALITY OR SOUL CARD
>   JUSTICE (11) AS PERSONALITY CARD
>   JUDGEMENT (20) AS HIDDEN FACTOR
>   FAMOUS 11–2'S
>   THE MINOR ARCANA TWO'S

If you are a 20–2, read:

>   THE HIGH PRIESTESS (2) AS PERSONALITY OR SOUL CARD
>   JUDGEMENT (20) AS PERSONALITY CARD
>   JUSTICE (11) AS HIDDEN FACTOR
>   FAMOUS 20–2'S
>   THE MINOR ARCANA TWO'S

THE HIGH PRIESTESS (2) AS PERSONALITY OR SOUL CARD

(This applies if you are a Single 2, 11–2, or 20–11–2.)

Personal Knowledge, Inner Truth

The HIGH PRIESTESS represents the inner mind, intuition, independence and self-sufficiency. As a card astrologically relating to the Moon, she represents its waxing and waning phases and the ebb and flow of the tides. She mirrors our present circumstances as reflections of previous events and memories, coded in symbols and projected to us (as on the veil behind her) through our dreams and feelings. Although she is also referred to as the Virgin Priestess, we must go back to the original significance of the word ''virgin'' to find that it means ''whole unto herself'' or ''not belonging to any man.'' She was a priestess dedicated to the Goddess, keeper of the knowledge of the mysteries of birth and death, of our past and future lives, and of our purpose in this lifetime. M. Esther Harding, in *Women's Mysteries*, virtually describes The High Priestess in this passage:

> The woman who is virgin, one-in-herself, does what she does—not because of any desire to please, not to be liked, or to be approved, even by herself; not because of any desire to gain power over another . . . but because what she does is true.[1]

As the second card of the tarot trumps, following the concept of the unity of self, she represents your realization of ''the other,'' of duality. She is like the infant who begins to realize that everything is not a part of itself, that it is separate from its mother. And so, as the interplay of the palms and the pomegranates (significators of sexuality and fertility) indicates, this card also represents the apparent duality of self and other, male and female, dark and light, etc.

As a High Priestess, you make choices intuitively and change them often. This is not because you are fickle, but because you recognize that circumstances are always changing, that energy ebbs and flows. You move with an inner rhythm that you have come to rely on and that cannot be hurried. Your ability to be calm is soothing to others, who often find themselves drawn to your serene demeanor. Other people talk freely to you about themselves and their worries because you are a good listener; you seem to know their innermost thoughts. In your nonjudgmental acceptance, they see their ideas and feelings mirrored back to them.

You are empathic and psychic, aware of the subtle undercurrents in a situation. You often experience something in your body before you know it in your mind. Being receptive to these impressions can create rapid mood changes. Often you experience other people's feelings as well as your own. The Justice card can help you separate your energies from those of others.

Being near water is essential to your mental and physical well-being. If nothing else, a warm bath with salt and soda in it will help clear your energy field. Your power is of water and the moon: cool, dark, and fluid. It needs to be contained.

Feminine qualities are highly developed, and women friends, mentors, and teachers are very important to High Priestesses. Since men often feel the need to repress this side of themselves, they may project their inner High Priestess qualities onto someone else. Therefore men with a High Priestess Soul Card have highly developed *animas*—inner images of the feminine—that they are always looking for in their outer world. The problem is that no real woman can live up to the perfection of this ideal image.

You are independent and self-sufficient. Solitude is important to you as an opportunity to reconnect with your spiritual source. You don't often reveal your true feelings and therefore attract others who find you mysterious and wise. Your feelings and emotions motivate you. Your mind compares and associates current situations with remembered ones from the past; your responses are strongly emotional.

If you have repressed your intuitive and psychic experiences, you may be skeptical of metaphysical beliefs—so much so that Shakespeare's line, ''The Lady doth protest too much,'' comes to mind. You will then find it hard to trust your intuitive feelings and attempt to justify everything you do with ''reason.''

Your dreams can be very important to you—write them down. They are an excellent means for accessing your intuition and getting advice from your inner self. By looking into your deep unconscious, you can come to know yourself.

The problematic side of The High Priestess comes from her essentially paradoxical nature. You can be pleasantly intriguing, or become involved in intrigue and lies. You can be flexible or fickle. You can be distrustful of logic, affecting disdain for it; or just the opposite, distrustful of intuition, creating a facade of logic and sophistry. You can pride yourself on your emotional sensitivity, or keep coolly distant from anything that affects your inner peace.

If you are a Single 2, with The High Priestess as both your Personality and Soul Cards, then both Justice and Judgement are your Hidden Factor Cards; read the descriptions of these cards next.

FAMOUS SINGLE 2'S

I know of no famous people who are Single 2's, because they only began being born again on December 31, 1957 (after a gap of 900 years). These people are of special interest because they have the potential to help our species connect with the deep currents of our collective unconscious. (See Chapter Thirteen for a discussion of ''The Age of The High Priestess.'') It is their task to help us with our dilemma of whether to hold to our present ways and possibly destroy ourselves, or to evaluate and change our ways in order to create awareness of our planetary kinship.

JUSTICE (11) AS PERSONALITY CARD

(This applies if you are an 11–2.)

Social Wisdom, Social/Public Truth

JUSTICE represents our social and cultural laws, which we create to maintain order and to compensate those who have been injured. The figure represents such goddesses of truth as Maat in Egypt and Themis and Athena in Greece, who seek to maintain the balance of nature and rhythm of life. Outer laws must accord with our inner nature to be just.

This card indicates that you believe it important to adjust yourself to others. You take responsibility for the way your judgments and decisions affect both yourself and others. You are aware that every action necessitates a reaction for which you must be responsible, so you look ahead to see the potential results of your impulses and actions. Or you look back to see what you did to warrant a specific result.

As a Personality Card, Justice refers to the need to be true to yourself, for neither justice nor mercy are possible without self-honesty. You learn through your mistakes by carefully evaluating the people, situations, and beliefs you trust. When these no longer have validity, nor bring appropriate results, you are able to sever your connections and free yourself from outmoded dependencies. With your sword you sacrifice the illusions, pretensions, and dreams that are in error. But you will strongly defend those ideas that represent to you the basic truths of existence. At the extreme, as Sallie Nichols points out in *Jung and Tarot*, you can get so caught up in wanting everything to be fair that you spend all your time "in court," or berating the system rather than working on yourself.

Your logical way of looking at the world means that you pay close attention to the law of cause and effect and prefer to rely on deductive thinking. Yet with The High Priestess as a Soul Card (note the two pillars appearing in both cards), you must learn to use both logic and intuition to balance your judgments (symbolized by the pillars being blended to grey). The Justice card tells you to apply the wisdom of The High Priestess when acting in the world.

You expect to pay for your transgressions, as well as benefit from your good deeds. When making decisions, you weigh all the pros and cons carefully (as in a set of scales) to be sure that balance is achieved. You seek harmony and stability by observing the rules. Be mindful that it is only through an awareness of the pain of chaos that equilibrium can be appreciated.

You make the most of memories, weighing and balancing them to achieve inner harmony. For this reason, many famous 11–2's are connected to children. They explore the relationship of childhood experiences to psychological development, or use the sword/pen to write down (and seek the meaning in) the memories and feelings of youth.

As an 11–2 you strive to maintain an even keel when buffeted by emotional tensions and unexpressed feelings. You might find writing to be a good outlet for those feelings and for your concerns about justice.

JUDGEMENT (20) AS HIDDEN FACTOR

(This applies if you are Single 2 or an 11–2.)

JUDGEMENT as your hidden factor indicates that change and transformation are essential but difficult. You feel the weight of order and authority judging you. You can be very critical of others, as well as yourself. You'd like to be in control, yet you see others as more powerful than you and perhaps feel yourself only able to react, and not initiate action. You may seek to obtain power in a situation by passive resistance.

You can learn from this teacher that *you* are the initiator of your own change and development; you are responsible for yourself. Trying to hold on passively only makes the change more difficult. Changes you originally felt to be destructive you can eventually see as liberating. You work to assuage fears and right injustices through the exposure of the truths that were formerly hidden or unacknowledged, especially those fears and injustices that you yourself once experienced.

In learning to take responsibility for transforming your life, the acceptance of your personal power opens new vistas of possibility. You eventually awaken to the social and/or spiritual significance behind individual and often isolated incidents.

FAMOUS 11–2'S

In this small group of 11–2's you'll find several people who have physically defended basic ideas of truth and freedom: Davy Crockett, Lord Byron, and Benjamin Spock. Crockett said in his autobiography, "I leave this rule for others when I'm dead, Be always sure you're right—then go ahead." Byron is known for the line, "Truth is always strange—stranger than fiction" (from *Don Juan*, XIV). The remainder of the people in this list studied early child development professionally or wrote children's books.

Davy Crockett (Frontiersman) 8/17/1786
Lord Byron (English poet and adventurer) 1/22/1788
Hans Christian Andersen (Danish writer of fairytales) 4/2/1805
Beatrix Potter (English children's author, illustrator) 7/28/1866
Llewellyn George (Astrologer) 8/17/1876
A. A. Milne (English children's author) 1/18/1882
Karen Horney (English psychologist) 9/16/1885
Anna Freud (Austrian psychologist) 12/3/1895
Benjamin Spock (Pediatrician and peace activist) 5/2/1903

JUDGEMENT (20) AS PERSONALITY CARD

(This applies if you are a 20-2.)

Cosmic Understanding, Spiritual Truth

JUDGEMENT represents resurrection or "awakening" in all the various forms of this card. In the Waite deck and most other decks, Judgement shows the resurrection of the dead from their coffins while an apocalyptic angel sounds the trumpet of life. In Crowley's Thoth deck, the corresponding Aeon card shows Isis (called "Giver of Life") with Osiris ("God of Death"), reminding us of how Isis found Osiris in a floating coffin on the waters of the Nile and brought him back to life. To complete the symbolism, Crowley's Justice card represents the Goddess Maat, who showed Isis the way to Osiris.

As a 20-2 you are aware that although the past has made you who you are, you can transcend those limitations. You will have many such awakenings in your life: jolts or "epiphanies" in which you suddenly recognize a purpose behind the events.

This is the card of synchronicities—that is, events that seem like "coincidences" but may have strong personal significance. The meaning is always there, only most of the time we don't bother to look. With Judgement as your Personality Card you will find that these synchronicities call attention to points of decision when your path branches in several directions.

20-2's seek to transform and take control of things around them. You are similar to the Plutonian people described by Robert Hand in his book, *Horoscope Symbols*: "They embody the forces of death and resurrection inherent in society . . . [taking] advantage of energies stirring within the culture." You are often involved directly in your generation's struggle for consciousness and identity. You see yourself embodying values that need to be brought into the world and shared.

20-2's can be healers, therapists, and those who teach techniques of self-transformation, or gurus and religious leaders who stress the roles of death and rebirth. You have an intuitive insight into the mass unconscious of your time, but especially your generation.

This card represents the process of perfecting yourself and therefore the necessity of leaving behind anything gross or imperfect that can hold you back. Like 20-2 Thomas Paine, you believe in going all the way: "Moderation in principle is always a vice."

The lesson you must learn is to use your personal power and influence on others, not for personal ends but to assist them in their own transformations. 20-2's have the potential to communicate with all parts of themselves, as shown by the three figures usually pictured rising from the coffins. In Transactional Analysis, for instance, they would represent the Parent, the Adult, and the Child; in Jungian terms, the Self, the Shadow, and the Ego. As a 20-2 you can help transform others with your understanding and vision. Most often you keep your visions quietly to yourself, affecting others through the integrity of your actions. You are socially oriented and good at bringing people together.

You can be a valued friend and loyal partner, while maintaining a strong sense of your own independence and self-worth.

With your strong Pluto-Moon relationship you are highly psychic, but because our culture does not value psychic development, you may deny this aspect of yourself and determinedly focus on the rational qualities of Justice, which is your hidden factor. (By hidden, in this case, I mean connected with repressed aspects of the unconscious and possibly liable to eruptions of inappropriate behavior.) Males in our culture tend to have problems acknowledging their intuitive feelings. If you do, your avowed rationality may be an illusion. Many 20–2's have heard an inner call, responding to an intuitive vision of what a harmonious world could be like.

JUSTICE (11) AS HIDDEN FACTOR

(This applies if you are a Single 2 or a 20–2.)

JUSTICE most often appears as a Hidden Factor Card. It indicates that you must learn to accept responsibilities when called to do so. You have a highly developed sense of personal right and wrong and can be overcritical of both self and others. Your judgments can separate you from others and destroy friendships. Paradoxically, you are very sensitive to criticism, even when unintentional.

You consider all sides of an issue or conflict, weighing the pros and cons carefully before acting. You feel it is important to be logical, even if inappropriate to the situation. In your desire to be fair you may rely on the "facts" alone, without acknowledging extenuating circumstances. Remember that most judgments are actually a matter of intuition. Reasons come afterward. Justice indicates that your actions depend on understanding the past as remembered by your inner High Priestess and using her intuitive knowledge in a practical way. Memories are your most instructive resources. Communication between your conscious and unconscious selves leads you to equilibrium.

Since your Hidden Factor Card is ultimately your teacher, you will find that by adjusting to circumstances and acknowledging the results, you can develop wisdom. By taking responsibility for your actions, you develop mercy, and by accepting that each person's values and needs are as valid as yours, you develop compassion. You must face the imbalances in your life and evaluate which side is true to your own nature. Only you can judge which memories to foster and which to deny, which actions to honor and which to castigate, which beliefs to uphold and which to cast down. Thus you can control the balance; it is your fate.

FAMOUS 20–2'S

You'll find people in this list who answered a call to devote themselves to establishing world harmony. There are many human-rights workers like Thomas Paine, Elizabeth Cady Stanton, Rosa Parks, and Julian Bond. And several famous psychics: Peter Hurkos, Sybil Leek, Marcia Moore, as well as two creators of feminist tarot decks. Also many imaginative romantics: Mozart, Poe,

Jules Verne, Graves—people who were able to actualize their inner visions. And there are renowned public figures with sensitivity to the group unconscious who provided the images needed by the masses, but not always the substance.

Elizabeth I (Queen of England) 9/17/1533
Thomas Paine (Writer on human rights) 2/9/1737
Wolfgang Mozart (Austrian composer) 1/27/1756
Edgar A. Poe (Author of mysteries and supernatural stories) 1/19/1809
Elizabeth Cady Stanton (Feminist) 11/12/1815
Jules Verne (Science-Fiction writer) 2/8/1828
Ramakrishna (Hindu mystic) 2/18/1836
Nikolai Rimsky-Korsakov (Russian composer) 3/18/1844
Claude Debussy (French composer) 8/22/1862
Frank Lloyd Wright (Architect) 6/8/1869
Robert Graves (Poet, author) 7/26/1895
Bob Hope (Comedian) 5/29/1903
L. I. Brezhnev (Russian leader) 12/19/1906
Mircea Eliade (Cross-cultural religious scholar) 3/9/1907
Katharine Hepburn (Actress) 11/8/1909
Ronald Reagan (U.S. President) 2/6/1911
Peter Hurkos (Psychic) 5/21/1911
Rosa Parks (Civil-rights activist) 2/4/1913
Edith Piaf (French cabaret singer) 12/19/1915
David Brinkley (TV journalist) 7/10/1920
John Glenn, Jr. (Astronaut and politician) 7/18/1921
Sybil Leek (Psychic and witch) 2/22/1922
Norman Mailer (Writer) 1/31/1923
Henry Kissinger (Political advisor) 5/27/1923
Gore Vidal (Writer) 10/3/1925
Art Buchwald (Newspaper columnist) 10/20/1925
Richard Burton (Actor) 11/10/1925
Eartha Kitt (Singer) 1/26/1928
Marcia Moore (Astrologer and psychic) 5/22/1928
Maya Angelou (Autobiographer) 4/4/1929
Jackie Kennedy Onassis (President's wife, society figure) 7/28/1929
Truman Capote (Writer) 9/30/1934
Julie Andrews (Singer and actress) 10/1/1935
Jim Brown (Athlete and actor) 2/17/1936
Lily Tomlin (Comedian) 9/1/1936
José Argüelles (New Age writer) 1/24/1939
Peter Fonda (Actor) 2/23/1939
Julian Bond (Civil-rights activist and politician) 1/14/1940
Paul Simon (Singer, songwriter) 10/13/1941
Ffiona Morgan (Creator, Daughters of the Moon Tarot) 11/21/1941
Bobby Fischer (Chess champion) 3/9/1943
Vicki Noble (Co-creator, Motherpeace Tarot) 4/13/1947
Jim Plunkett (Football athlete) 12/5/1947
Charles (Prince of Wales) 11/14/1948
John Travolta (Actor) 1/18/1954

THE MINOR ARCANA TWO'S

The TWO'S represent your lessons and opportunities, your gifts and whatever blocks you from expressing the highest qualities of The High Priestess.

When dealing with any aspect of the Constellation of The High Priestess, we are usually faced with a decision. The minor arcana cards show how we might handle that choice-making process: blending together (Cups), choosing one over the other (Wands), indecision (Swords), or choosing them both (Pentacles).

Angeles Arrien uses the Two's to represent types of intuition: Swords are telepathic, Cups are empathic, Wands are perceptual, and Pentacles are kinesthetic.

The TWO OF WANDS indicates that when you are in charge you are comfortable making decisions and will stand by them. Although you may not be able to give logical reasons for your decisions, you feel confident enough to act on them. You seldom turn to someone else for direction, preferring to do things in your own way and taking responsibility for the outcome.

You need equilibrium between mind and body, so you don't act until you need to. This self-discipline, combined with your intuition, can bring success to your enterprises. Boredom—lack of a new direction or stimulus—is your greatest problem here. Your faults include thinking that only you have the answers.

The TWO OF CUPS indicates that you are a compassionate and caring person. You understand the healing powers of love and the importance of relating with others. The two entwined snakes and the strange red-winged lion head suggest a spiritual dimension to your passion and a passionate drive toward spiritual expression. Acceptance of your own inner masculine or feminine self (the opposite of your actual gender) is one of your primary tasks.

This card shows that your conscious and subconscious dimensions can work together and that seeming oppositions can be reconciled. Your faults can include becoming oversentimental and empathizing with others so strongly that you forget whose feelings are whose. Quell your urge to comfort and heal everyone you come in contact with.

The TWO OF SWORDS indicates that in your desire to be a peacemaker, you can be reluctant to express an opinion unless forced to. Wanting order and stability can lead you to blind conformity and rigidity. Although you seek to maintain calm through balanced rationality, it also makes you deny your intuitions. When you are uncertain of your objectives, you procrastinate. Conflicts between your own opinions and those of others can cause stalemates and indecision.

When you are unable to see your options, rationality (Swords) is of no help. Don't try to force things to happen prematurely. By listening to the swell of your emotions, you will know when the tide turns and it is time to act.

The TWO OF PENTACLES represents your ability to handle two or more situations at once. Travel and change can regenerate you, but too much makes you feel restless and unstable. Being near water is very healing for all Two's, as is time out for recreation. Take time to remember your childhood and let yourself play. Being flexible and venturesome provides scope for your intuition.

You are adaptable and easy-going with friends and associates, but in danger of being easily influenced by individuals or mass opinion. When you feel that life is pushing you around, and you don't know where you're going, look around for synchronicities; you may discover a deeper meaning to your experience and find new direction.

NOTE

1. Esther Harding, *Women's Mysteries: Ancient and Modern* (New York: Harper Colophon, 1971), p. 125.

FROM THE MOTHERPEACE TAROT

This constellation demonstrates that creativity means combining elements in such a way that they are more than just the sum of their parts—as with love, a jump is made that transcends the simple physical properties of the components to become something else altogether. Love supplies the urge for union which brings the parts together, while the imagination takes the leap into new realms of possibility.

CHAPTER SIX

THE CONSTELLATION OF THE EMPRESS: 21–12–3

THE WORLD (21)   THE HANGED MAN (12)   THE EMPRESS (3)

6 OF WANDS   6 OF CUPS   6 OF SWORDS   6 OF PENTACLES

THE PRINCIPLE OF LOVE AND CREATIVE IMAGINATION

THE EMPRESS	THE HANGED MAN	THE WORLD
Venus	*Neptune*	*Saturn*
Personal Love	Unconditional Love	Universal Love
Giving Birth to Body	Giving Birth to Soul	Giving Birth to Spirit

Keywords: Creativity. Nurturance. Sacrifice. Surrender. Form. Relatedness. Fertility. Limitation. Imagination.

If you are a Single 3 (3–3), read:

> THE EMPRESS (3) AS PERSONALITY OR SOUL CARD
> THE HANGED MAN (12) AS HIDDEN FACTOR
> THE WORLD (21) AS HIDDEN FACTOR
> FAMOUS SINGLE 3'S
> THE MINOR ARCANA THREE'S

If you are a 12–3, read:

> THE EMPRESS (3) AS PERSONALITY OR SOUL CARD
> THE HANGED MAN (12) AS PERSONALITY CARD
> THE WORLD (21) AS HIDDEN FACTOR
> FAMOUS 12–3'S
> THE MINOR ARCANA THREE'S

If you are a 21–3, read:

> THE EMPRESS (3) AS PERSONALITY OR SOUL CARD
> THE WORLD (21) AS PERSONALITY CARD
> THE HANGED MAN (12) AS HIDDEN FACTOR
> FAMOUS 21–3'S
> THE MINOR ARCANA THREE'S

THE EMPRESS (3) AS PERSONALITY OR SOUL CARD

(This applies if you are a Single 3, 12–3, or 21–3.)

Personal Love, Giving Birth to Body

THE EMPRESS is related to the goddesses Demeter and Ceres—bountiful, fertile, growth-producing. She represents the union of the first two cards in the major arcana, The Magician and The High Priestess. Their combination is The Empress, shown pregnant with a totally new being, that is, something more than the sum of the parts. As a card relating to Venus, she signifies love and beauty. She is the feminine energy that provides a nurturing environment for the growth and well-being of those around her. She is the archetypal Earth Mother and seeks to connect all opposites, to banish disharmony.

With The Empress as your Personality or Soul Card, your sense of aesthetics, harmony, and balance is innate. You recognize and enjoy beauty in all its forms. Thus you will be drawn to hobbies or jobs that let you express these talents. You can be fertile with creative ideas, yet you may lack the discipline necessary to give them practical form, or the aggression necessary to market them. Your power comes from love, and you rule through understanding the needs of others.

You thrive in comfortable surroundings, finding ugliness distasteful, and from your point of view, unnecessary. Food is a possible metaphor for the expression and fulfillment of your qualities—growing it in gardens, aesthetically preparing it, and nurturing others with it. But because you enjoy the delights of a well-prepared meal so much, watch your weight.

Mothering is another central issue for you. You may have close ties with your own mother; she was probably the more significant parent in the formation of your basic character. Whether you are a man or woman, you want to "mother," to take care of others. If this is not expressed through actual child-bearing or child-rearing, then you will project that instinct onto other people and interests in your life.

You have a deep regard for the relatedness of all things. You experience this as a feeling of allegiance with the earth, with Spirit, your country, your group, your work, or with individuals. Although you can be very regal and commanding, you feel you can sway others best through love. Your primary task is to make connections. Through your creative imagination you find new solutions that bring people and things together.

You have a strong sense of reality, functioning primarily through your physical senses. You like to touch and handle situations directly. You like to know where your food and clothes come from, for instance, to assure that they are healthy or well-made.

Negatively, you fear letting go of those you feel connected to. You can be smothering and even devouring in your care. Jealousy and vindictiveness are among your less pleasing traits, but these come from a need to preserve your home and loved ones, or from not wanting to entrust them to another's care. You feel devalued when you are not "needed."

If you are a Single 3 (that is, with The Empress as both your Personality and Soul Card), then both The Hanged Man and The World are your Hidden Factor Cards. Read descriptions of these cards next. They are found later in this chapter.

FAMOUS SINGLE 3'S

Since there have been no Single 3's for the last several hundred years until their recent appearance, beginning January 31, 1958, I have only one famous person on my list.

Brooke Shields (Model, actress) 5/31/1965

THE HANGED MAN (12) AS PERSONALITY CARD

(This applies if you are a 12–3.)

Unconditional Love, Giving Birth to Soul

Since the end of the 19th century, THE HANGED MAN has appeared most frequently as a Hidden Factor Card. There will now be more and more young people born with The Hanged Man as a Personality Card during the next two generations.

As a 12–3 you can devote yourself so completely to your work, art, or cause that you become oblivious to yourself. Hanged Man personalities can merge totally with their calling. When you sacrifice yourself with confident abandon to the requirements of your chosen path, you unify with its spirit. You give without thought of receiving. Others may feel you have lost your mind; you seem to have given up common sense, but you are only seeing something that escapes others, and with this vision you can accomplish wonders.

You might do things diametrically opposed to other people and thus find yourself in conflict with the world (as indicated by The World card being your hidden factor). Your actions may be misunderstood and misinterpreted. The Hanged Man corresponds to Neptune, sensitizing you to the wrongs of the world and the injustices done to humankind. However, you express your realizations in ways that may seem extremist and disorganized.

You must learn to give up all expectations and sidestep the rules. Even during periods of enforced inactivity when nothing seems to be happening, try to understand that vital growth is taking place within. Accept your circumstances with humility and you will discover new possibilities. Your interludes of loneliness and helplessness allow you to value love and relationships.

Ironically, 12–3's find their inspiration in the depths of helplessness. Realization of your own powerlessness actually spurs you to action. When you are truly bereft, you finally must turn to some greater power and allow it to work through you.

You experience time subjectively, depending on whether you are totally involved in what you do or just hanging around waiting for something to happen.

The Hanged Man as number 12 symbolizes both the clock (hours) and the year (months). You realize you are fated to obey not your own will, but the impersonal dictates of time.

This is the card of the mystic, the shaman, the dreamer. 12–3's see things that are not of this world. You gather in the impressions of your imagination and surrender to your vision. You can act for others by uniquely expressing through your own life the inner needs and dilemmas of the masses. By describing what you see through writing, film or paintings, or through some other creative medium, you give others a new perspective on their own experience.

Taken to the extreme, 12–3's can totally sacrifice themselves for their loved ones or a beloved cause. They may blind themselves to the imperfections of others, or feel incapable of withdrawing from a difficult situation. Sometimes this leads to imprisonment, or bondage to a person, lifestyle, or ideal. Thus, 12–3's need to be wary of whatever fascinates them.

THE WORLD (21) AS HIDDEN FACTOR

(This applies if you are a Single 3 or a 12–3.)

THE WORLD as your Hidden Factor Card indicates that you fear restriction of any kind. Form and structure tend to limit you, and you deliberately try to escape from them. Time, as a kind of form, is an enemy holding you back; later in life, as The World becomes your Teacher Card, you learn that time can be used with grace and precision.

You fear your life being out of control. You want to ''dance'' freely but are somehow restricted from doing so, and thus freedom becomes a major issue. You feel incomplete in yourself, and a sense of wholeness eludes you in the physical world. It is only through transcendent mystical experience, or the immersion of yourself in your work, that you find a sense of wholeness.

The wreath encircling the dancer in The World card represents containment of energies to prevent their dissipation. With The World as your hidden factor, a lack of boundaries is dangerous: it leads to confusion, such as that experienced by undisciplined mystics or psychics who cannot tell whether their images and emotions are their own or another's. 12–3's may have trouble with their identity, although struggling with this ''problem'' helps formulate a strong and unconventional sense of self.

FAMOUS 12–3'S

Each person on my short list of 12–3's below represents a variation of the description above. Dali's surrealist paintings depict his dreams with bizarre images and wild techniques—one of his most famous, ''Persistence of Memory,'' deals with time in the form of melting clocks. He was also fascinated by religious subjects, especially by the crucifixion theme. Nat Turner was a deeply religious natural preacher who believed himself divinely appointed to lead his fellow slaves to freedom. Alfred Hitchcock was known for his suspense movies (in which everyone is suspended, hanging onto their seats). Alice Bailey was a mystic and psychic channel. Colette often wrote with nostalgia of her mother and delicately observed the little things that others rarely notice. Charles Dickens felt the sorrows and imprisonment of his fellow beings strongly and through his imagination let others experience them too. The childless Emma Goldman was selflessly dedicated to her cause of anarchy and overturning the power structure, yet was known to close friends as ''Mommy.'' Eva Braun is a classic example of a tragic 12-3, a helpless dreamer and captive of cheap novels and trashy films. Hitler's chauffeur said, ''She spent most of her life waiting for Hitler.''

Nat Turner (Slave leader) 10/2/1800
Charles Dickens (English writer) 2/7/1812
Alice Bailey (Metaphysician) 6/16/1880
Colette (French writer) 1/28/1873
Emma Goldman (Anarchist) 6/27/1869
Eva Braun (Hitler's mistress) 2/6/1912
Salvador Dali (Spanish artist) 5/11/1904
Alfred Hitchcock (Film director) 8/13/1899

THE WORLD (21) AS PERSONALITY CARD

(This applies to 21-3's.)

Universal Love, Giving Birth to Spirit

THE WORLD card literally indicates your strong connections to the earth. Nature thus gives you a profound love of beauty and sensitive aesthetic appreciation.

THE WORLD.

As a Personality Card, The World indicates that you must learn to work within structure. The card shows a woman suspended in air, a braided wreath forming a ring around her—I call this learning to dance on your limitations. As the card is associated with Saturn (known as the Great Liberator), the wreath can be seen as the boundary of the personality, which manifests as the structures we live within. Many of those structures, such as genetic inheritance and our language and culture, we cannot change. Nevertheless, these frameworks do not limit our experience of freedom; they only channel it. In like manner, you find that your need to develop your potential self-expression, although circumscribed by your society, is not necessarily limited by it.

You learn to know the medium that you work with so well that it does not hamper your creativity. For instance, as a musician you learn the notes, scales, and fingering of your instrument in order to be able to create and improvise with complete freedom. The same with painting—you must know the possibilities and limitations of your brush, colors, and surface before you are free to create with them.

21-3's need to establish personal discipline if they wish to accomplish something. Only in this way can you use your penchant for being drawn to many different areas of endeavor to become a well-rounded individual. Remember that discipline, combined with what 21-3 John Wayne called his ''favorite four-letter words: hard work,'' gives you the basic tools with which to express your creative imagination and give it form.

The figures in the corners of the card represent the four fixed signs of the zodiac: Scorpio (eagle), Aquarius (angel), Taurus (bull), and Leo (lion), and also symbolize the four directions, four winds, four seasons, etc. They represent your ability to locate yourself in space and time. You synthesize the wholistic thinking of the intuitive with the four-square rationality of the scientific thinker. This synthesis can also be apparent in a career that combines two different aspects into a new expression.

Just as your Soul Card, The Empress, represents physical birth, so The World represents your ability to give birth to yourself and your ideas, in this world. The scarf flowing around the figure, which has been called both winding sheet and birthing sheet, conceals the dancer's hermaphroditic qualities, which are also indicated by the double-tipped wands and infinity signs on the wreath, like those of The Magician and Strength. Your ultimate creation, represented by this, the last trump, is your ability to integrate masculine and feminine characteristics within you, giving birth to the wholeness of being human.

21–3's tend to use wholistic thinking that enables them to sense the larger picture. This is also why you probably focus your "mothering instinct" on planetary or even cosmic issues. Because they focus on functioning within limitations, 21–3's stretch our concepts of what is humanly possible in all fields. Also, many 21–3's break through the previously accepted ideas of what is appropriate for their gender, such as Amelia Earhart and Indira Ghandi for women, or Bill Cosby for men (as a nurturer).

Since 21 is the last number in the major arcana (The Fool is an unnumbered "nought"), it is also a card of completion. In this case completion implies freeing yourself from inhibition and seeing things from a wholistic perspective. Once you conceive what is possible and see it in all of its dimensions, the process of actualization becomes automatic.

THE HANGED MAN (12) AS HIDDEN FACTOR

(This applies if you are a Single 3 or a 21–3.)

THE HANGED MAN represents self-sacrifice and submission of the self to higher ideals. For many people with an Empress need-to-mother, this represents the desire to hold onto someone; for instance, someone who talks about their sacrifices in order to receive recognition of love. You need to ask yourself, How and why am I being a martyr? One of your lessons to learn is humility.

If not already focused on family and children, you may devote yourself to an equal or greater cause. However, this devotion can be overwhelming, turning a normal life upside down and becoming greater than any personal relationship.

The Hanged Man literally represents your "hang-ups," things you try to hang on to, and whatever you are hung up on. You fear being alone and powerless. Yet it is often through bafflement and confusion that spiritual growth can take place. Mythologically, the figure on the card represents the son/lover of the Goddess, who is sacrificed yearly after impregnating Her. It is also the scapegoat, which was historically an actual goat on which was symbolically placed all the blame for old feuds, angers, and anything that went wrong during the year. When it was killed, all blame died with it, so that the community was cleansed and renewed and made sacred again. Some 21-3's seem to take on the woes of the world, or act out the myths and dreams of the masses. When such a role becomes too great to handle, you may turn to drugs, drink, or overwork to escape the pressure, which ultimately only intensifies the problems. These Neptunian qualities of The Hanged Man may also emerge in flights of fancy and imagination, or become lost in illusion.

In its teacher aspect, The Hanged Man shows you how to make noble and unconditional sacrifices. You will be forced to release your preconceptions, especially in Hanged Man Years. It is also the pattern breaker, turning upside down any habits that limit you from realizing your highest self.

FAMOUS 21-3'S

Among the 21-3's are several people whose lives express the fantasies and dreams of specific groups of people: Arthur Rimbaud represents for poets of past and present the extremes of passion for the Muse. Jack Kerouac followed in his footsteps, and both of them sought their release from reality through substance abuse. We have Neil Simon, whose plays examine the details of love in contemporary relationships. Bill Cosby is not afraid to be identified with children and food and thus has become an image of the male ability to nurture. The work of many of these people shows their ability to be highly disciplined and creative in several fields.

Johann Goethe (German poet and playwright) 8/28/1749
Victoria (Queen of England) 5/24/1819
Arthur Rimbaud (French poet) 10/20/1854
Evangeline Adams (Mother of American astrology) 2/28/1865
William B. Yeats (Irish poet and occultist) 6/13/1865
Harry Houdini (Magician) 4/6/1874
Amelia Earhart (Pilot and adventurer) 7/24/1898
F. Scott Fitzgerald (Novelist) 9/24/1898
Margaret Mead (Anthropologist) 12/16/1901
John Wayne (Actor) 5/26/1907
Wernher von Braun (German physicist) 3/23/1912
James Hoffa (Union leader) 2/14/1913
Indira Gandhi (Prime Minister of India) 11/19/1917
Judy Garland (Singer and actress) 6/10/1922
Jack Kerouac (Novelist) 3/12/1923
Phyllis Schlafly (Anti-feminist) 8/15/1924
Robert Kennedy (Politician) 11/20/1925
Miles Davis (Musician) 5/25/1926
Neil Simon (Playwright) 7/4/1927
Fats Domino (Musician) 2/26/1928
Anne Frank (Dutch diarist) 6/12/1929
Barbara Walters (TV journalist) 9/25/1931
Germaine Greer (Feminist) 1/29/1935

Carol Burnett (Comedian) 4/26/1935
Bill Cosby (Comedian) 7/12/1937
David Bowie (Singer and actor) 1/8/1947

THE MINOR ARCANA THREE'S

These are the gifts, challenges, and opportunities of the Principle of Love and Creative Imagination. They represent four aspects of the creative imagination and the tests of love.

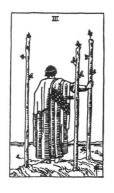

The THREE OF WANDS indicates that you have the ability to envision new possibilities, often long before they become actuality. Your mind is fertile and receptive to new things and foreign ideas. You travel farther in your mind than some people ever do in physical reality, and therefore have many unusual experiences—sometimes even astral traveling. You require a broad perspective and a sense of the entire terrain before you begin anything. You get excited by your vision and are able to communicate your enthusiasm to others. However, determining the specific steps necessary to actualize your creative ideas is difficult for you. Sometimes you remain too distant from where things are happening, with no conception of how to get down to work or put your ideas into action.

In love relationships this is the test of time and distance. You may already have a partner, yet still want the freedom to look around. It shows an ability to love more than one person at once. One of the dangers of the Three of Wands is that by always wanting something out of reach, you may fail to appreciate fully what is close at hand. Even with your need for free expression of your feelings, you are still steadfast and dependable. Like a mother waiting up for her children or watching over their lives from a distance, your love and care for the people in your life is strong.

The THREE OF CUPS indicates the gifts of friendship and hospitality. You are social and love a party as an opportunity to get together with others and celebrate your mutual accomplishments. You work well with other people and can bring out the best in them, so that they reveal aspects of themselves that they normally couldn't share. Your natural grace, rhythm, and harmony make you enjoyable to be around. Like the Muses, you inspire others with your belief in them and their capabilities.

As a challenge, this card can represent dissipation and overindulgence. As in the children's story in which the grasshopper is interested only in frolic, you may find bleak and difficult times when winter sets in. The lessons of discipline come hard but are essential. The Empress must learn to cultivate her garden or many potentials will be sacrificed to the wild growth of weeds.

The THREE OF SWORDS indicates the gift of sorrow. It is the ability to experience your emotions fully, even pain and heartbreak, so that you don't get blocked. It is the cleansing and purifying process of grief, through which you let your feelings wash over you and release any anguish that has built up. It says that even in the most loving of relationships there are times of conflict, hurt, and separation.

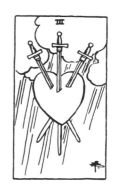

It also represents painful memories, usually of old hurts triggered by fears in current relationships. Jealousy, the ultimate block to love and creativity, is actually a mental (Swords) process in which you use your creativity to imagine the betrayals of a loved one, or to play back old scenes. You may either quietly bear your pain as a martyr or get hung up in your jealousy, whether based on reality or imagination. The card also shows how conflicting ideas may seem to cancel each other out, making you think all your heart's labor is for naught; your center is pierced. Often this stage of despair comes just before a major creative breakthrough.

Your opportunity with the Three of Swords is to express your melancholy feelings through some creative form. This deals with old patterns in a new way, releasing their constraining energy so that healing is possible.

The THREE OF PENTACLES indicates love of your work. It is a card of the craftsperson, and its gift is in working together with others. It shows the harmony that can result when you use your best skills in cooperation with other capable partners. This card also shows your ability to create and work out practical plans for any project. You are able to advance step by step when you recognize and value the role of each person in the endeavor, and you ground your vision in the practical world through physical effort. You have the discipline to work long and hard when you understand the overall plan; otherwise you get caught up in the drudgery of meaningless exertion, or hung up in the details. Stand back periodically to take a look at the whole and form a mental picture of the completed project.

The major challenge in this card is in thinking you can do everything. This leads to workaholism, which is just as devastating to love and creativity as any other excess, and you'll end up sacrificing many things for the sake of one. Your opportunity with the Three of Pentacles is to demonstrate and share your work with others, which satisifies your need for their feedback and approval. Whatever your vocation, you go farther with the active support and encouragement of those around you.

FROM THE HANSON-ROBERTS TAROT

This constellation features the characters of Fool and King found in ancient folktales from around the world that teach that wisdom does not always wear a fine robe and a white beard, and that rags and tatters will conceal knowledge and power from those who look no further than the surface. Whatever the King builds will eventually collapse, yet from the death of the old springs new life and continued existence.

CHAPTER SEVEN

THE CONSTELLATION OF
THE EMPEROR: 22–13–4

THE FOOL (22=0)		DEATH (13)		THE EMPEROR (4)
4 OF WANDS	4 OF CUPS	4 OF SWORDS		4 OF PENTACLES

THE PRINCIPLE OF LIFE FORCE AND REALIZATION
OF POWER

THE EMPEROR	DEATH	THE FOOL
Aries	*Scorpio*	*Uranus*
Realization of		
Paternal & Worldly Power	Life Power	Eternal Power
Physical Force	Vital Force	Spiritual Force
Generation	Release	Regeneration

Keywords: Completion and Transition. Establishing and Building. Releasing. Mortality and Immortality. Rites of Passage.

If you are a Single 4 (4–4), read:

> THE EMPEROR (4) AS PERSONALITY OR SOUL CARD
> DEATH (13) AS HIDDEN FACTOR
> THE FOOL (22) AS HIDDEN FACTOR
> FAMOUS SINGLE 4'S
> THE MINOR ARCANA FOUR'S

If you are a 13–4, read:

> THE EMPEROR (4) AS PERSONALITY OR SOUL CARD
> DEATH (13) AS PERSONALITY CARD
> THE FOOL (22) AS HIDDEN FACTOR
> FAMOUS 13–4'S
> THE MINOR ARCANA FOUR'S

If you are a 22–4, read:

> THE EMPEROR (4) AS PERSONALITY OR SOUL CARD
> THE FOOL (22) AS PERSONALITY CARD
> DEATH (13) AS HIDDEN FACTOR
> FAMOUS 22–4'S
> THE MINOR ARCANA FOUR'S

THE EMPEROR (4) AS PERSONALITY OR SOUL CARD

(This applies if you are a Single 4, 13–4, or 22–4.)

Realization of Paternal and Worldly Power, Physical Force, Generation

THE EMPEROR.

THE EMPEROR represents power that comes with establishing, building, and doing. As a card relating to Aries, you are at the forefront of new projects and activities, but as a 4, you demand that structure and order be found in them. You are fact-oriented. You rely on reason and "using your head." You also take pride in "fathering" things—in inventing, initiating, and promoting them. You want to immortalize yourself through your creations. You are assertive, positive in outlook, forceful in your beliefs, and dynamic about getting things done.

As an Emperor you like the security that can be found in rules of order and underlying structures. Once order reigns, you begin to find yourself bored and confined. It is the act of discovering principles, defining laws, and mapping domains that interests you. You seek to understand and comprehend the forms in nature. By naming things, you feel you gain the power to use them constructively.

Because you strive to master your situation, it is difficult for you to work under others. Most Emperors eventually find themselves either in business for themselves, or if they work for others, need to be in charge or with positions of authority. Since you understand the purpose of rules and corporate gamesmanship, you can move quickly up the ladder of success if you apply yourself.

If you are a Single 4 you feel comfortable within your boundaries. You need security and stability in your life and want to act with power and authority. If your social situation makes you relatively powerless, you might tend to project your images of power onto the authority figures in your life, thus giving parents, political leaders, employers, or cultural idols more importance than warranted. You are most fulfilled by being a leader, even if over a small and personal domain. You need to "wield the scepter" in order to feel a sense of achievement.

Your greatest problem could be your need to find a reasonable explanation for anything before accepting its validity or even its reality. You want to rule situations by discovering an order in them. In the extreme you can become dictatorial.

With Death and The Fool as your hidden factors, you seek immortality through the creations you "father" and the structures you produce. Change, disruption, lawlessness, humor that pokes fun at the things you stand for, the "unexplained"—all confuse or even frighten you, and yet they offer your best opportunities for growth and self-understanding. You always seek a method in the "madness" around you and perhaps will find real solutions to some of humankind's problems. You deny there are any limits to reason and therefore continually push back those limits to pioneer new frontiers. You can be an architect of the spirit, a builder of new worlds.

If you are a Single 4 (with The Emperor as both your Personality and Soul Card), then both Death and The Fool are your Hidden Factor Cards. Read the descriptions of these cards next, found later in this chapter.

FAMOUS SINGLE 4'S

Before 1959, there had been no Single 4's born for over 600 years (since 1298). The current reappearance will last until 2018. I haven't yet come upon any famous Single 4's.

DEATH (13) AS PERSONALITY CARD

(This applies if you are a 13–4.)

Realization of Life Power, Vital Force, Release

DEATH represents an end but is also a new beginning, a cutting away that leads to new growth. It is destruction and renewal, immortality and regeneration, as well as dismemberment and severing. Relating it to its sign Scorpio, it eliminates anything restrictive or no longer of service. I like to think of it as the "compost card," the decaying dead matter out of which comes rich, fertile soil that gives the opportunity for new growth.

As a Personality Card, Death refers to letting go of old ways and thoughts in order to be transformed or renewed. "It is enough" were the last words of 13–4 philosopher Immanuel Kant. 13–4's tend to learn by facing their mortality, even taunting it, orchestrating their lives to take them to the very brink of death or discorporation. Krishnamurti, a 13–4, welcomed the dying process as a way of life. He said, "Each day I die a little."

You plunge deeply and totally into your experiences, putting such passionate feeling into your beliefs that you are not always aware of the consequences of your actions. As another 13–4, Benjamin Franklin, said, "Experience keeps a dear school, but fools will learn in no other."

Your natural leadership attracts followers to you, and you must eventually come to terms with your desire for power for its own sake. You bring passion and depth to whatever you do, for nothing is taken lightly.

You are a transformer, working to dismember outworn policies, to set free new human possibilities, to liberate potentials. You have no qualms about dissociating from whatever states cannot continue to exist. Your sexuality is either very active and passionate or consciously sublimated into your work. "Intellectual passion drives out sensuality," said Leonardo da Vinci, a 13–4.

THE FOOL (22) AS HIDDEN FACTOR

(This applies if you are a Single 4 or a 13-4.)

THE FOOL as your hidden factor indicates fear of being considered foolish and immature. And you will often be seen by others as living your life foolishly, throwing away your life potential, or as working on something that others deem a waste of time. It may be hard for you to see yourself as an unlimited being. But confronted by the spirit within, you learn to trust your own natural potentials. You fight to maintain independence although you are often incongrously cast into the role of leader. You admire freedom of thought above all else. Ignorance is limitation to you, and so you always seek the meaning or purpose behind things. Others may think you've lost your reason or gone mad, but you are simply discovering your infinite potential.

Your fascination with diverse topics makes you seem scattered, but you should trust that your natural instincts are steering you right. You need to understand, not necessarily control, your own desire for anarchy.

Just as The Fool has no real number value, so you fear being counted insignificant, a nothing; yet, as does the zero, you increase whatever you combine with. Therefore, while you fear loss of self, you work well with others, encouraging them to achieve their potentials.

As your teacher, The Fool helps you let go of other people's opinions and trust in your own processes. The Fool shows you vistas that others rarely see and encourages you to take risks, plunge off into the unknown, and enjoy every minute to its fullest.

FAMOUS 13-4'S

Famous 13-4's have been responsible for shocking revelations of deeply hidden things—for revealing the undercurrents of passion, power, and the potential for good and evil in all of us. Several, such as Harriet Beecher Stowe, with *Uncle Tom's Cabin* (credited with starting the Civil War), J. R. Oppenheimer, with the atomic bomb, or Immanuel Kant in philosophy, have exploded the myths of their time, resulting in a worldwide reconstruction of the basic assumptions we live by. Many have used death as the theme of their greatest works, such as J. D. Salinger in *Catcher in the Rye*, the English poet Shelley, and the German composer Richard Wagner. Some have courted death, even flaunting it, such as William Burroughs with his drug sagas, Haile Selassie of Ethiopia, or Thor Heyerdahl, sailing the high seas in a tiny raft of reeds. Immanuel Kant was so concerned about dying due to frail health that he never varied his rigid physical regimen and never married. He is known for his *Critique of Pure Reason* (a very Emperor topic) and for developing the theory that individual freedom lies in obedience to moral law within, a perfect example of the interplay of Emperor and Fool.

Leonardo da Vinci (Florentine artist and inventor) 4/24/1452
Benjamin Franklin (Statesman) 1/17/1705

Immanuel Kant (German philosopher) 4/22/1724
Percy B. Shelley (English poet) 8/4/1792
Harriet B. Stowe (Humanitarian and novelist) 6/14/1811
Joseph Smith (Founder of Mormon Church) 12/23/1805
Richard Wagner (German composer) 5/22/1813
Jiddu Krishnamurti (Spiritual teacher) 5/12/1895
William Burroughs (Writer) 2/5/1914
Haile Selassie (Emperor of Ethiopia) 7/23/1891
J. D. Salinger (Novelist) 1/1/1919
Thor Heyerdahl (Norwegian anthropologist and explorer) 10/6/1914
J. Robert Oppenheimer (Atomic bomb project leader) 4/22/1904
Harold Wilson (Prime Minister of England) 3/11/1916

THE FOOL (22) AS PERSONALITY CARD

(This applies if you are a 22–4.)

Realization of Eternal Power, Spiritual Force, Regeneration

THE FOOL represents your childlike and spontaneous nature. As your Personality Card, it indicates that you need to develop greater trust, innocence, and lightheartedness. You will gain wisdom only when you realize how much you don't know.

As a 22–4 you always live with the paradoxical nature of wisdom and foolishness. Your purpose is to establish self-control and set the standards in your field, yet you must be prepared to admit ignorance, cast your fate to the winds, and make wild leaps of divine inspiration. As Sallie Nichols says in *Jung and Tarot*, "The job of the fool is to remind us of our folly and keep us from hubris —overwhelming pride." But few 22–4's have the wisdom to play the fool with grace and humility.

One of the problems of 22–4's is their belief that they are exempt from the rules they make. They will accept no discipline from without and can be irresponsible and even amoral. 22–4's often have the attitude, if not appearance, of youth and vigor. In old age they are constantly surprising others with their ability to integrate the new, unexpected, and strange.

Emperor-Fools can be quite different at different stages of their lives. There is the stage of being totally The Fool—usually when you are young—of doing things on a whim, of being the vagabond. Then you settle down and become The Emperor; very organized and practical, establishing businesses and a home. But occasionally you need to break out and be footloose again in order to rejuvenate yourself. When these two qualities are combined, you can be creative and even innovative. You take risks but get results. You are the pioneer, the inventor. But when this inner contrast is not well integrated, you want to be The Emperor, yet are afraid you are The Fool. You are then unable to let go of inhibitions and cannot truly look at yourself or your own processes. You must learn to laugh at yourself for taking your situation too seriously.

As a 22–4 you may have a finely developed sense of humor based on the ironies of life and a poignant appreciation of human foibles. You know all too well the situations into which we are led by unruly passions, but can see their comic side.

The Fool represents your spirit before manifestation, between incarnations. The cliff on the card represents your jumping-off into life, into the manifested world of The Emperor. Death represents being released again so that you can freely experience your limitless self. After accepting Death as your teacher, you realize the polarity of wisdom and folly and recognize that death is only a mechanism of eternal life.

In *Tarot for Your Self* I said that The Emperor was the Personality Card and The Fool was the Soul Card. Although in this book I say the opposite, it is primarily to keep the process here consistent. Emperor-Fools tend to resist all categorization. In tarot philosophy The Fool is to be found nowhere and everywhere.

DEATH (13) AS HIDDEN FACTOR

(This applies if you are a Single 4 or a 22–4.)

DEATH as your hidden factor indicates that you deny death, experiencing it as an idea that limits and binds you. One outcome is that you strive (perhaps a bit fanatically) to produce works (or children) that will live after you are gone, to carry on your name and perpetuate your existence. You can be a dictatorial parent, demanding that your child follow in your footsteps. Or you may feel that in the face of death, life becomes meaningless and thus suffer from existential angst.

Death becomes a thing to fight, something to prove yourself against. Humans are the only creatures aware of the fact that they die, and thus death can become the measure by which all action and creations are judged. But the more you hate death, the more you will hate the life around you. Death means totally losing your sense of ego, and so many people with Death as a hidden factor will work to make their ego strong and well-known—an indelible identifying mark. As 22–4 Mark Twain reported in a famous telegram, ''The reports of my death are greatly exaggerated.''

Since death, in symbolic and vernacular terms, has long been considered a metaphor for orgasm—the ''little death''—4's and 22–4's may experience their fear of the loss of self through sexual release. It used to be said that each orgasm shortens one's life by a day. You will either ''foolishly'' and joyfully embrace that death, or run from it. Fascination with this subject is evidenced by the famous 22–4, Sigmund Freud. Death becomes the Teacher Card when you realize that coming to terms with death is true liberation. You can then die to those rules that constrict your freedom of spirit.

FAMOUS 22–4'S

There are several threads to follow when looking at famous Emperor-Fools. Many of them were revolutionaries or radicals, such as Annie Besant with her birth-control campaign, Marie Curie, who had to flee Poland for her student activities, Fidel Castro, and even Eugene McCarthy and George McGovern. Freud was a 22–4 who took his shadow as his teacher by digging up repressed sexuality and death-wishes from the unconscious. Others were charged with unconventional behavior and insensitivity to criticism, like Marie Antoinette (a queen known for her disregard for anyone's opinions), J. P. Morgan, Butch Cassidy, Hugh Hefner, Kate Millett, and Marshall McLuhan. Another major tendency seems to be the urge for immortality as a driving force, to prove themselves physically and reach the peak of their respective fields. There are numerous humorists and even out-and-out fools: Marcel Marceau, Woody Allen, Mark Twain, Ed Sullivan, and Ingmar Bergman, who always blended humor with his death-wish imagery. Woody Allen is a model 22–4. He once cited *The Denial of Death* by Ernest Becker as the most important book he had ever read. Also, one of his great lines is about wanting to achieve immortality, not through his work, but by not dying. Mark Twain was, of course, known for his humor and his stories of those American vagabonds and fools, Tom Sawyer and Huck Finn (his personae in novelistic guise). Violence also seems to be an undercurrent here (hidden factor of Death) with Manson, Castro, Cassidy, Bergman, and Peckinpah.

Marie Antoinette (Last Queen of France, beheaded) 11/2/1755
Annie Besant (Social reformer, Theosophist) 10/1/1847
J. P. Morgan (Financier and sportsman) 4/17/1837
Sigmund Freud (Austrian father of psychoanalysis) 5/6/1856
Butch Cassidy (Outlaw) 4/6/1866
Mark Twain (Writer, humorist) 11/30/1835
Marie Curie (Polish chemist, discovered radium) 11/7/1867
Ingmar Bergman (Swedish film director) 7/14/1918
Hugh Hefner (Publisher of *Playboy*) 4/9/1926
Marshall McLuhan (Professor, writer) 7/21/1911
Ed Sullivan (TV show host) 9/28/1902
Woody Allen (Film director, writer, humorist) 12/1/1935
Fidel Castro (Revolutionary, Cuban leader) 8/13/1927
Marcel Marceau (French mime) 3/22/1923
Eugene McCarthy (Professor, politician) 3/29/1916
George McGovern (Professor, politician) 7/19/1922
Sam Peckinpah (Film director) 2/21/1925
Joe Frazier (Boxing champion) 1/12/1944
Charles Manson (Cult leader) 11/12/1934
Kate Millett (Feminist) 9/14/1934
Luciano Pavarotti (Opera singer) 10/12/1935
Paul McCartney (Beatle) 6/18/1942
Nadia Comaneci (Rumanian Olympic gymnast) 11/12/1961
Arnold Schwarzenegger (Bodybuilder, actor) 7/30/1947

THE MINOR ARCANA FOUR'S

The FOUR'S represent stabilization after the creative interaction of the Three's, a time to consolidate what has come before. In metaphysical philosophy, Four's represent completion, similar to that of the Ten's (because $1 + 2 + 3 + 4 = 10$). Like The Emperor, they deal with your ability to locate yourself in time and space. Four's are the gifts or challenges relating to your personal power. They represent opportunities to release outworn modes and stabilize change. They picture the situations you experience in establishing a firm base for your activities and in developing your leadership.

The FOUR OF WANDS indicates the sense of completion and welcome renewal that comes when opposing energies harmonize; for instance, at the change of seasons, or when day and night are equal. You treat such times as rites of passage: cleansing, celebrating, and being generous with the fruits of your labor. You show appreciation for those who have supported you, you give thanks for your bounty, you enjoy what you harvest.

The first gift of the Four's is, therefore, your ability to celebrate life. This card pictures the rewards that come from moving through each developmental stage in your life and your acceptance of responsibility at new levels.

The FOUR OF CUPS is both gift and challenge. You have the ability to let things take their course, trusting the cycles of change. You recognize the need for letting situations lie fallow in order to regenerate. By resting and meditating, you receive new insights and messages from your unconscious.

As a challenge, though, the Four of Cups represents your inertia when you lack focus or a sense of purpose. Indulging in your feelings, as in the Three of Cups, often leads to dissatisfaction, lethargy, or exhaustion. Go slowly in emotional matters. You get bored only when your curiosity has not been piqued, or self-indulgence has become meaningless. Take time to be with nature, observing its natural rhythms, and you will be rejuvenated.

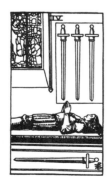

The FOUR OF SWORDS indicates that stress is a large factor in your health. Because of the weight of your responsibilities, there are times when you need to ask for advice, either from your higher self or from a professional counselor. Taking everything on yourself makes matters worse.

When you feel burdened or stressed, pull back into solitude in order to consider the details calmly. Put your thoughts in order and determine priorities. Suspend action on all issues but one, which you can then ask your unconscious to work on, and sleep on it. Through centering and meditation practices, you can create the objectivity required to see all sides of an issue. From this experience something useful and powerful can emerge.

The FOUR OF PENTACLES indicates that you have the gift of drawing to you the resources you need. You consolidate your power so that you can act with assurance. You need to feel secure in your sense of worth, for only then can you have a sense of humor about yourself.

This card also represents the dangers of grasping material accumulations too tightly. This is the constipating aspect of Scorpionic Death. Miserly protectiveness of your possessions closes you off to personal development. The transitions pictured in the Four of Wands can no longer take place, nor can the new experiences in the Four of Cups and the release from the stresses of responsibility in the Four of Swords. Think about the positioning of the pentacles in the Waite-Smith image, which illustrates the posture of personal power, or miserliness. To experience the power pictured in the card, balance a pentacle above your head, ground your feet firmly on the two pentacles below, and finally, center the last pentacle in your hands. When you feel completely centered and stable, bring the last pentacle inside your body—this is your point of personal power. Having found your security within, you no longer need to hold onto anything out in the world.

FROM THE AQUARIAN TAROT

This constellation shows two methods of handling life's problems and dis-ease. On one hand, we can take our problems to the authorities and ask what we "should" do, believing that there is a right way and a wrong way. On the other hand, we can strive through the experience of trial and error to redress our mistakes and heal our wounds. It also speaks about direct experience versus dogmatic faith.

CHAPTER EIGHT

THE CONSTELLATION OF THE HIEROPHANT: 14-5

TEMPERANCE (14)		THE HIEROPHANT (5)	
5 OF WANDS	5 OF CUPS	5 OF SWORDS	5 OF PENTACLES

THE PRINCIPLE OF TEACHING AND LEARNING

THE HIEROPHANT
Taurus
Social/Cultural Education
Freedom of Choice
Learning from Authority

TEMPERANCE
Sagittarius
Spiritual Education
Freedom of Action
Learning by Experience

Keywords: Testing. Counseling. Training. Assimilating and Integrating. Healing. Guidance. Bridging. Translating, Interpreting, and Channeling. Arbitrating.

If you are a Single 5 (5-5), read:

> THE HIEROPHANT (5) AS PERSONALITY OR SOUL CARD
> TEMPERANCE (14) AS HIDDEN FACTOR
> FAMOUS SINGLE 5'S
> THE MINOR ARCANA FIVE'S

If you are a 14-5, read:

> THE HIEROPHANT (5) AS PERSONALITY OR SOUL CARD
> TEMPERANCE (14) AS PERSONALITY CARD
> FAMOUS 14-5'S
> THE MINOR ARCANA FIVE'S

(Note: If a card from 14 through 18 is your Personality Card, you will not have a separate hidden factor. As a "nighttime card," the shadow aspect is contained within the Personality Card itself.)

THE HIEROPHANT (5) AS PERSONALITY OR SOUL CARD

(This applies if you are a Single 5 or a 14-5.)

Learning from Authority, Freedom of Choice, Social/Cultural Education

THE HIEROPHANT represents teaching and learning the laws set down by The Emperor. Hierophant means "Speaker of Mysteries." In this capacity you

THE HIEROPHANT

become a spokesperson for the powers that be and in effect translate information to make it accessible to the general public. For instance, if you are a scientist with specialized knowledge, you can communicate it to others who would not otherwise understand. Artists like Van Gogh and Cézanne (both 5's) saw the world in a very particular way, yet were able to give us some insight into what they saw through their ''interpretations'' on canvas. You are a bridge-maker. As Hierophant you communicate what is mysterious or strange to others, so that they will have the opportunity to experience it too. Many 5's are known as storytellers. Any incident can become an adventure in your eyes.

Like the two acolytes pictured in the card, you are either an active learner, searching and questioning the validity of what you learn, or you are the submissive learner who accepts what you are taught by those considered to be authorities. Often Single 5 Hierophants will be rebellious against authority while young, but as they grow older they become authorities themselves; they have discovered their niche—what they have chosen to stand up for.

Whether you officially do any teaching or training, you love to give advice and help people with problem-solving. As a matter of fact, people often come to you for assistance because they respect your expertise and knowledge and know that you are willing to help them. You are able to separate complex directions into simple components and don't give information that is extraneous or too difficult to understand. In problem-solving situations you choose between going to an authority and following instructions or testing techniques for yourself, trusting your intuition for guidance.

You can be a good listener, recognizing that what's on the surface does not tell all. The figure on the card has two fingers of the right hand upright, indicating what is said, while the three closed fingers indicate understanding of what is not said. The Bishop's cross demonstrates the four levels (including the top circle of spirit) of every statement. There are also four ways to teach or learn anything (hearing, doing, reading words, and seeing pictures or diagrams). You are the fifth element, the one who understands. You can adapt your teaching to the needs of those you teach.

Your greatest problem is that your knowledge can become codified into dogma that may no longer be appropriate in current situations. When you refuse to continually question your beliefs, they become dogma and thus limit your possible experiences.

Just as your adherents swear by your teaching, so you in turn admire and even idolize the teachers and models you trust. The danger in this is in accepting what they say as ''God's own truth.'' As teachers, Hierophants come to expect unswerving submission and adherence to the doctrines they teach.

Single 5's are afraid of making mistakes, and therefore you want to be sure before you do anything. Rather than being ridiculed, you would prefer not to try at all if you think you might fail. You believe there is a right and wrong way of doing things, and blame yourself when something goes wrong. Yet Hierophants learn best through their mistakes. One of the challenges for Single 5's is to learn to be your own authority, based on realizations arrived at through trial and error, experimentation, and experience. You will face this lesson over and over until you develop the flexibility to accept your problems and mistakes as teachers. Being "wrong" can be good if it points out the need for readjustment or completely new methods.

Five's have highly developed consciences—that is, a strong sense of morals and values determines your actions. Watch your tendency to be self-righteous. Follow your own conscience but dedicate yourself to right-minded living.

You search for a purpose that is larger than our mortal order. You yearn for a quintessential truth that ties everything meaningfully together. Oswald Wirth, in *The Tarot of the Magicians*, says, "In your own way formulate your own knowledge and in your heart conceive the religion which convinces you." With the Hierophant as your Soul Card, your purpose is to develop your own authority via an inner self that speaks with the innocence of a child and the wisdom of your inner High Priestess. When you act in accord with your highest potential, you transmit information from the higher self into the physical world.

TEMPERANCE (14) AS HIDDEN FACTOR

(This applies if you are a Single 5.)

With TEMPERANCE as your hidden factor, you can be rigid and temperamental. Especially when you are young you think that mistakes are wrong; you judge yourself to be bad if you make them. This can hamper your willingness to take risks and try things out. Single 5's always want to do things the "right" way and always follow the directions as learned. By coming to terms with Temperance as shadow, you learn give-and-take and the importance of trial-and-error learning from your mistakes. The challenges of life may appear as "problems" until you temper your nature through learning patience and good timing.

You may find it difficult to value your spiritual resources or trust your natural empathy. You may even feel that sensitivity and displays of emotion are weaknesses. Thinking of yourself as a pragmatist, you disguise your sentimentality with cynical humor and wisecracks. With maturity, as you accept Temperance as your teacher, you become more flexible, easing up on your judgments of yourself and others.

FAMOUS SINGLE 5'S

Famous Single 5's are somewhat difficult to classify because they are quite individualistic. They have tremendous idealism and require perfection of themselves and their models. An example is Bertrand Russell, who describes the beauty of mathematics in *The Study of Mathematics* as "without appeal to any part of our weaker nature, sublimely pure, and capable of stern perfection." Hierophants take themselves and their ideas seriously. While many of them are revolutionaries and iconoclasts in their youth, they tend to quickly find an ideal they can believe in, and spend the rest of their lives in the role of "authority," promoting, teaching, and following their beloved ideal. One of Blake's *Proverbs from Hell*, ''A truth that's told with bad intent/Beats all the lies you can invent,'' indicates the 5's moral attitude toward truth.

William Blake (English artist, poet, mystic) 11/28/1757
Maximilien Robespierre (French revolutionary) 5/6/1758
Friedrich Engels (German Socialist) 11/28/1820
Clara Barton (Founder, American Red Cross) 12/25/1821
Paul Cézanne (French artist) 1/19/1839
Pierre Auguste Renoir (French artist) 2/25/1841
Vincent Van Gogh (Dutch artist) 3/30/1853
Bertrand Russell (English philosopher) 5/18/1872
James Joyce (Irish novelist) 2/2/1882
Malcolm X (Religious leader, revolutionary) 5/19/1925
Johnny Carson (TV personality) 10/23/1925
Coretta King (Freedom fighter) 4/27/1927
Clint Eastwood (Actor, politician) 5/31/1931
Werner Erhard (Founder of est) 9/5/1935
Dick Cavett (TV personality) 11/19/1937
Rudolf Nureyev (Soviet ballet dancer) 3/17/1938
Lee Harvey Oswald (Presidential assassin) 10/18/1939
Julie Christie (English actress) 4/14/1940
Mick Jagger (English rock musician) 7/26/1943
Bette Midler (Singer, actress) 12/1/1945
Kareem Abdul Jabbar (Basketball player) 4/16/1947
Mikhail Baryshnikov (Soviet ballet dancer) 1/27/1948

TEMPERANCE (14) AS PERSONALITY CARD

(This applies if you are a 14–5.)

Learning by Experience, Freedom of Action, Spiritual Education

TEMPERANCE represents healing, tempering, adjusting, and redistribution. As a 14–5 you seek to creatively combine contrary forces into a new whole that is more than the sum of its parts. For these reasons, the figure on this card is often called The Alchemist. After the dismemberment and blackening melancholy of death (the ''nigredo'' stage of alchemy) comes the creative reconstitution of the purified self. Temperance promises that there is a solution to every problem.

14–5's look inward to find personal resources and creative materials with which to aid not only their own growth but that of others. You are a humanist, filled with compassion for the feelings and failings of others because you recognize them first in yourself. Many 14–5's actively seek to describe the human condition in new ways, uncovering and delving into the shadowy realms that are rarely acknowledged socially in order to bring these forgotten parts back into ourselves. You work actively to promote the circulation of ideas.

To 14–5's teaching is healing. Illness is the deterioration of a perfect whole that needs to be reassembled and understood on an entirely new level. Your problems don't exist in a void, but are connected to everything else in your life. You seek to assist others in seeing the whole picture and the connections between the parts. You heal others (individually and socially) not only by lending your own strength, but also by your loving acceptance of who they are, with sympathy for their plight. You seek to heal both physical and psychic wounds.

When you trust the deeper currents of life and value your inner experiences, they bring new insights and reveal new dimensions of experience. Yet you must always work to reconcile the world of your dreams with that of your daily life, to mix inner knowledge with the appropriate physical expression.

In the extreme, you desire to purify by wiping out undesirable qualities, or to simplify things to their essence (like Mao Tse-Tung, Georgia O'Keeffe, Yukio Mishima). You are a purist. 14–5's are often not moderate. Hitler, a 14–5, is well-known for his excessive desire to purify the Aryan race, summed up in this remark: "I shall stop at nothing and crush anyone who opposes me." You may need to learn moderation and to temper your idealism in order to deal with contingencies. But learn you will.

14–5's, as if washed in the fountain of youth, maintain a certain impetuosity, often accompanied by a tendency to look and act younger than your age.

Right timing is essential to problem-solving, and 14–5's often achieve their greatest successes by being in the right place at the right time. You recognize the importance of seasonal change and renewal and of yielding when appropriate. If the time is not propitious, you will still seek the right gradient or catalytic agent and trust that through trial and error you will eventually arrive at a workable solution.

But because 14–5's carry their own shadow within them (Temperance is a "nighttime card"), you are just as likely to be in the wrong place at the wrong time. You must recognize timing as being the key to manifesting results on the physical plane. Otherwise you may be unsure of what you stand for, or perhaps feel out of place, born too soon or too late. You are caught between the land and the sea. You may be unrealistic about where to focus your talents and energies, squandering them in time-consuming and fruitless tasks. You may also be giving up your own autonomy and personal ideals in order to live by the dictates of those you consider your superiors (bosses, religious and secular authorities, etc.), living by their standards rather than your own.

If such is the case, you need to recognize that your beliefs form the basis of the reality you experience, whether valid or not. Like the two cups, they are the only things you have to juggle with. You create your world in the image of your thoughts. This idea was scientifically stated by consciousness researcher John Lilly (a 14–5) as follows: "What one believes to be true either is true, or becomes true within limits to be determined experimentally." Opportunity therefore comes when you are confronted with conflicting beliefs that you normally experience as stress. Instead, treat them as a creative challenge: make something more out of them than either belief would warrant by itself. You can accomplish whatever you set out to do, and you are capable of solving intricate problems. Believe in yourself. Take care not to get scattered; keep yourself focused on the task at hand and on your image of success.

FAMOUS 14-5'S

There is a tendency for famous 14-5's to step out of the world of the mundane and into the world of myth and mysticism, although always with the purpose of exploring and describing the human condition. They often tap into such deep, numinous sources that they become spokespersons for, or even representatives of, archetypes of their time. There are notable freedom-fighters here, such as Che Guevara, Simon Bolivar, Mao Tse-Tung, and Abraham Lincoln. There is a fascination with the macabre and mysterious apparent in the work of Diane Arbus, Aubrey Beardsley, Cagliostro, Manly Hall, Jorge Luis Borges, Yukio Mishima, Adolf Hitler, and even Charles Darwin. Many of them have found that out of bones and decay comes a purity of truth and beauty undiscerned by others. Note also the three pairs of "twins" in this list: Lincoln and Darwin, born the same day in 1809; Alan Watts and John Lilly, born the same day in 1915; Marlon Brando and Doris Day, born the same day in 1924.

Theresa of Avila (Spanish saint and mystic) 4/7/1515
Cagliostro (Italian occultist) 6/2/1743
Simon Bolivar (South American "liberator") 7/24/1783
Charles Darwin (English naturalist, evolutionist) 2/12/1809
Abraham Lincoln (U.S. President) 2/12/1809
Aubrey Beardsley (English illustrator) 8/24/1872
Helen Keller (Freedom-fighter for the blind and deaf) 6/27/1880
Georgia O'Keeffe (Artist) 11/15/1887
Adolf Hitler (German dictator) 4/20/1889
Eileen Garrett (Founder, Parapsychology Foundation) 3/17/1893
Mao Tse-Tung (Communist Chinese leader) 12/26/1893
William Faulkner (Southern writer) 9/25/1897
Jorge Luis Borges (Argentine author) 8/24/1899
Clark Gable (Actor) 2/1/1901
Manly Palmer Hall (Metaphysician, author) 3/18/1901
Gary Cooper (Actor) 5/7/1901
Marlene Dietrich (Actress) 12/27/1901
John Steinbeck (Writer) 2/27/1902
Ellen Yoakum (Faith healer) 8/2/1903
Albert Camus (French existentialist writer) 11/7/1913
Howard K. Smith (TV news commentator) 5/12/1914
Alan Watts (Mystic and writer) 1/6/1915
John Lilly (Interspecies communications researcher) 1/6/1915
Walter Cronkite (TV news commentator) 11/4/1916
Al Hirt (Trumpet player) 11/7/1922
Diane Arbus (Photographer) 3/14/1923
Marlon Brando (Actor) 4/3/1924
Doris Day (Actress) 4/3/1924
Yukio Mishima (Japanese author) 1/14/1925
Che Guevara (Cuban revolutionary) 6/6/1928

THE MINOR ARCANA FIVE'S

The FIVE'S upset stability and stagnation. Each of the Five's gets us out of the rut of the Four's by overthrowing complacency, and creating challenges to be met creatively. It is through such testing of our fears that we learn to activate our potentials.

Wands present you with the test of ideas, in which you must face your fear of strife, resulting in stress. Cups present you with the test of love, in which you must face your fear of disappointment, resulting in sorrow. Swords present you with a test of will, in which you must face fear of defeat, resulting in defensiveness. And Pentacles present you with a test of belief, in which you must face the fear of insecurity, resulting in worry.

The Five's teach you temperance; that is, combining your abilities with right timing.

The FIVE OF WANDS indicates that you find your ideas tested through conflict and disagreements. Question authority! Such arguments or discussions can be invigorating and give you the opportunity to contribute your ideas and teach what you know. Temperance stresses the need to balance and temper individual ideas until something new can be formed out of the variety of experiences—a broader picture than just one individual (or point of view) can offer. This kind of synergistic process is one of the major ways in which to learn.

When this confrontation of differing ideas takes place within you, like an inner committee with five different voices rattling on in your head, producing too many things to think of at once, it can create confusion over what to do. You may find that the basis of the problem is in conflicting beliefs. The Temperance card suggests finding a concept or overview that will bridge varying beliefs, allowing for each to coexist with the others.

The FIVE OF CUPS shakes you from the complacency of the Four of Cups. You don't sufficiently appreciate something until you have lost it. Cups teach you about grief and how to transcend loss. When something you put your heart into has not worked out, you experience disappointment. The three spilled cups can represent a loss of harmony, or beliefs that used to sustain you. This can be a friendship turned sour, a physical loss, or plans overturned. You wrap a black coat of sorrow about you and turn inward with your grief. This is appropriate for a time. The two cups remaining are in the hands of the Temperance angel; thus healing can take place if you throw off sorrow and pick up the remaining cups. Renewing your interactions with loving friends, focusing on a new project, and "crossing bridges when you come to them" are ways out of heartache.

The Temperance angel reminds you that nothing is really ever lost. All energy continues, taking on new forms. The eternally pouring water symbolizes the continuity of the life force. When you experience disappointment, remember there is a time and season for everything. Let your tears flow; realize that time will bring healing and that creation itself is never-ending. Ask yourself what you can learn from this experience.

The FIVE OF SWORDS represents difficulty in communicating your ideas to others. Thinking is fragmented and decisions are difficult, bringing confusion and doubt. Others try to impose their ideas on you, but you must rely on your own inner voice. Or perhaps your own thinking is so rigid that there is no room for other opinions. Avoid willful confrontations. Accept input from others but do not let it destroy your own perspective. This is not a situation of right and wrong, but of needing to look at all possibilities and rejecting none. The preceding Four of Swords retreats from such issues and attempts to deal with them in solitude. Here, in the Five of Swords, you are ready to clash with others.

Such circumstances are no-win situations. Or you win the battle but lose the war; you make your point but lose your best friends. Trying to prove that you are right is not going to change their minds. Arguments and stormy scenes arise from a dogmatic stance.

When you have been injured and hurt from such an encounter, you need to heal. When you are fragmented like the scattered swords, you need to be made whole again. Don't let such experiences limit you to a desire for revenge. Instead call on the angelic, spiritual being inside you for guidance. Most of the great healers gained their gift from a personal wounding that they transcended, and then assisted others in this process.

The FIVE OF PENTACLES represents the challenges of deprivation, insecurity, and exclusion. It is everything that the Four of Pentacles is holding out against. It shows the upset of every effort towards stability. As a 5 or a 14–5 you learn by being denied everything you wanted to hold on to. This technique is sometimes deliberately used in spiritual teachings to help you recognize the transitory nature of physical and material desires. Such austerity and even poverty is felt to channel all your thoughts into your spiritual development.

But you can also find yourself in such a situation through your iconoclastic questioning of the powers that be. In rebelling against the norms of society, you may choose to live the life of the ''outsider''—upholding the beliefs that you value with a few like-minded friends.

Motherpeace

When your home, work, or other form of security is threatened, you have to choose how to handle it. If you feel powerless, you might seek sanctuary or accept welfare—perhaps an appropriate first step. But, as the Motherpeace Five of Disks (a woman kneading clay or bread) and Temperance card both suggest, you can work at your situation slowly and steadily, trying different things until you get a combination that holds together. Despite the hardships, this is a card of progress toward a goal. The reward will be as great as your belief in what you can achieve.

FROM THE XULTUN TAROT

This constellation is about creative choice, involving first a need to discriminate differences among things, and then discern how they are all part of a greater whole. In this constellation we become aware of all the connections that exist between us and everything else around us. With The Lovers you must face the other half of yourself and accept it; with The Devil you turn away and project your fears or needs onto others.

(Xultun Tarot is available from Arcana Publishing Co., PO Box 2, Wilmot, WI 53192.)

CHAPTER NINE

THE CONSTELLATION OF THE LOVERS: 15–6

THE DEVIL (15)		THE LOVERS (6)	
6 OF WANDS	6 OF CUPS	6 OF SWORDS	6 OF PENTACLES

THE PRINCIPLE OF RELATEDNESS AND CHOICE

THE LOVERS	THE DEVIL
Gemini	*Capricorn*
Urge to Unite	Urge to Separate
Choice to Love	Choice to Fear
Ourselves in Relation to Others	Ourselves in Relation to the World

Keywords: Attraction and Division. Synergy and Separation. Exchange. Sharing and Relating. Reciprocity. Vitality. Sensuality. Connectedness. Ability to Discriminate between Good and Evil. Temptation. Obsession.

If you are a Single 6 (6–6), read:

> THE LOVERS (6) AS PERSONALITY OR SOUL CARD
> THE DEVIL (15) AS HIDDEN FACTOR
> FAMOUS SINGLE 6'S
> THE MINOR ARCANA SIX'S

If you are a 15–6, read:

> THE LOVERS (6) AS PERSONALITY OR SOUL CARD
> THE DEVIL (15) AS PERSONALITY CARD
> FAMOUS 15–6'S
> THE MINOR ARCANA SIX'S

THE LOVERS (6) AS PERSONALITY OR SOUL CARD

(This applies if you are a Single 6 or a 15–6.)

Urge to Unite, Choice to Love, Ourselves in Relation to Others

THE LOVERS represents synergy, reciprocity, and learning from others. This card has very different pictures in the French and English schools. The French school shows a man standing between an older woman and a young woman, thought to represent vice and virtue, or his mother and his wife, or as Barbara Walker suggests in *The Secrets of the Tarot*, the picture could be of a respected elder in the act of marrying the man and woman. Eros shoots his arrow from

Marseilles

above their heads. In the English school, beginning with the illustrations by Pamela Colman Smith, the picture is of Adam and Eve in the Garden of Eden with the snake of wisdom and the fiery archangel Michael above.

Both designs focus on an initiation—a choice being made to experience knowledge that was previously denied. This knowledge is couched in carnal terms. We see the severing of the previously unquestioned protective restrictions and an acceptance of the resultant power of procreation—to allow you to become a god, a creator in your own right. The individual leaves the mother and/or father, to cleave to the lover. Unity is broken, and from the separation comes the desire to reunite in order to create something new, separate from the originator.

As a card relating to Gemini and the Journey of the Twins myths, you have two sides to yourself that you attempt to reconcile. This can be the split perceived between the ''good'' and ''bad'' parts of yourself, the reflective and the dynamic, the passive and the active, the masculine and feminine, or your personal independence and your desire to be in a relationship.

Ultimately your task is to unite these two aspects of yourself. When these two parts work together in harmony, you experience tremendous power and pride in your knowledge and abilities. You can then use your rational mind (Logos) to look to the inner world where you connect with Spirit, as well as the outer world. In thus relating intuitive awareness to focused consciousness, you are able to perceive a meaning that transcends them both.

With The Lovers as either your Personality Card or your Soul Card, personal relationships are of primary importance to you. You learn most about yourself through the people with whom you have relationships: your family, friends, coworkers, lovers. Unrestricted and honest communications are vital to you. You look for a partner with whom you can communicate your deepest feelings and aspirations and prefer people with interests similar to your own. The central issue for you is: ''What do I want and need in relationships?'' However, since relationships of any kind fascinate you, you are also intensely curious about how anything ''works''—whether animal, vegetable, or mineral. You may take mechanical things apart and are always figuring out and tinkering with the relationship of things and people to one another, on both micro and macro levels.

Many 6's work with or share a hobby with a partner they probably consider to be their best friend. If you are ''unattached,'' you are probably attracted as much by conversation and friendship as anything else.

With The Lovers, the people you relate to mirror your own self-image. The best way to see yourself is to look at who you have drawn into your life. The qualities you cannot see in yourself, often called your shadow, you project onto others; you are unusually sensitive to, annoyed by, or envious of these traits in others. While this happens with everyone, for Lovers this is a major way in which you learn about yourself. Your relationships reflect this self-image until you learn to take back and ''claim'' for yourself all your projected traits.

The Lovers is a card of choice, symbolic of separating ourselves from the Garden of Eden, from our parents, from our security bases—in order to choose our own experiences and thus achieve knowledge. For Lovers, though, the choices are based on the two basic emotions of love and fear, from which all others arise. At every junction in the path, you must ask yourself which of these is determining your choice. Is your action motivated by love, or to avoid what is fearful? This question is related to another of your characteristic dilemmas, that of choosing between your belief in freedom and your need for attachment. Because you tend to think in terms of "we" rather than "I," the influence of others is felt in all your decisions, drawing you even closer into relationships.

THE DEVIL (15) AS HIDDEN FACTOR

(This applies if you are a Single 6.)

THE DEVIL

THE DEVIL as your hidden factor indicates that you tend to hide your untamed instincts, even from yourself. Thus your sexuality in particular, and your vivacity in general, can feel overwhelming to you at times. You either see yourself as a basically sexual creature motivated by your desires and obsessed with your needs, or you repress these feelings in yourself with accompanying inhibitions and taboos.

If you grew up in an environment with rigid standards that allowed you little freedom, you may harbor doubts about your self-worth. If you experienced your situation as oppressive, you may have felt punished for transgressing in ways you did not understand. You may have internalized many personal qualities as being "bad" because of these repressive attitudes. For instance, you might have felt or been told that sex was forbidden or repulsive. If you were a "good" child you tried to make sure you never did anything to be ashamed of, hiding even from yourself thoughts and feelings that were not sanctioned.

Single 6's as children open themselves to others with total trust. You intensely desire relationship and reach out freely to others. When this trust is betrayed, you end up feeling the guilty and responsible one. You may have been abused either physically or mentally by someone exerting power and control over you. Girl children accused of being flirts or teases, for instance, are particularly susceptible to self-blame.

You then grow up either feeling guilty about sex, repressing your natural instincts and sublimating them into a need for power, or you see sexuality as an expression of your personal power. Being sexually desirable can become a way of proving your own importance and self-worth. You may feel you have things to hide—some "dirty" secret. If anyone found out, they couldn't possibly love you. Alternatively, you may turn this feeling into suspicion of others and their motivations. At the extreme, unable to face your own sense of guilt or blame, you may project it onto others. You find scapegoats for your own sense of powerlessness, or try to manipulate your relationships as the only way of getting what you need.

The key to this card is mirth! Don't take manipulation and other people's power trips seriously. See the humor in the situation. This is how to break through obsession, manipulation, and overweening pride. Nietzsche, who was a Single 6, said: "Man alone suffers so excruciatingly in the world that he was compelled to invent laughter.'' Bedevilment shakes you out of a fixed way of seeing things and allows for new perspectives. Like the tricksters and coyotes of myth, you shake things up; you emphasize new connections instead of accepting previous divisions and discrimination. You need to learn there are no sins, only errors —and these are rectifiable. Union with self comes through learning to forgive yourself.

After your Saturn Return (about age 30), as The Devil becomes your teacher, you become more comfortable with the natural power and magnetism that draws others to you. You discover that you can activate tremendous creativity when you trust your instincts and face the things that terrified you previously. This can become a desire to explore hidden traditions and places and taboo subjects, or a fascination with the powers of the dark and mysterious.

Eventually you realize that ultimate power lies in being able to choose your own values. You find that all those secrets and manipulations assumed power over you by obsessing you. By admitting your fears and taking them from the shadows, you gain the personal power to laugh away constrictions and liberate your full creative potential.

FAMOUS SINGLE 6'S

Among the well-known Single 6's, John Lennon, Charles Schulz, Stephen King, H. G. Wells, and Jonathan Swift all use satire and humor to expose the hidden fears of the human species. Einstein's research released the power and, in his term, ''menace'' of the atomic bomb, but he also said (rightly or not), ''It may intimidate the human race into bringing order into its international affairs, which, without the pressure of fear, it would not do.'' Nietzsche believed in the full expression of our ruthlessness, courage, and pride in order to access our true power. Swedenborg rejected the limitations of structured religion to communicate directly with Spirit. He said, ''Love in its essence is spiritual fire.'' It was John Lennon, famous love-lyricist, who said, ''In the end the love you take is equal to the love you make.''

Jonathan Swift (English author, satirist) 12/10/1667
Emanuel Swedenborg (Swedish scientist and mystic) 2/8/1688
Sarah Bernhardt (French stage actress) 9/25/1844
Friedrich Nietzsche (German philosopher) 10/15/1844
H. G. Wells (English author, social thinker) 9/21/1866
Nikolai Lenin (Russian Communist leader) 4/22/1870
Sergei Rachmaninoff (Russian composer) 4/1/1873
Albert Einstein (Physicist) 3/14/1879
William Randolph Hearst (Publisher) 4/29/1863
Charles Schulz (Cartoonist) 11/26/1922
Joanne Woodward (Actress) 2/27/1930
Ed Buryn (*Vagabonding* author, photographer) 5/29/1934
Vanessa Redgrave (English actress) 1/30/1937
John Lennon (Beatle) 10/9/1940
Jesse Jackson (Civil-rights leader) 10/8/1941
Goldie Hawn (Actress) 11/21/1945

Stephen King (Writer) 9/21/1947
Michael Jackson (Musician) 8/29/1958

THE DEVIL (15) AS PERSONALITY CARD

(This applies if you are a 15–6.)

Urge to Separate, Choice to Fear, Ourselves in Relation to the World

THE DEVIL represents raw, untamed power and creativity. This lord of the material world, feared as dangerous to self and society, is represented by the devil as pictured in the middle ages—a composite image taken from the gods of supressed religions, demonstrating that it is easier to twist and distort such a force than to get rid of it. This figure was concocted out of bats that fly at night, randy goats, the talons of a bird of prey, and our nightmares and fears of what others might discover about us.

Therefore The Devil represents what you as a 15–6 try to keep hidden or repressed. Characterized as a card associated with the earth sign Capricorn, you prefer to find a structured form that can contain your fears and thus keep them separate from your sense of self. This card also represents the part of yourself considered "worldly," base, or material—the part that western culture has tried to separate from the spiritual, and with which, since your Soul Card is The Lovers, you will always strive to unite.

You can be ambitious and willing to go to both the heights and depths of experience in the service of that ambition. You sacrifice your own needs and those of others you love to the ideals that obsess you, making yourself difficult to live with. You work hard and play hard. You appear distant and cold, presenting an air of formality to those who are unaware of the passionate commitments you hold. Your pride is beneficial in that you recognize your abilities, and harmful in that it promotes artificial distinctions between yourself and others. 15–6 Robert Browning recognized this when he wrote in an album, "As if true pride/Were not also humble!"

Feeling ultimately alone in your freedom to choose a purpose for your life, you either become a bold romantic, upholding a strict moral ethic as a method of keeping society together, or you struggle with the despair and bewilderment of a meaningless universe that neither rewards nor punishes you and therefore makes all action absurd.

You probably grew up within a rigid but satisfyingly structured view of the world, in which certain behaviors were correct no matter what was actually happening beneath the surface. Later you became painfully aware of the contrast between this world of social etiquette and the real world, with its underlying deceit and lack of deep connectedness in personal relationships. "Human kind/Cannot bear very much reality," said 15–6 T. S. Eliot.

You may see yourself as some sort of dupe or clown who tries to imagine yourself free, when you know yourself to be constricted by the boundaries of self, society, and the natural world—things outside your control. You dissect social conditions and human character in an attempt to discover who you are. You feel that if only you can have control over a situation, you will be free.

15–6's often work to uncover the hidden aspects of our culture. Elizabeth Kubler-Ross has exposed our fear of death and dying. Mike Wallace, Vance Packard, and Eleanor Roosevelt strove to uncover consumer fraud and state our human rights.

Many 15–6's, such as Ibsen and T. S. Eliot, have portrayed humans as responding to life in a constricted world with a sense of separateness and labelling lack of responsibility as freedom—thus ultimately sinning through our failure to love.

The central question for 15–6's is in their relationship to the universe. What is the place of human beings? How do we fit into the structure? At various times we have perceived ourselves differently: sometimes we think we are as gods, sometimes we see ourselves in the image of a devil or monster, and sometimes we are even aware of our foolish self-importance in thinking that we are made in the image of anything, rather than by just pure chance. What is the nature of man—to be god or beast? 15–6 Ram Dass in his book, *Grist for the Mill*, concludes, ''We are in training to be nobody special. And it is in that nobody-specialness that we can be anybody.''

You either take yourself too seriously or you see yourself ironically, laughing at your all-too-human foibles and the hidden beastliness that keeps you from being somebody.

For 15–6's the challenge is to maintain godly honestly and inner freedom in relationships, while being devilishly surefooted in the world.

FAMOUS 15–6'S

Note how many 15–6's (Sartre, Beckett, Genet, Antonioni, Fellini, Pinter) have written for the theatre and film, and especially for what is known as the ''Theatre of the Absurd,'' which portrays our existential dilemma of having choice in a meaningless universe during our brief appearance on this stage called earth.

Others, such as D. H. Lawrence, Isaac Asimov, Franz Mesmer, and Buckminster Fuller, each in their own unique way, have hoped that we could eventually find fulfillment through union with nature and acceptance of ourselves as natural beings.

Christopher Columbus (Italian explorer) 10/30/1451
Elizabeth B. Browning (English poet) 3/6/1806
Robert Browning (English poet, playwright) 5/7/1812
Henrik Ibsen (Norwegian playwright) 3/20/1828
Lewis Carroll (English children's writer, mathematician) 1/27/1832
Eleanor Roosevelt (Humanist) 10/11/1884
D. H. Lawrence (English novelist) 9/11/1885
T. S. Eliot (Poet and playwright) 9/26/1888
Buckminster Fuller (Design engineer) 7/12/1895

Jean-Paul Sartre (French philosopher, playwright) 6/21/1905
Howard Hughes (Financier, playboy) 12/24/1905
Samuel Beckett (Anglo-French playwright) 4/13/1906
Jean Genet (French playwright) 12/19/1910
Michelangelo Antonioni (Italian film director) 9/29/1912
Richard Nixon (U.S. President) 1/9/1913
Joe Louis (Boxing champion) 5/13/1914
Mike Wallace (TV commentator) 5/9/1918
Aleksandr Solzhenitsyn (Russian novelist) 12/11/1918
Iris Murdoch (English novelist) 7/15/1919
Isaac Asimov (Biochemist, science-fiction writer) 1/2/1920
Federico Fellini (Italian film director, writer) 1/20/1920
Ray Bradbury (Science-fiction writer) 8/22/1920
Elizabeth Kubler-Ross (Writer on dying) 7/8/1926
Harold Pinter (English playwright) 10/10/1930
James Dean (Actor) 2/8/1931
Ram Dass (Richard Alpert) (Spiritual teacher) 4/6/1931
Francis Ford Coppola (Film director) 4/7/1939

THE MINOR ARCANA SIX'S

The SIX'S show how to sustain relationships. They are the gifts and challenges that those in the Constellation of the Lovers must face in relating to others and the world around them. All of the minor cards seek a reciprocal balance of energies.

The SIX OF WANDS represents the gift of victory that can come from working with others to achieve a goal. Both the leader and the followers are victorious. From the struggle of ideas in the Five of Wands there emerges a dominant theme and a leader. But the leader can do nothing without the support and backing of the followers. This shows the necessary reciprocal relationship that exists between any leader and followers, between the chairman and the committee, if they are to succeed.

This card shows the self-confidence and pride that comes from creatively solving a problem. When your work is recognized, you feel elevated above those around you. But your pride can make you forget where you came from and those who helped you get where you are.

When you have skills or influence that can assist others, you have a responsibility to be of service to them, using your abilities to bring victory to all concerned. In making your choices you need to consider whether you act out of love, which takes you to freedom through understanding, or out of fear that takes you to guilt and bondage.

The SIX OF CUPS represents the exchange of love and pleasure that two people can bring to each other. You take advantage of your opportunities to let dear ones know how you feel. Don't hold back, or you will regret it at some later time.

You are a romantic who will always fall for the hearts-and-flowers routine. You enjoy being showered with love and are hungry for tender words and a caring touch.

After the disappointment and hurt of the Five of Cups, the Six of Cups poses the real test. Are you willing to accept an apology, to forgive and let go of your pain? Can you be the one to ask first for forgiveness? Are the memories of your happiness together strong enough to sustain you through separations? Those with The Lovers for their Personality or Soul Card must learn to love with the trust and receptivity of a child.

The SIX OF SWORDS represents the gift of support in adversity. It is the ability to stick with someone when their luck has run out, or to help them through difficult times and transitions to new phases. It is also the challenge of maintaining personal perspective and mental tranquillity during times of turmoil.

This card indicates that you must be willing to "cross the water" to see the other person's point of view. In resolving arguments you must "lay all the swords on the table" in order to achieve clarity and unruffled communications. When caught up in the obsessions, fears, and panic of The Devil, you need to make your way to someplace (inner or outer) where you can clear your mind and order your thoughts.

In situations in which there has been mental or physical abuse, you need distance and support to gain perspective. With distance it is possible to rise above the particular situation so that you can begin to see the larger pattern and determine some meaning behind it and what actions are necessary. There are times when you must leave others behind, to break through relationship patterns that obsess and bind you.

The SIX OF PENTACLES offers the gift of success in relationships, achieved through generosity of spirit and sharing your resources. Each person's wants and needs must be considered equally. At its best, love gives you a feeling of abundance that you share magnanimously, with no fear of running out. Benevolence is an infinitely renewable resource.

Many of our personal as well as global relationships are based on dynamics between those who have and those who don't. Doling out your attentions, promises, "sexual favors," or finances can be a manipulative means of keeping people bound to you. Your challenge is to give with no conditions, according to your ability, and contrariwise, to receive what is freely given. Only then will you find true stability and security in your relationships.

When success is measured in terms of what you give, everyone shares in it. When it is measured in terms of what you get, then you are chained to the need for more.

FROM THE NEUZEIT (NEW AGE) TAROT

In The Chariot card, the will of Spirit seeks to dominate and control the forces of nature and the animal instincts. But in the The Tower card, Nature shows herself to be powerful by unleashing natural disasters ("acts of God"), which still have the power to destroy whatever man builds. The lesson of this constellation lies in the experience of reconciling these two energies.

CHAPTER TEN

THE CONSTELLATION OF
THE CHARIOT: 16–7

THE TOWER (16)		THE CHARIOT(7)	
7 OF WANDS	7 OF CUPS	7 OF SWORDS	7 OF PENTACLES

THE PRINCIPLE OF MASTERY THROUGH CHANGE

THE CHARIOT
Cancer
Mastery
Controlled and Directed Energy

THE TOWER
Mars
Breakthrough
Illuminating Energy Unleashed

Keywords: Starting. Causing. Stimulating. Control. Breakthrough. Self-Development. Insight. Building Up and Letting Go. Conflict and Trials.

If you are a Single 7 (7–7), read:

THE CHARIOT (7) AS PERSONALITY OR SOUL CARD
THE TOWER (16) AS HIDDEN FACTOR
FAMOUS SINGLE 7'S
THE MINOR ARCANA SEVEN'S

If you are a 16–7, read:

THE CHARIOT (7) AS PERSONALITY OR SOUL CARD
THE TOWER (16) AS PERSONALITY CARD
FAMOUS 16–7'S
THE MINOR ARCANA SEVEN'S

THE CHARIOT (7) AS PERSONALITY OR SOUL CARD

(This applies if you are a Single 7 or a 16–7.)

Mastery, Controlled and Directed Energy

THE CHARIOT represents self-mastery and control and thus victory. It is a card relating to Cancer, but Aleister Crowley calls it Mars in Cancer, which gives a better description of the contrary energies found here. The Chariot is like the crab in his shell, armored and protected so that his soft inner emotions and intuitions are not exposed. On the other hand, he is posed outwardly as the dynamic protector of others, the warrior who fearlessly drives to meet his opponent. With the Chariot, you are both the warrior and the crab.

107

You take your job and other personal roles very seriously. For instance, if you are a business person you cloak yourself in an executive suit as if it were the charioteer's armor. After work you change clothes to go off dancing or sporting. You are not afraid of danger, but rather of someone getting under your skin. You have an outward appearance that says you can take care of yourself. However, you're prone to being annoyed or distracted and may carry a chip on your shoulder, as the moons on the charioteer's shoulders suggest.

You like being in the driver's seat, exerting control over situations. With your mind firmly fixed on your destinations, you move quickly and surely toward them. Without a sense of purpose, you can get mired down and become inflexible. Unexpected events and emotional scenes are disrupting. You wear your armor to protect yourself from a fall or from criticism, or to keep others from knowing your true feelings.

You have high ideals and can elevate your consciousness above the mundane. Your motivating force comes from your questioning mind, just as the Sphinx was known to question travelers. You are always looking to find the answers. Your emotions and instincts are often in conflict about which direction to take you, so it is only through the firm use of your will, focused on your goal, that you are able to harness your conflicting perspectives to move forward. Sometimes it seems as though your conflicts and feelings could tear you apart.

With Cancer as your astrological significator, you have strong roots in your family, your people, and your country. You see yourself as their defender. Although you like to travel, you still keep connected to your source. Your roots provide nurturance, security, and a comforting flow of feelings. Yet you must move outward to prove yourself and develop your own mastery. So while part of you wants to keep the values and ideals of your origins, another part of you urges you toward self-development and individuation.

Marseilles

Many of your tasks involve tearing up old foundations that are inconsistent with new ideas, or confronting and destroying whatever stands in the way of "progress."

Seven's have a "breakthrough" consciousness, the ability to see old things in exciting new forms and thus revive their usefulness. Whatever cannot be shaped to new concepts, you tear down. Your sphinxes (or horses in some decks) pull in two different directions, between the desire for progress and the desire to leave things intact. You are not passive when challenged, but will fight back actively.

Eventually you need to establish equilibrium, so that all parts of yourself are properly harnessed, with your will holding the reins. Your task is to develop a firm identity keyed to an inner guiding principle. Some form of meditation or centering practice, perhaps a martial art, will help you in doing this.

THE TOWER (16) AS HIDDEN FACTOR

(This applies if you are a Single 7.)

THE TOWER.

With THE TOWER as your hidden factor, you are afraid of being thrown off course, losing control, or otherwise being left vulnerable and unprotected. Changes in mid-course or abandonment of plans can shake you to your very roots. Then you dig in until you can assess the damage. You either lose your temper frequently to let off steam or control your feelings so tightly that you think you never get angry.

You may be afraid of your own fury and what you might do if you express it. On the other hand, you may have unconsciously discovered that displaying your anger is an effective way of breaking up resistance, although you would deny that it is a modus operandi. Sometimes 7's have an out-and-out violent temper, usually released when their normal controls are affected by drinking, drugs, or emotional upheaval.

When opinions or work have to be thrown out, you might lose your temper but you will also find the way cleared for you to begin building anew. You are afraid that people may see through your armor, possibly exposing you as a weakling. As The Tower becomes your teacher, you will welcome the opportunity to rebuild a more appropriate "front."

You keep sexual release tightly under control, and can learn to direct and focus your energies through tantric practices. Or contrariwise, you prove your virility by directed sexual prowess. War and sex, anger and passion stimulate you, but your task is to direct them always to a higher purpose. Learning patience with your own impetuosity is important.

Ultimately you learn to respect power and recognize the need to release it, whether through anger or lightning insights. Attempting to stop these disintegrative forces will only lead to personal disaster or to becoming totally rigid. Because you are goal-focused, you may not realize the extent to which you have built up an inflexible inner structure. Then you need either a flash of insight or some kind of shock that releases you from the prison of yourself.

As The Tower becomes your teacher, you learn to channel its light as a healing force. You also learn to accept your defeats, to clear out the debris of what is no longer necessary. Whether you do this through a cleansing fast, a house cleaning, by throwing out old clothes representing old roles and personalities, or by letting go of people and places that are not good for your continuing development, it is necessary for your continuing quest of self-discovery.

FAMOUS SINGLE 7'S

You might say a key phrase for this small sampling (many more 7's have been born since 1950) is, "no one tells me what to do." On my list there are three members of the Order of the Golden Dawn (OGD), whose tarot tradition I follow, and a fourth person, Jim Wanless, who has written a book on Crowley's

OGD-inspired tarot deck. Most of these people were notorious for their disruptive attitudes and shattering of social conventions, as well as for their highly individual lifestyles.

Just as I was completing this section I received a letter from a friend who is a Chariot Personality and Soul. He is a Vietnam veteran, known for his quick temper and accident-proneness. Where he is you'll usually find trouble. He is also very psychic, a dedicated healer, and consistently a warrior for those in need. He writes from a medical mercy ship in Central America: "No longer am I afraid of my violence—it has departed. What remains is pure energy so intense that, as a channel, my healing gifts have returned. What many perceive as the power of the cosmos I see as the Light of God. There is no sex or shape or essence to it, just a blinding, spiritual Light which I call God . . . Total concentration is the key that opens the doors of perception—to disturb that concentration is to disrupt the flow of energy. This energy is sacred, so sacred that we guard it and treasure it as if it were our very Life Force." This is a Chariot whose Tower has become his teacher.

Nichiren Daishonin (Buddhist spiritual teacher) 2/16/1222
Ben Jonson (English playwright and poet) 6/21/1573
Pierre Curie (French scientist) 5/15/1859
Maud Gonne (Irish freedom fighter, OGD) 12/20/1865
Erik Satie (French composer) 5/17/1866
Marcel Proust (French novelist) 7/10/1871
Gertrude Stein (Author and arts patron) 2/3/1874
Aleister Crowley (Occultist, tarot author, OGD) 10/12/1875
Paul Foster Case (Founder BOTA, tarot author, OGD) 10/3/1884
Max Ernst (German artist) 4/2/1891
Richard Chamberlain (Actor) 3/31/1935
Bruce Lee (Actor, martial arts expert) 11/27/1940
James Wanless (Creator, Voyager Tarot) 4/22/1943
Demetra George (Astrologer, author) 7/25/46
Uri Geller (Israeli psychic) 12/20/1946

THE TOWER (16) AS PERSONALITY CARD

(This applies if you are a 16–7.)

Breakthrough, Illuminating Energy Unleashed

THE TOWER represents insight that strikes your crown and shatters whatever is rigid and unyielding. It represents the natural disasters of your life that move you to constantly build new and more appropriate structures or to find a haven out of the storm. As a 16–7 you weather these storms well, because you have to. You often find yourself up against great odds and acting counter to public opinion, and yet you continue with determination. As 16–7 Dostoevsky scornfully said, "Taking a new step, uttering a new word, is what people fear most." You have strong force of character, are willing to be an individual, and can take abuse without letting it dissuade you from your task. You take upsets in stride. You are looking for the big breakthroughs, and know that if you shirk your task they will never happen.

Often major changes in your life circumstances catapult you into a whole new direction or change the circumstances of your life. Your way is filled with emotional ups and downs.

You are able to cut through all opposition and you burn through your tasks. Like Thomas Huxley, a 16–7, you believe that "The great end of life is not knowledge but action" (from *Technical Education*). You are not afraid to show anger and don't bother to hide your temper, realizing that its expression is healthy and clears the air quicker than holding it in.

With a nighttime Personality Card, 16–7's contain their own shadow in the qualities of The Tower. Your shadowy aspects are pride, arrogance, and a belief that you are beyond the rules that govern others. Your towering intellect and drive to the heights of ambition are fraught with the risk of setting you up for a fall. You might come to feel yourself a victim—innocent but punished nonetheless. Your personal intensity and passion, and your urge to "burn the candle at both ends" can exhaust you, leaving you depressed and alienated.

Still, you have the potential to learn to use the force of light for healing. And you can be a ray of inspiration, a beacon to others to follow.

FAMOUS 16–7'S

Examples of famous 16–7's include Wilhelm Reich, who wrote about how we psychically armor our bodies and the need to break through it. Galileo performed many of his experiments from towers, including his famous one at Pisa. Both of these men were publically disgraced and had much of their "inflammatory" work burned. Many 16–7's, such as Dostoevsky, Eliot, Baraka, and Le Guin, are also concerned with the relationship between individual and cultural neurosis and how to release pent-up energies without pathological or destructive results. And Dylan Thomas cried out in a poem to his father, "Do not go gentle into that good night. / Rage, rage against the dying of the light."

Sir Francis Bacon (English writer, statesman) 2/1/1561
Galileo Galilei (Italian inventor, astronomer) 2/25/1564
Oliver Cromwell (Lord Protector of England) 5/5/1599
George Sand (French novelist) 7/5/1804
George Eliot (English novelist) 11/22/1819
Feodor Dostoevsky (Russian novelist) 11/11/1821
Louis Pasteur (French chemist) 12/27/1822
Thomas Huxley (English biologist, educator) 5/4/1825
William Morris (English poet, painter, designer) 3/24/1834
C. C. Zain (Church of Light Tarot) 12/12/1882
Hermann Goering (Hitler's right-hand man) 1/12/1893
Nikita Krushchev (Chairman, Communist party, Russia) 4/17/1894
Joseph B. Rhine (ESP researcher) 9/29/1894

Wilhelm Reich (Psychiatrist, biophysicist) 3/24/1897
George Gershwin (Composer) 9/26/1898
Joseph Campbell (Writer on myth) 3/26/1904
Lillian Hellman (Playwright, novelist) 6/20/1907
Dylan Thomas (Welsh poet) 10/27/1914
Arthur Miller (Playwright) 10/17/1915
John F. Kennedy (U.S. President) 5/29/1917
Peter Sellers (Actor) 9/8/1925
William F. Buckley, Jr. (Writer, editor, lecturer) 11/24/1925
Marilyn Monroe (Actress) 6/1/1926
Ursula Le Guin (Science-fiction writer) 10/21/1929
Imamu Baraka (Playwright, poet) 10/7/1934
Joan Baez (Folksinger) 1/9/1941
Muhammad Ali (Boxing champion) 1/17/1942

THE MINOR ARCANA SEVEN'S

The minor arcana SEVEN'S are the gifts and challenges for developing self-mastery, breaking through obstacles, and dealing with anger. Since the number 7 relates to Initiation, the minor Seven's represent the trials and tests that must be passed to prove yourself. They show how you seek dominion over your environment. They are the ordeals over which you triumph, using the potentials inherent in The Chariot and The Tower.

The SEVEN OF WANDS represents the need to test your mettle, to prove yourself in combat or against competition. Only then will you know whether you have mastered your lessons. Your gift is having the nerve, sense of purpose, and determination to meet such challenges. It is a willingness to stand up to opposition without backing down. When you are fired up about something, you speak your ideas and stand up for your values. You have the courage to face odds and overcome obstacles. Your opponents test your limitations, but you build your mastery.

When you achieve a position of leadership like that pictured in the Six of Wands, there will always be others who crop up to challenge you. The Seven of Wands depicts such competition: it is the jealousy of others who want what you have. As a warrior, you will encounter situations in which it seems everyone is against you. You need to be realistic about the odds you face and not let rage back you into a corner.

The SEVEN OF CUPS represents your ability to conjure up visions, fantasies, and dreams. You are able to visualize possibilities, seeing them clearly in your mind. After the pleasures of the Six of Cups, you see only good things for the future. With your skills and abilities so well developed, you now have to decide where to use them. In your mind you explore the potentials, but you need to beware of slipping into unrealistic dreams.

The challenge lies in allowing yourself to experience your emotions—to know what you really want, but at the same time not get caught up in fantasies. At the extreme, you may wallow in indecision or let your emotions swamp you. Your test here is to look at your deepest desires and then choose one upon which to focus. Allowing them all to break your attention will eventually tear you apart. Or you may choose, only to find your choice vanish like smoke. You need to learn to recognize which goals have enough meaning and power to sustain you.

The SEVEN OF SWORDS indicates that you have wit and cunning, with the ability to create plans and strategems. When the odds seem to be against you, you find a way to disarm the enemy. You can also take the potential sting out of a situation by forethought and preparation, using your ability to take care of details.

Since you are able to out-think others, your challenge is to use such abilities honorably. Being so goal-oriented, you may come to believe that the end justifies the means. If so, you can then find yourself involved in stealing, lying, scams, and "con jobs," possibly even with the best of intentions. When dealing upfront seems futile, you think it justified to sneak around. When you get angry you can become vindictive.

As a test of your mastery, this card can mean "counting coup": doing something daring that proves your bravery, skill, speed, and cunning. By applying mental energy to every task, you prepare the ground for later action.

The SEVEN OF PENTACLES indicates that no matter what you do, there is a certain point at which you have to wait for the results. You must allow the fruit to ripen in its own time. While you wait, thoughts arise of sudden storms or other natural disasters that can destroy all your work. So your challenge is to face and move through the self-doubts that raise your fear of failure and your apprehension that your work will be for nothing.

This card also refers to the responsibility for being the reaper, cutting off the fruit for some personal purpose. Even in the face of such overwhelming odds as man versus Nature, you still seek to submit these elemental forces to your labors and your will. To do this you must calculate the odds and sow the seeds most likely to grow. But ultimately, you must let go of your expectations and cultivate patience.

FROM DAUGHTERS OF THE MOON TAROT

Strength demonstrates "power within," or power in harmony with your own nature. The Star represents Nature's regenerative and sustaining powers. Thus, this constellation deals with having the strength to actively partake in your destiny or "fate," and to persevere with hope in the face of difficulties.

(Daughters of the Moon Tarot (originals 5" round) deck and book are available from Box 888, Willits, CA 95490.)

CHAPTER ELEVEN

THE CONSTELLATION OF
STRENGTH: 17–8

THE STAR (17)   STRENGTH (8)

8 OF WANDS   8 OF CUPS   8 OF SWORDS   8 OF PENTACLES

THE PRINCIPLE OF COURAGE AND SELF-ESTEEM

STRENGTH
Leo
Courage of Your Convictions
Acknowledging the Power Within

THE STAR
Aquarius
Courage to Be Yourself
Acknowledging the Power from Source

Keywords: Self-Confidence. Fate. Perseverance. Power. Force. Kundalini
Energy. Hope. Grace. Balance.

If you are a Single 8 (8–8), read:

STRENGTH (8) AS PERSONALITY OR SOUL CARD
THE STAR (17) AS HIDDEN FACTOR
FAMOUS SINGLE 8'S
THE MINOR ARCANA EIGHT'S

If you are a 17–8, read:

STRENGTH (8) AS PERSONALITY OR SOUL CARD
THE STAR (17) AS PERSONALITY CARD
FAMOUS 17–8'S
THE MINOR ARCANA EIGHT'S

STRENGTH (8) AS PERSONALITY OR SOUL CARD

(This applies if you are a Single 8 or a 17–8.)

Courage of Your Convictions, Acknowledging the Power Within

STRENGTH represents the balance and integration of opposites. Like The Magician, the woman in this card has the *lemnescate* (infinity sign) over her head. She is the female magician or witch, sometimes called the enchantress because of her ability to charm the beasts and animals. Her power to do this comes from a recognition of the similarities in our natures rather than the differences. She exemplifies how we can accomplish anything we set our minds to by acknowledging our linkage with the world and working *in harmony with its principles*. Strength represents being attuned to your own inner nature, not denying it.

115

She demonstrates the belief that Will and Desire are not at odds and shows that they can work together. By gentling the wild animal within rather than "breaking it," its will is not subjugated and its spirit remains free.

As a witch/enchantress with astrological correspondence to Leo, you are an overtly emotional person. Part of your task is to understand your emotions, not suppress them. Your passionate feelings can be used to charge your hopes with the energy that will actualize them. You need to express yourself in your own unique way, allowing the vitality and vision within you to emerge. This takes courage, for people will try to pressure you into conforming. You have to struggle between your own inner needs and the demands of work and society.

You are a midwife, which means you are "with the wife" at the birth, assisting in that natural, inevitable process. You are also the one in labor. You know that the life force moves through you with a great surge of energy, and through your breathing and pushing, you simply work with and become part of those natural forces. You are a healer who assists the body's own mechanisms in maintaining health. You know about working with your own resources and are instinctively aware of your regenerative abilities. Trusting in the power of love and the healing qualities of touch, you do not shy from direct contact with whatever needs your understanding.

As your soul purpose, Strength means that you must engage your heart in whatever you create. Therefore, you must learn self-acceptance and come to terms with your nature. As in those stories where the wild animals assist the heroine, you need to let your instincts play a part in whatever you do. If you are to have the fortitude to express yourself and use your abilities, you must learn to love what society may call ugly or ungainly in yourself. Face your fears by expressing them. Look bravely at the worst that can happen. Often, once the "worst" is voiced, you can see that behind its dreadful aspect it is endurable, if not beneficial.

You are a survivor. Your inherent lust for life is felt by others as steadfast strength and perseverance, as never letting the odds get you down. In any struggle, you have the advantage of being able to empathize with your adversaries so that you know what they are feeling and thinking. You also recognize that life's jailers and murderers are your shadow-self, and that by hating them you become them. By learning to love what you fear in yourself, you can begin to befriend it and find the strength to endure.

When you refuse to give voice to your emotions, they can burst upon you unawares, breaking bonds in a destructive way or resulting in sins of passion. Your unexamined feelings can swallow you whole, making you fearful of life itself. At its worst, Strength becomes caught in a battle with life that is perceived as overwhelming and frightening. Or you refuse to take responsibility for the effects of your passions, thinking that your own feelings are all that count, resulting in self-centeredness and isolation.

You can be calm and collected in emergencies, for you possess an instinctive understanding that showing fear is dangerous. Instead, you use firmness and gentleness to handle the situation, first calming the panic, then examining the needs.

While The Chariot focuses on progress, Strength seeks to cultivate and civilize. As with the feeding and pruning of a rose garden, you cultivate your desires and with perseverence produce rewarding results. Like using a waterfall to generate electricity, you civilize by changing raw energy into power for work.

Some people can readily identify with the "power of love" and giving of oneself to the forces of life that this card represents, but others sometimes project this outside of themselves, onto the image of another, as "fascinating." This has become part of the myth of the female enchantress. For instance, for men with this image in mind, there is a fear of women and their life-giving power, as well as a fascination; an attraction and repulsion that sees women as either devouring and overwhelming or as soothing and humanizing. This fascination frightens these men so that they want to run away but can't. They either idealize women or characterize them as "bitches"; if the latter, they fear the feminine within themselves. It is from such paranoia that the horrors of the witch-burnings arose.

THE STAR (17) AS HIDDEN FACTOR

(This applies if you are a Single 8.)

With THE STAR as your hidden factor, you tend to hide your bright shadow from yourself. That is, you don't acknowledge your own abilities and accomplishments, or you may go to the other extreme and insist on being the "star of the show." You think yourself superior to others and may rage when they don't appreciate your vision and achievements. You feel insulted when called on to perform menial tasks.

Like the witches of history, you may feel you have to hide your true self and not let your power show (represented by keeping your hair bound and out of sight). You cannot see your own good qualities, believing yourself to be ugly and graceless, while admiring the beauty of others. You may even deny your own abilities to heal or to be creative. You are afraid of being revealed as the coward you think you are.

You may be afraid of squandering your emotions or wasting your energy. This can manifest as hypochondria—being plagued by ailments because you are unable to see yourself as whole and healthy. You sometimes lack objectivity and distance from your feelings so that your own emotions color everything. You may believe only what your senses tell you, becoming insular and landlocked.

The worst fear associated with The Star as a hidden factor is a lack of hope and lack of belief in the future. This is expressed in pessimism and self-doubt. Yet the positive force of The Star is so powerful that most 8's learn to overcome such doubts.

The Star as your teacher shines out in the darkest of times. It becomes a drive to bring hope into the world and a need to help others recognize and develop their highest capabilities. It awakens a rage against injustice and a dedication to preserving life and our natural resources. You come to believe strongly in the future and wish to leave something for the generations that follow.

FAMOUS SINGLE 8'S

I have very few Single 8's on my list of famous people, but they will shortly be more abundant than 17–8's. In this group we have innovators like Beethoven, Montessori, and Wright, all of them looking for more freedom. Both Montessori and Cayce encouraged the development of one's own natural abilities beyond what was thought possible at the time. There are also two stargazing astrologers and Grace Slick of the "Starship," who have the 17–8 connection to the stars.

Ludwig van Beethoven (German composer) 12/16/1770
Edgar Cayce (Psychic, astrologer, and healer) 3/18/1877
Maria Montessori (Italian educator) 8/20/1870
Orville Wright (First aviator) 8/19/1871
Juno Jordan (Numerologist) 6/8/1884
Noel Tyl (Astrologer) 12/31/1936
Grace Slick (Rock vocalist) 10/30/1939
Joe Namath (Football player) 5/31/1943
Maharaj Ji (Spiritual leader) 12/10/1957

THE STAR (17) AS PERSONALITY CARD

(This applies if you are a 17–8.)

Courage to Be Yourself, Acknowledging the Power from Source

THE STAR represents hope in a vision of the future. As the card that follows The Tower, it shows the individual freed from all masks and restrictions, being replenished by the waters of the unconscious. It represents the regeneration of life after the Great Flood. The card pictures Isis Unveiled, sky-clad, using the elements to link the purposes of heaven and earth: "As above, so below." She is both Earth and Star Goddess fully revealed, signaling the rise of the waters of the Nile, bringing fertility to the land and hope to the people.

As a card relating to Aquarius, it means that 17–8's are innovative. You are way ahead of your time, an inventor and visionary. As an experimenter, you are willing to try anything at least once. As a visionary, you are able to see possibilities far in the future or off in the distance, yet don't always know how to relate them to the here and now or to your immediate circumstances. For instance, you can envision a way for us to have peace and happiness on the planet, but may have trouble keeping peace with your neighbor.

One of the major learning tasks for a 17–8 is to reveal yourself and be receptive. It is only through the uninhibited expression of your hopes and visions, when you are stripped clean of all pretensions, that you can begin living out your destiny unimpaired.

As a 17–8, your sense of destiny or fate is very strong. When you look in the mirror, you see not only yourself but a reflection of something much larger than yourself, a feeling of personal fate as part of a universal design. 17–8 William Wordsworth knew this when he said, "There's not a man/that lives who hath not known his godlike hours'' (in ''The Prelude''). When you seek to live in accord with that destiny, finding the inner meaning of the events and even the disasters in your life, you draw from the patterns a font of strength and a sea of potential with which you can inspire others. You may be willing to work for a long-term goal not accessible in your lifetime.

Although you present a cool, even distant, exterior to others, inside you burns the light of inspiration. You are not swayed by your emotions to the same degree as the Single 8's. You have a scientific, objective mind that seeks expression through causes, and a commitment to reflecting society back to itself. Your sense of self is strongest when identified with something external to and greater than yourself. While the desire for fame and recognition is strong, and you are very ambitious, you prefer being known for your works and causes rather than for your personal life.

As the personality aspect of the witch archetype, you are a ritualist, finding that through repetitive actions and personal discipline you perceive order in your world and can experience serenity and a feeling of connectedness with the universe. For this reason a regular meditation practice, or the opportunity to get away from it all, is helpful. Nature is a source of comfort and healing to you, and many 17-8's return that gift with an involvement in ecology or world peace.

With a talent for seeing the inner light and the possibilities inherent in people, you can be inspiring, although you often expect too much of specific individuals in your life; they may feel unworthy of your image of them. The Star represents the focus of your longing for an unattainable goal of perfect happiness.

You have a personal sense of grace which, when called upon, can spark into charisma. You believe in yourself and your capabilities. When you have been blessed with the recognition and rewards you feel you deserve, you will try to give back some of your gifts to the world, usually through some altruistic cause. You want to help redistribute wealth and resources, and succeed in situations that allow you to do so.

With a nighttime Personality Card, you carry your own shadow within. This manifests when you get so involved in helping others and with ideals of kinship that you can't connect on an individual level. Your concern with causes is seen as a personal issue, inseparable from your sense of self. You may be extraordinarily sensitive to other people's opinions of you. 17-8 Oscar Wilde's comment is pertinent: ''There is only one thing in the world worse than being talked about, and that is not being talked about'' (from *The Picture of Dorian Gray*).

Another shadow aspect is to be so convinced that there is an abundance of resources that you squander them, with the mistaken belief that they will never run out. Or you may believe they are yours to use because the generations that follow will be able to develop new technologies—perhaps out in the stars. Ultimately your lesson is to open yourself to the gentle voice of intuition, which like the bird on the card, sings the song of your spiritual destiny. Only then will you find your personal resources ever renewed, and yourself able to bear the scrutiny of public recognition.

FAMOUS 17–8'S

The 17–8's on my list are only exceeded in number by the 18–9's. We find visionaries and inventors like Catherine the Great, Betsy Ross, Mary Shelley (author of *Frankenstein*), Alexander Graham Bell (who used the universal air waves for communication), and Timothy Leary, with his futurist ideas. There are also many outstanding women who were innovators presenting ideas way ahead of their time, like Mary Wollstonecraft, Mary Baker Eddy, and Eleonora Duse (who created the "natural" style in acting). And several more astrologers and taroists add up to a significant total for the constellation as a whole (see the Single 8's).

Rembrandt van Rijn (Dutch artist) 7/15/1606
Catherine the Great (Czarina of Russia) 5/2/1729
Mary Wollstonecraft (English women's rights advocate) 4/27/1759
William Wordsworth (English poet) 4/7/1770
Mary Shelley (English author) 8/30/1797
Brigham Young (Mormon elder) 6/1/1801
Mary Baker Eddy (Founder, Christian Science) 7/16/1821
Andrew Carnegie (Industrialist, philanthropist) 11/25/1835
Alexander Graham Bell (Inventor) 3/3/1847
Paul Gauguin (French artist) 6/8/1848
Oscar Wilde (Irish writer) 10/16/1854
Eleonora Duse (Italian actress) 10/3/1858
Pablo Picasso (Spanish artist) 10/25/1881
Taylor Caldwell (Novelist of past lives) 9/7/1900
Eden Gray (Tarot author, astrologer) 6/9/1901
Grant Lewi (Astrologer) 6/8/1902
George Orwell (English novelist, *1984*) 6/25/1903
Isaac Bashevis Singer (Writer) 7/14/1904
Anne Morrow Lindbergh (Writer) 6/22/1906
Laurence Olivier (English actor) 5/22/1907
Tennessee Williams (Author, playwright) 3/26/1914
Jonas Salk (Physician, developed polio vaccine) 10/28/1914
Timothy Leary (Neuropsychologist, futurist) 10/22/1920
James Baldwin (Writer) 8/2/1924
Rocky Marciano (Boxing champion) 9/1/1924
Paul Newman (Actor) 1/26/1925
Stanley Kubrick (Movie producer, director) 7/26/1928
Helen Frankenthaler (Artist) 12/12/1928
Grace Kelly (Actress, Princess of Monaco) 11/12/1929
Neil Armstrong (Astronaut) 8/5/1930
Mickey Mantle (Baseball player) 10/20/1931
Elizabeth Taylor (Actress) 2/27/1932
Peter Balin (Creator, Xultun Tarot) 6/5/1932
Peter O'Toole (English actor) 8/2/1933
Judy Blume (Author) 2/12/1938
Carole King (Singer) 2/9/1941
Bob Dylan (Song writer, musician) 5/24/1941

Aretha Franklin (Singer) 3/25/1942
Barbra Streisand (Singer, actress) 4/24/1942
George Harrison (Beatle) 2/25/1943
Joni Mitchell (Singer) 11/7/1943
Diane Keaton (Actress) 1/5/1946
Stephen Arroyo (Astrologer) 10/5/1946

THE MINOR ARCANA EIGHT'S

The minor arcana EIGHT'S are the gifts and challenges relating to developing self-esteem, accessing your potential, and finding and living your personal destiny. Since 8 is the number of balance and renewal of energies, the minor Eight's represent the trials and tests that must be passed in order to transform hope into actuality. The balance of energies required in Strength must be integrated into the self.

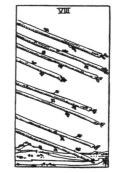

The EIGHT OF WANDS represents your ability to express your energies creatively once you have found a focus. You dynamically release them toward your goal with the assurance that you will succeed. Your enthusiasm can sweep people off their feet and get them moving with you. Freedom of speech and personal expression is vital to you. When unleashed, your imagination flows unchecked. Such a burst of energy can be felt as an urgency to get moving or as a frenzy of activity. At times you need to gentle these impulses with quiet meditation or an effort of self-control.

To you there is no joy like that of running free or traveling light. You fall in and out of love at the drop of a hat. You probably prefer telephone calls to letters because of the instantaneous communication possible. You can get carried away with new ideas, but be careful lest you lose your perspective. Your challenge is to not lose your self-confidence, but to take sudden infatuations and new ideas in stride.

The EIGHT OF CUPS represents the ability to go deep within yourself to regenerate your energies. Your passionate nature and lust for life can lead to overindulgence in sex, alcohol, drugs, or work to the point of burn-out. Then you must find the courage to retreat and heal yourself, even when your loved ones are there to nurture you. You may find that you are dissatisfied with outer fulfillment, recognition, and even demonstrations of affection. You may have plenty of love, care, and support, but there are times when you feel that something is missing and you don't know what it is. You sense that there is something more that draws you into the unknown. This could be a spiritual search for meaning or for a purpose that is worthy of your total commitment and dedication. Since the moon is shown full *and* waning, it seems that you actualized something with the full moon and now must move on as it fades.

Your basic fortitude and hope for the future are strengths that others may depend on. Some people may be too needy, making you feel manipulated or used without a return of energy. Avoid such a psychic drain; take time out to care for your own needs.

The EIGHT OF SWORDS represents a major challenge to the development of your potentials. You fear success and power, perhaps because of a refusal to accept the beast within. You figuratively blindfold yourself so that you can't see your abilities and then manage to "get tied up" so that your passions won't be loosed. You restrain yourself from activity as a way of avoidance, convincing yourself there are no alternatives.

This card represents a sense of destiny turning into a feeling of choiceless predestination. The swords represent beliefs that keep you hemmed in and reasons why nothing will work. You think you will be swamped by your emotions if you take a step. You hope that a knight in shining armor will rescue you, so you wait. Or you feel only temporarily stuck, or blocked by giving away your power to someone else. The challenge is to realize that you have done this to yourself. The situation shows in a negative way the power of what you can visualize, but you can use that same power to transform the situation. Begin by recognizing *right now* where in your life you *do* have power. Begin with that, for by activating your sense of power in any area you will be rebuilding self-confidence.

This card indicates tremendous potential for focusing on innovative ideas and then releasing a burst of energy. It is what I call the Houdini card, or backing yourself into a corner. You deliberately get yourself in an apparently impossible situation in order to force a really creative solution. You use your intuition and ingenuity, rather than brute force, to liberate yourself.

The EIGHT OF PENTACLES represents your ability to develop and refine your skill or craft. In the Seven of Pentacles the work was in doubt; here you are sure of your purpose. When a goal is clearly defined, you keep working on it even if it seems tedious. Some situations call on all your energy to keep going. You might be hoping for things to get better. Still, repetition of activities in a ritualistic way gives you a sense of security. You want to be recognized for your craftsmanship and are willing to undergo an apprenticeship to develop your strengths.

You do things with the belief that they are worth your time and effort. You look forward to the future, plan your moves, and prudently prepare things in advance. This is one form of taking care of yourself and your own needs.

One of the greatest skills of a craftsman is knowing both your medium and your message so well that you work in harmony with their natures, so that they function together at their best.

FROM THE MYTHIC TAROT

With this constellation we complete the Patterns of Personal Destiny, and appropriately, that is the task of the 9's and the 18–9's. These patterns emphasize the inner processes (rather than outer actions) that come when you have no one to turn to but yourself. As the minor arcana Nine's indicate, the inward search of Moon-Hermits to find their personal truth is a lonely journey, in which they must accept not only their accomplishments and gains but their despair and isolation.

CHAPTER TWELVE

THE CONSTELLATION OF THE HERMIT: 18–9

THE MOON (18)		THE HERMIT (9)	
9 OF WANDS	9 OF CUPS	9 OF SWORDS	9 OF PENTACLES

THE PRINCIPLE OF INTROSPECTION AND PERSONAL INTEGRITY

THE HERMIT	THE MOON
Virgo	*Pisces*
Completing Karma through Service	Completing Karma through Evolution
Looking Within	Journeying Within
The Seeker	The Source

Keywords: Completion. Perfection. Patience. Integrity. Authenticity. Illusion (Delusions vs. Reality). Karma. Culmination. Journey into the Unknown. Prudence. Reason vs. Instinct.

If you are a Single 9 (9–9), read:

> THE HERMIT (9) AS PERSONALITY OR SOUL CARD
> THE MOON (18) AS HIDDEN FACTOR
> FAMOUS SINGLE 9'S
> THE MINOR ARCANA NINE'S

If you are an 18–9, read:

> THE HERMIT (9) AS PERSONALITY OR SOUL CARD
> THE MOON (18) AS PERSONALITY CARD
> FAMOUS 18-9'S
> THE MINOR ARCANA NINE'S

THE HERMIT (9) AS PERSONALITY OR SOUL CARD

(This applies if you are a Single 9 or an 18–9.)

Completing Karma through Service, Looking Within, The Seeker

THE HERMIT represents introspection, solitude, personal integrity, and prudence. It is a card relating to Virgo and the harvest of the grain. (Some decks include the wheat symbol on the card itself, or show The Hermit holding a scythe.) When ripened grain is cut, it is sacrificed so that it can be transformed

into bread, feeding and serving others. Yet in spring the grain, after a dormant period under the earth, will sprout with new life. Thus The Hermit as Soul Card is a metaphor for how you can serve others with the knowledge you have gathered, which has ripened and been transformed into a palatable form. Likewise, after the long periods of introspection that you need as a Hermit, you too will emerge with new life.

You need to be alone, to have time to yourself. You feel you must work through your own problems and can only make decisions for yourself, yet you are available to assist others. You always have some feeling of isolation but also an inner strength that comes from facing the unknown alone.

''Showing the way'' is your characteristic action, and you will eventually serve as some kind of a teacher or role model for others. Since you are circumspect and discreet, people come to you with their troubles because you don't betray their trust. You know how and when to keep secrets. Your insights into the problems of others help them learn to look within themselves. You teach best by living what you believe in, but you are a perfectionist and may expect others to live up to the same standards. Thus you can be difficult to live with, one of the many isolating factors in your life.

You have strong role models in your own life, and you learn from their actions: not what they say, but what they do. You stand by what you believe in, trusting wisdom that comes from experience and has stood the test of time. This can be a problem if you refuse to take risks or accept anything new. If anything, you are over-cautious, needing to know exactly where you are going, resistant to change, and needing to do things your own way.

Your prudence can make you hesitant with untried solutions and suspicious of iconoclastic behavior. You have no desire to stand out in a crowd or to be flashy or loud. You probably follow social mores and exhibit good manners primarily to escape notice and because it makes the way go smoother. Since you think for yourself, you may actually be quite unconventional, but you are quietly so, preferring to act circumspectly.

Your social detachment and objectiveness draws you to humanitarian service. You project your high ideals into works that will benefit everyone. It is only through such service that you as a Hermit can realize yourself fully. You cannot work successfully for self alone, but must act for the benefit of humanity.

Hermits like to travel but usually do so by themselves. Yet your desire for solitude and sobriety hides an exaggerated need for love and personal acceptance. Since you rarely express this need, you may pretend to be emotionally self-sufficient and even rebuff those who attempt to get too close (as a test to see if they really care).

You have mediumistic gifts and psychic abilities that are of primary importance to your quest for inner understanding, but you like to appear logical and fact-oriented and take pride in an analytical approach to problem-solving. This is a well-developed and possibly unconscious ploy to cover up an almost instinctive awareness of situations. Although your intuitions cannot be explained, you eventually learn to trust them.

As the last of the prime numbers, 9 represents completion. Thus, Hermits usually have something to complete in this lifetime. You have the wisdom of many previous incarnations, which may emerge as easily developed talents and skills. You have little difficulty understanding concepts and probably appeared "older than your years" as a child. Responsibilities and decision-making are thrust on you quite early by your parents—or you impatiently want to be allowed to go your own way. You are here in this lifetime to share what you have learned and thus release it so that you can continue your own development unencumbered by old tasks.

Thus, many Hermits feel that they have a "purpose" and decide on a direction early in life. You have strong creative energies, especially for synthesis, which you apply to definite goals. You plan thoroughly and can clearly visualize the results you want.

You are likely to have friends and relatives whom you feel you've known for a long time. However, you can also easily release old relationships, so don't be surprised by your ability to make deep connections for a short time and then move on without looking back.

Hermits find it hard to ask others for assistance because their natural tendency is to turn within. Yet by allowing others to assist you, you teach while at the same time letting go of your limiting sense of self-importance.

Periodically you will need to turn away from the outer concerns of life. This is necessary in order to consolidate knowledge for completing the task at hand. This task involves looking within, no longer projecting onto others, and simply accepting yourself. A 9, mathematically as well as personally, always returns to itself.

THE MOON (18) AS HIDDEN FACTOR

(This applies if you are a Single 9.)

With THE MOON as your hidden factor, you have some deeply hidden emotions and an inability to see part of yourself—perhaps because you fear that your feelings and psychic abilities will overwhelm you. There can be latent alcoholism or dependency on drugs and mind-altering substances, supported by denial of your blind spots. However, Maurice Maeterlinck, a Single 9, accepted this in saying, "Men's weaknesses are often necessary to the purpose of life" (from *Joyzelle*).

Your shadow reveals its presence by the feeling that there is something inside you, something much bigger than yourself—and you are not sure if it even belongs to you. You feel an unfulfilled urge to be doing something. Somewhere, something is calling to you, but you can't see it. By comparison, everyone else will seem to know just where they are going and what they are doing. You will probably feel confused until you chance upon a goal or task that suddenly feels right. Or you may experience what probably appears to be a series of coincidences, and then find yourself moving swiftly in unplanned directions. Eventually you learn to trust this process.

You tend to be suspicious of others and fear that people are talking behind your back, or that they don't really like you. Thus you may affect an exterior attitude of not caring about anything. Actually you are very sensitive and hunger to be liked and accepted. You want to please those you care about to the extent of being chameleon-like; then you don't understand if they later say you were not being honest.

As The Moon becomes your teacher, you learn to trust in some inner guiding process. You realize that the walls between you and other levels of awareness are very thin. You finally come to realize that your earlier suspicions were other people's self-conscious fears and anxieties, which were acutely sensed by you but rarely directed at you. So you develop compassion and understanding for the human condition. You recognize the suffering that others feel and find ways to alleviate it.

You may have a strong interest in the occult and in reclaiming hidden traditions. You intuitively understand symbolism and may have mystic experiences, especially if you are religiously inclined. Your psychic gifts and strong ability to visualize, if developed, enable you to help others access their own inner worlds. You can be a mirror serving to reflect the hopes, needs, and visions of a group of people. Being very suggestive yourself, you can influence individuals around you, reflecting what they find unable to express. Thus, you can act as a catalyst for people, a potent ability that can have unforeseen results when unconsciously activated but can be consciously channeled to the public good, especially to bring out unexpressed currents and intentions.

FAMOUS SINGLE 9'S

There are currently very few Single 9's in my list of famous people, but we will begin seeing them during the next few years and throughout the 21st century.

Maurice Maeterlinck (Belgian author and playwright) 8/29/1862
Imogene Cunningham (Photographer) 4/12/1883
Evonne Goolagong (Australian tennis champion) 7/31/1951

THE MOON (18) AS PERSONALITY CARD

(This applies if you are an 18–9.)

Completing Karma through Evolution, Journeying Within, The Source

THE MOON represents intuition and delving deep into the unconscious, where the veils between worlds are very thin. With this influence we become aware that reality is a dream, that time and space (as well as our physical bodies) are merely conceptions, and therefore all can be changed. 18–9's don't have abilities that the rest of humanity lacks; they just tend to be more curious about them. As a Moon-Hermit you are fascinated by the unseen and the unknown, the strange, and even the macabre.

THE MOON.

The Moon relates to past lives, to magic and mystery. It involves working with hidden forces and factors and learning to function in the realm of the subconscious. Imagine yourself at night on a forest path during the dark of the moon; you can either make your way slowly along the path, stumbling as you go, or by drawing on your intuitive sense of where you are going, run swiftly and surely without trying to "see" your way. This is activating a sense of inner "knowing" that Hermits must learn to trust. Your life as an 18-9 tends to revolve in cycles like the phases of the moon, moving into periods of heightened psychic awareness, when you find yourself where you "should" be, and then into periods in which you fear that you have been deceived by your insights. You must learn that the cycle has its own correct natural rhythms. The confusion, illusion, and delusion of The Moon comes in part from trying to do something when it is not the right time in the cycle.

Your purpose as an 18-9 is to evolve into a higher being. You are here to deal with specific karmic responsibilities. These can involve making actual genetic changes to help in the evolution of the human race. This is possible through capabilities biologically and psychically inherent in you as an individual, and within the potentialities of all life on the planet. It is through the imagination that you can make subjective experience objective. By mirroring your desire in your mind, you can restructure the particles of energy in order to bring about the outer objective change. You believe, as 18-9 Gandhi did, that "The highest moral law is that we should unremittingly work for the goal of mankind."

The Moon relates to the use of intuitive functions rather than rational ones. This knowledge is often experienced through the body rather than through the brain. And in ancient writings the seat of the brain was either in the gut or the heart. Knowledge was something that came from deep within the body—an inner wisdom that people trusted. As the rational faculties developed, intuitive thinking was no longer valued or trained. The Delphic Oracle fell silent. Fewer and fewer people had access to this knowledge, and it came to be distrusted. For the last several thousand years, the world of the unconscious has been seen as a delusional trap. Yet it is only by the marriage of both lunar and solar consciousness that unity of spirit can be born.

The Moon represents divination, whose language is signs and symbols and whose meaning is not always immediately apparent. You need insight and patience, as indicated by your Soul Card, The Hermit. The moon does not represent deception; it is the "glamour" in which we humans wrap ourselves that deceives us. You probably respect the unseen and unprovable experiences of others as valid experiences from which we can learn. And 18-9's have historically unveiled the realities of both our inner and outer lives.

Just as the crayfish in the card devours all that is decomposing and from this builds its house, so you realize the importance of digesting your past, your fears, and what you have hidden from yourself in order to experience a moral and psychic regeneration. Accepting your destiny, you must leave the crusty shelter that is your past and instinctively take refuge in the pool of your habits. Otherwise you will be caught in nostalgic reveries, in a passive attitude resulting from unfulfilled aspirations. Break out of your shell of old ways of thinking that lock you inside. Pass by your wild desires (the wolf) and your domestic breeding (the dog); walk between the towers of lofty thought and human technology, following the path to the high mountain of spiritual intuition.

Your thinking mind sometimes resists the expansion necessary to take in new concepts. When beyond the control of ordinary perception, there could be a panic reaction that makes you feel as if you are ''going crazy.'' This is probably entry into new levels of awareness, but it can be most unsettling while you are actually experiencing it. This happens very often to the elderly in our society (who are in a Hermit/Crone developmental stage), who go through rapid change and expansion in preparation for their ''crossing,'' only to be labeled ''senile'' as a result.

FAMOUS 18-9'S

To me, diarist Anaïs Nin best characterizes the inner process of an 18-9: ''There is the whole mystery of growth, of expansion, of deliverance from the traps which life sets us, because life loves the drama of entrapping us and seeing whether we can get out. It's a game, a game of magic. Every difficult situation into which you are sometimes thrown has some way of opening somewhere, even if it is only by way of the dream'' (from *A Woman Speaks*).

There are more 18-9's in my total list of over 700 famous people than in any other constellation pattern (many are omitted from this list for the sake of brevity). There are several tendencies in the 18-9's, including a large number of people with interests in ''other realities.'' Of these, many have worked specifically to create ways that others could use to explore these realms, functioning as guides and ''ones-who-show-the-way.'' There is also a surprising number of novelists who I would characterize in general terms as ''imaginative realists'': Nabokov, T. H. White, Uris, Vonnegut, Grass, O'Connor, Updike, Jong. And I want especially to mention Bessie Smith, Billie Holiday, and Ella Fitzgerald, who might have a special understanding of Nin's quote above.

Nostradamus (French astrologer and physician) 12/24/1503
Johann S. Bach (German composer) 3/31/1685
Louis Daguerre (French inventor, photography) 11/18/1789
Dante G. Rossetti (English artist, poet) 5/12/1828
Mother Jones (Mary) (Union organizer) 5/1/1830
Johannes Brahms (German composer) 5/7/1833
John Muir (Naturalist) 4/21/1838
Auguste Rodin (French sculptor) 11/12/1840
Ambrose Bierce (Humorist) 6/24/1842
Nikola Tesla (Serbian scientist, inventor) 7/9/1856
Rudolf Steiner (Austrian metaphysician) 2/27/1861
Mohandas Gandhi (Mahatma, India) 10/2/1869
Virginia Woolf (English writer) 1/25/1882
Kahlil Gibran (Syrian poet, artist) 1/6/1883
Roberto Assagioli (Founder, Psychosynthesis) 2/27/1888
Bessie Smith (Singer) 4/15/1898

Henry Moore (English sculptor) 7/30/1898
Vladimir Nabokov (Russian-American novelist) 4/23/1899
Erich Fromm (Psychoanalyst, writer) 3/23/1900
Bing Crosby (Actor, singer) 5/2/1901
Anaïs Nin (Novelist and diarist) 2/21/1903
Israel Regardie (Metaphysician) 11/17/1907
Billie Holiday (Singer) 4/7/1915
Ella Fitzgerald (Singer) 4/25/1915
T. H. White (Author) 5/6/1915
Kurt Vonnegut (Novelist) 11/11/1922
Leon Uris (Novelist) 8/3/1924
Flannery O'Connor (Author) 3/25/1925
Rock Hudson (Actor) 11/17/1925
Carlos Casteneda (Anthropologist, shaman) 12/25/1925
Allen Ginsberg (Poet, publisher) 6/3/1926
Günter Grass (German novelist) 10/16/1927
Ray Charles (Musician) 9/23/1930
John Updike (Novelist) 3/18/1932
Yoko Ono (Musician, writer) 2/18/1933
Gloria Steinem (Magazine editor, writer) 3/25/1934
Shirley MacLaine (Actress, writer) 4/24/1934
Van Cliburn (Pianist) 7/12/1934
Elvis Presley (Singer, actor) 1/8/1935
Robert Redford (Actor) 8/18/1936
Dustin Hoffman (Actor) 8/8/1937
Jack Nicklaus (Golf champion) 1/21/1940
Erica Jong (Writer) 3/26/1942
Jimi Hendrix (Acid-rock musician) 11/27/1942
Angela Davis (Revolutionary writer) 1/26/1944
Mary Katherine Greer (Tarot author, teacher) 10/14/1947
Robin Williams (Comedian) 7/21/1952

THE MINOR ARCANA NINE'S

The minor arcana NINE'S are the gifts and challenges relating to developing introspective insight, personal integrity, and completion of our lessons. Since the number 9 is usually associated astrologically with the Moon or with Neptune, dreams and delusions play a role in these cards.

The NINE OF WANDS presents the opportunity to face your greatest fears with the gift of strength of purpose. You meet your future with an unshakable stance. You are prepared to protect and support others who are in need. You find spiritual strength in facing your fears. With the Nine of Wands you must complete a spiritual or creative task.

The Nine of Wands also carries a warning that the barriers you have set up to protect you can also become your cage. This concept is a reminder that The Moon corresponds to Pisces, and the symbolic Piscean fish swims both ways.

Rather than completion, this can be a card of following old habits, suggesting inflexibility of outlook. You have risked so much through the previous eight wands that when you come to this one, with its relative safety, you may be afraid to go on. If you fear facing the beasts outside the stockade, you'll be stuck. But the very feeling of being fenced in can force you to the next stage, the Ten's: in the Ten of Wands, the same person has taken down the fence. He is carrying his experiences with him, but is no longer afraid to move on.

The NINE OF CUPS presents the opportunity to create your own reality with the gift of creative imagination. You have dipped nine cups into the pool of the unconscious and have successfully faced all terrors to take the path home. Now you know how to come and go from the land of The Moon (the unconscious) with ease. This card represents working with dreams and intuitive techniques. You can visualize what you desire (the red hat) with such clarity that it comes into being. You have the resources and the knowledge to nurture others along the same path you have traveled.

The problem comes when you begin to think that this is all there is. You become complacent and self-satisfied. Although the tasks are completed, you may not want to move on; you get stuck in sensuality or gluttony, or wrapped up in your fantasies and illusions. This then is the vision of Maya (Hindi for ''illusion''), that is attributed to the Moon.

The NINE OF SWORDS presents the opportunity to grieve, face the demons, or weather the nightmares through the gifts of time and patience. With the Nine of Swords as a Lessons and Opportunities Card, you face the self-cruelty aspects of your idealism and perfectionism. You can find endless faults with yourself, mostly projections of your own fears. Your dreams and memories remind you of the things you should have done, or those things you once had but now are lost. Also, as a highly empathic 18–9, you might be taking all the sorrows of the world on your own shoulders.

And yet, confronting fears and experiencing grief are ways of purging ourselves. The Nine of Swords is essential before any process can be complete. You must transform your pain, first by re-experiencing it, then by identifying the source of the emotion in order to know what to change. When you find yourself in the midst of stress or depression, realize that it is part of a larger cycle of events and is usually the last despair of your rational mind before new possibilities break through from the unconscious.

The NINE OF PENTACLES presents the opportunity to complete the ''work'' of self-development through confidence in your self-discipline and patience. You are in harmony with nature around you. Just as the grapes will ripen in their own time, you know everything will bear its fruit. Although the woman keeps a hawk to remind her of her instincts and intuitions, she knows to keep such a wild creature hooded when not in use. You are alone here, as you are in each of the other Nine's, indicating that you have had to turn to yourself to reap the reward of self-development.

The Nine of Pentacles is called ''gain'' and indicates everything you can gain from your work and skills, including the luxury of leisure and solitude. Another aspect of this card is the loneliness that can come from cutting yourself off from your emotions and personal contacts. In your struggles to reach the top, you may lose your ability to be wild and free. Do you feel confined in your grape orchard, hooding your desire for free expression as the bird is hooded, and, as with the gloved hand, keeping your personal contacts at a distance?

YOUR YEAR CARDS

For each year of your life you have a major arcana card called the Year Card. It represents the tests and lessons you experience in any given year. Some major arcana cards will appear as your Year Cards over and over, while others you will never get. The events that happen to you in any year offer you the opportunity to master new skills and discover more about yourself and your needs. The Year Card points out what that learning will be about. It indicates the kind of archetypal energies that are constellated in that year, suggesting personal qualities you can work with, such as assertion, compassion, relating. Knowing your Year Card makes you more aware of the overall situation at your disposal and the kinds of learning opportunities it presents during that year.

FINDING YOUR YEAR CARD

Following this example, add the month and date of your birth to the current year, and reduce it to 22 or less.

Month of Birth	12
Day of Birth	20
Current Year	<u>1987</u>
	2019 = 12 The Hanged Man

In determining the Year Card, always keep the highest number under 23 and don't reduce it!

Find your own Year Card by adding:

> The month of your birth: _____
> The day of your birth: _____
> The CURRENT YEAR: _____
>   Equals: _____   = _____(Year Number)

For the current year _____, my Year Number is _____, which corresponds to the major arcana card: _____.

THE COMMENCEMENT OF YOUR TAROT YEAR

The first question is: "When does my Year Card begin, on January 1 or on my birthday?" The answer is both! There are two different cycles that overlap to an extent, depending on how late your birthday is in the year.

Your year begins on January 1 in terms of *events happening to you*. You then begin to learn the lesson of the year through experiences that require you to face the issues represented. This is an *outer, event-oriented* cycle.

By your birthday, you have integrated the lessons to the extent that you begin *acting out that energy*. In this way, you have a birthday-to-birthday *inner experience* cycle.

People with birthdays at the beginning through middle of the year will have little trouble using the January-to-January cycle for most purposes. It is often easiest to recognize and identify the outer events that happen to you (January-to-January), rather than your inner motivations and modes of expression (birthday-to-birthday). Those with birthdays in the last two months might find most of their associations with a card falling in the following calendar year. For instance, at the beginning of a Hermit Year all your friends seem suddenly unavailable. At parties you can't seem to connect, etc. Thus you are forced into spending more time alone. By your birthday you've realized how much you can accomplish, as you enjoy the time to complete things and do some reflecting. Then as you move into a Wheel of Fortune Year in January (outer cycle), you are thrown into the whirl of social events and sudden opportunities. You react at first with the prudence and circumspection that you came to trust in your Hermit Year, while wishing that those peaceful moments of solitude would return.

THE *YEAR CARD CHART*

*In Tarot for Your Self there is a chart on which you can graph your cards to get a sense of the flow of the cycles of your life.

It is well worth calculating your Year Cards for your entire life: 90 or 100 years.* The *Year Card Chart* on the following page was designed by Bay Area taroist Twainhart Hill and can be used to quickly determine your Year Card for any specific year. The chart also makes it easy to find the Birth Cards and Year Cards of your friends. This is a good chart to photocopy.

To use the *Year Card Chart*, add up the month, day, and year of your BIRTH. The sum before you reduce it to a tarot card number is _____. I call it your four-digit Base Number. Find this number on the chart; the number corresponding to your Personality Card will be next to it; mark it as ''0 years old'' or ''Born.'' You will not be one year old until the following year. Take the four-digit Base Number from your Year Card calculations and find this number on the chart, with your Year Card number next to it. Write your *age on your birthday this year* in the space next to it. From the present year you can easily count backward or forward.

Look at your last five Year Cards. Lay the cards out on a table or the floor; ask yourself how each of these cards represents lessons you needed to learn in that year. While simple, this system can tell you a great deal. I am surprised at what I learn about myself just by considering the significance of each card. Each year I dialogue with my Year Card, asking it, ''What do I need to learn from you this year?'' But it may take awhile to gain enough perspective to see the real learning, which is why it helps to look at your past cards—to see trends via hindsight. It will also help to refine your foresight in future years.

Make a list of your Year Cards. Next, write a sentence for each year, telling what happened to you in that year and why it was significant. (Don't worry if there are years in which you remember nothing—that's normal; you'll probably remember something else to add whenever you look at your chart.)

CHART 11
YEAR CARD
CHART

Left-hand columns = Base Numbers; Right-hand columns = Year Cards											
1880	17	1916	17	1952	17	1988	8	2024	8	2060	8
1881	18	1917	18	1953	18	1989	9	2025	9	2061	9
1882	19	1918	19	1954	19	1990	19	2026	10	2062	10
1883	20	1919	20	1955	20	1991	20	2027	11	2063	11
1884	21	1920	12	1956	21	1992	21	2028	12	2064	12
1885	22	1921	13	1957	22	1993	22	2029	13	2065	13
1886	5	1922	14	1958	5	1994	5	2030	5	2066	14
1887	6	1923	15	1959	6	1995	6	2031	6	2067	15
1888	7	1924	16	1960	16	1996	7	2032	7	2068	16
1889	8	1925	17	1961	17	1997	8	2033	8	2069	17
1890	18	1926	18	1962	18	1998	9	2034	9	2070	9
1891	19	1927	19	1963	19	1999	10	2035	10	2071	10
1892	20	1928	20	1964	20	2000	2	2036	11	2072	11
1893	21	1929	21	1965	21	2001	3	2037	12	2073	12
1894	22	1930	13	1966	22	2002	4	2038	13	2074	13
1895	5	1931	14	1967	5	2003	5	2039	14	2075	14
1896	6	1932	15	1968	6	2004	6	2040	6	2076	15
1897	7	1933	16	1969	7	2005	7	2041	7	2077	16
1898	8	1934	17	1970	17	2006	8	2042	8	2078	17
1899	9	1935	18	1971	18	2007	9	2043	9	2079	18
1900	10	1936	19	1972	19	2008	10	2044	10	2080	10
1901	11	1937	20	1973	20	2009	11	2045	11	2081	11
1902	12	1938	21	1974	21	2010	3	2046	12	2082	12
1903	13	1939	22	1975	22	2011	4	2047	13	2083	13
1904	14	1940	14	1976	5	2012	5	2048	14	2084	14
1905	15	1941	15	1977	6	2013	6	2049	15	2085	15
1906	16	1942	16	1978	7	2014	7	2050	7	2086	16
1907	17	1943	17	1979	8	2015	8	2051	8	2087	17
1908	18	1944	18	1980	18	2016	9	2052	9	2088	18
1909	19	1945	19	1981	19	2017	10	2053	10	2089	19
1910	11	1946	20	1982	20	2018	11	2054	11	2090	11
1911	12	1947	21	1983	21	2019	12	2055	12	2091	12
1912	13	1948	22	1984	22	2020	4	2056	13	2092	13
1913	14	1949	5	1985	5	2021	5	2057	14	2093	14
1914	15	1950	15	1986	6	2022	6	2058	15	2094	15
1915	16	1951	16	1987	7	2023	7	2059	16	2095	16

(Designed by Twainhart Hill, based on the work of Angeles Arrien.)

Rather than making predictions for cards in the future, determine where you are in a cycle. For instance, people often make major choices in a Lovers Year (6). In the following year, which is usually a Chariot Year, they act on that choice, focusing on moving ahead along the path set in the previous year. And then in the Strength Year (8), they need to reevaluate whether their heart is still in it. If not, they may lack the fortitude to persevere through the two years until the Wheel of Fortune (10) again brings change.

In the following chapter I suggest possible meanings for your Year Cards. For more specific information and direct guidance, use the dialogue technique described in Chapter Three. Ask the card directly what meaning it has for you and how to obtain the most from your year.

USING THE *YEAR CARD CHART*

If you examine the *Year Card Chart*, you will begin to notice several interesting things:

The two columns on the right run in clear ten-year cycles. But note that the other columns also run in ten-year cycles if you realize that the lower numbers like 5, 6, and 7 are actually reduced 23's, 24's, and 25's continuing after the previous 22. The ten-year cycles are marked by double lines. So every ten years you jump to a new cycle of numbers, usually beginning one number higher than the last cycle. If you are young, or if the sum of your birth month and day is a high number (like 12 + 29 = 41), you will not experience the higher numbered major arcana cards. Nevertheless, they are quite common for most of the famous people listed as examples of each constellation pattern. Each historical "age" has its own characteristic pattern of Year Card numbers, which indicates its stage in the cyclical ebb and flow of our "Christian Era" (or "Common Era" as some people prefer to call it) as defined by the Gregorian calendar. Remember that the Year Cards, like the Personality and Soul Cards, give us a look at ourselves in a mirror colored and blurred by this Western Anglo-European society we live in. Perhaps we need a spiritual lunar calendar such as the ancient Mayans used, in which we might see a clearer reflection of our soul's true potential.

People born in any one year could have any of 42 possible four-digit Base Numbers, but these reduce to a far more limited range of cards, depending on the year. For example, people born in 1992 can only have Personality Cards between 2 and 13, or 11 of the 22 constellation patterns. Someone born in 1959 can only have one of 15 possible cards. A person born in 1892 could have any of 18 possible cards from 5 to 22, but not Single 2's, 3's, or 4's—which did not become possible until January 1, 1957. After 1991 there will be no more 19–10–1's or 22–4's until the close of the 21st century, yet these numbers have grown steadily in frequency throughout the last five hundred years until now. These give us our generational factors.

In a lifetime of 80 or so years, the average person will experience the majority of the major arcana cards as Year Cards. Look through your chart to determine which cards (and therefore lessons) you will *never* experience. These are not necessarily for you in this lifetime, representing qualities probably already well developed. Which cards will you receive most often? These are your greatest lessons to learn and probably the most difficult, but you are not alone—your entire generation has a similar focus.

YOUR KARMIC YEAR

The four-digit Base Number that is the sum of your birth month, day, and year *before reducing* can itself be read as if it were a year, and is important to you. It represents a year that especially tests and challenges you to develop your potential. I call it your Karmic Year because unfinished issues from the past that express "soul" themes come up in that year, giving you an opportunity to complete them, or at least recognize your task and begin that process. An example of this is pertinent to us all on a world-wide level: According to the Mayan Calendar, we are completing its Great Cycle of 5,125 years in 2012 A.D., which according to their legends indicates a great shift in world consciousness and communication. José Argüelles, author of *The Mayan Factor: Path Beyond Technology*, says that this date is preceded by what he calls "Harmonic Convergence" on August 16–17, 1987. He describes this as "the moment at which acceleration phases into synchronization. Following that moment will be the rapid unfolding of the stage of planetary civilization leading to galactic climax, 2012 A.D."[1] It is interesting to note in our context here that 8/17/1987 adds up to the four-digit number 2012! Reducing this number, we find that its card is The Hierophant (5), and therefore it is a year of teaching and learning, of new knowledge to be revealed.

GETTING IN TOUCH WITH YOUR SOUL PURPOSE

Look at your *Year Card Chart* again. Every ten years you will have experienced your Personality, Soul, or Hidden Factor Card as a Year Card. Circle these years on your chart and note their actual calendar year and your age. During these years you were probably drawn to and involved in the things that are especially important to your soul purpose in this lifetime. You were probably doing or directly searching for something in which you could express your highest potential. Look at your achievements, actions, travels, relationships, studies—how you spent your time and what you hungered to do. Where did your fantasies and dreams lead you in those years? These are the things that are probably most in line with your soul purpose.

Occasionally you will find that in one or more of these personally important years, you felt your greatest frustration and pain. This happens when you feel powerless to follow your own needs and instincts or to develop your interests. You might then project your own potentials onto someone else who awes you with their ability, or perhaps you resist their influence and thus reject the qualities and learning that the card represents. This happens when your task seems too powerful for you. When you project your potentials onto a powerful person outside yourself, that person actually indicates the possibilities accessible to you, which you can gradually assimilate and eventually express in your own lifework and personality. Each time your Personality, Soul, or Hidden Factor Card appears as a Year Card—in ten-year cycles—you will have particular opportunities to work with the constellated energies of your destiny.

MILESTONES AND TURNING POINTS

To find the significance of any major event in terms of your personal development, look at your *Year Card Chart* to see when that event happened. Then look at the card for that year to see the nature of its energy. For instance, if you married in a Lovers Year, it would be obvious that you learned about your wants and needs in a relationship and how another person mirrors your own self-image. But people get married under the auspices of all the different Year Cards. So, if you were married in an Emperor Year and you are a woman, you might have taken the initiative. You might also have been learning to organize and establish a firm foundation. Or, if you felt uncomfortable asserting yourself, you might have chosen an older father-figure as your mate to teach you what The Emperor energy is about. Whereas a Wheel of Fortune Year would have emphasized lessons of change and expanding horizons that you experienced as a result of the marriage. The Year Card associated with your marriage or any ongoing commitment will generally characterize your entire involvement in it.

THE AGE OF THE HIGH PRIESTESS

Waite-Smith

Near the middle of the *Year Card Chart* you will find the four-digit Base Number 2000. At this point a whole new kind of cycle begins. This ushers in a period during which The High Priestess can appear as a Single 2; that is, as both Personality and Soul Card (instead of only in combination with an 11 or a 20). Most people who are adults in the second half of the twentieth century will experience The High Priestess once in their lives as a Year Card. Quite a few people born from December 31, 1957 through January 1, 1998 will have her as their Personality Card. The High Priestess has not figured as a Personality or Year Card for the last 900 years, since January 1, 1098 A.D. She will not appear as a Birth or Year Number again for approximately 8,000 years!

Marseilles

It is interesting that she appears just before a period that has been marked by the prophecies of native peoples all over the world as the time of the possible destruction of the world. Most of these myths allow for a choice or decision to be made by human beings about how to relate globally in order to save our planet.

Hanson-Roberts

At the end of the last millennium, it was necessary to integrate the lessons of The Magician into western culture—that is, among those of us who agree to use this calendar to mark our time and progress. I believe that this had to do with the rise of individual consciousness. The Magician as Personality, Soul, or Year Card was only possible between the years 958 A.D. and 998 A.D., for a period of forty years and a day. It was during this period that England, Hungary, and Poland first had a king over an entire unified country, and that many countries established Christian rulerships (Poland, England, Sweden, Hungary, and Kievan Russia). Most importantly, this period heralded (in the Christian world) the end of the millennium after the birth of Christ, bringing universal fear of the Last Judgment (20) and the end of the world. All of Europe was on the move as people left their homelands on pilgrimages so that they could meet their end at one of the holy sites of Europe or in Jerusalem.

Aquarian

As Europe moved into the next century (the 11th) and the world was not destroyed, there began a period with many changes and signs of a new aeon. This was the period of the last appearance of The High Priestess as a Personality, Soul, or Year Card, or 900 years ago—lasting from 958 A.D. (Dec. 31, 958 = 1001) to January 1, 1098 A.D. At this time, food was more abundant than ever before, due to the advent of new plows with wheels, and so the population drastically increased. Famines were still periodic, but this was before the times of the great plagues. The Eastern Orthodox and Western Roman Churches were making their final break with each other. Gregory VII was cleaning up the excesses of the previous profligate popes of Rome. And in 1054 a minor star in the constellation Taurus exploded in a supernova visible for 23 days by daylight and for two years by night, creating what we call today the Crab Nebula.*

Mythic

*An interesting synchronicity associated with the creation of the Crab Nebula in Taurus during the last High Priestess period is that The High Priestess corresponds astrologically with the Moon, which "rules" Cancer (symbolized by the crab) and is "exalted" (that is, finds its highest expression) in Taurus.

In keeping with The High Priestess influence, it was a time of strong women rulers, such as the Byzantine Empresses Zoe, Theodora, and Eudoxia Macrimbolitissa. Women physicians studied, worked, and taught at Salerno, Italy and other centers where Greek, Latin, Jewish, and Arabian medical teachings were being revived. Women scholars also taught and wrote in the universities of Muslim southern Spain, while El Cid was driving the Moors out of northern Spain. Women held and administered an historical high of 25 percent of the land, either in their own names or in trust for heirs. Men were often identified in town registers only by their mothers' names. Many of these were the children of priests and not able to take their fathers' names. However, Rome was becoming determined to bind the priesthood to itself through celibacy, and in 1074 all married priests were excommunicated. The 12th and 13th centuries saw the rise of a civil bureaucracy that allowed no posts for women, lowered their status and legal rights, and blocked them from fulfilling important decision-making roles.

Motherpeace

In 1095 the new pope, Urban II, declared the First Crusade to free the Holy Land. Yet before any official army could gather, an unprecedented People's Crusade began marching toward Constantinople to take the Black Sea route to the infidels of the Levant. Peasants, tramps, and common people set off toward the East in a stream that has been likened to a modern gold rush. These people were inspired by wandering "mad" preachers, the pressures of an increasing population, and some kind of mass dream. Unfortunately, their wild fervor and unrest led them to massacre whole communities of Jews in Germany and France, as well as fellow Christians, when they reached lands with foreign languages and customs. Most of these Crusaders were killed or died before they ever reached the Black Sea or saw a single Muslim.

Daughters of the Moon

Now once again we have the opportunity to learn the lessons of the High Priestess. The High Priestess as the number 2 suggests the idea of a choice between two options. She is also pointing to a reawakening of the Goddess. In no other period of women's written history has there been such a widespread interest in women's spirituality. New appearances of the Virgin Mary are inspiring miracles and pilgrimages. This has happened since people have begun experiencing the High Priestess as a Year Card. In my experience, I have found that most women have significant spiritual awakenings in their High Priestess Year. This is a year when they often become involved in psychic, intuitive, or healing studies. They will often literally discover the myths and religion of the Great

Thoth

Voyager

Neuzeit

Goddess in their 2 Year. There is usually increased independence and self-reliance, strong friendships with women, and a compelling need to be near water or out in the country where the cycles of the moon can be observed.

Men in a High Priestess Year will often be drawn to women who represent an ideal in their lives. The woman, actual or imaginary, can be a muse, confidante, or spiritual teacher, but often is mysterious or unapproachable in some way, maintaining her independence. If she falls from this status and wants a more personal human relationship, the man may feel disillusioned. Actually, a 2 Year is an opportunity for a man to open up to the artistic, psychic, and intuitive aspects of himself, as well as acknowledging and getting to know his inner feminine aspect, or *anima*, as it is called by Carl Jung. It could be the emergence of The High Priestess (who represents the sacred *qadishtus*—translated incorrectly as prostitutes—of the Temples of the Goddess) that has allowed so many men and women to explore non-procreative sexuality and erotic love with their own sex.

Native American

Those people who were born with The High Priestess as both Personality and Soul Card, or who had the High Priestess in their early childhood, will have had an opportunity to integrate many of the High Priestess qualities into their whole outlook on life. Because of their extreme psychic sensitivity and openness to the other planes of reality, they sometimes find it difficult to be practical and down-to-earth, or to deal with the input of too many people. They are often quiet and withdrawn. Although probably aware of the undercurrents and invisible aspects of life, they may have limited scope for their experiences in our society. From a sense of self-preservation, they may attempt—without realizing it—to close down their psychic centers and thus appear (and even be) uncaring and insensitive to others. This could result in the dangerous combination of someone who is sensitive to the dreams of the masses, yet has hardened to the feelings of individuals. We can see this effect in Ronald Reagan, who as a 20–2 (Judgement-High Priestess) embodies the fantasy President desired by the public, yet in reality is a callous practitioner of George Orwell's *1984* vision of "double speak." Seemingly believing his own lies, he preaches right to life, peace, and freedom while promoting war and public debt, cutting social services and individual liberties, and actually perpetrating the death and destruction of peoples through both official (CIA) and unofficial terrorist organizations.

Morgan-Greer

Xultun

Tarot Classic

MOON MEDITATION

The following moon meditation is especially effective in a High Priestess Year, or for anyone with a special connection to The High Priestess. At the time of the first sliver of the new (waxing) moon, begin or conceptualize a project that you want to work on. Go outside and look at the first tiny sliver and commit yourself to its growth. Every night thereafter, try to catch a glimpse of the moon, and as it grows note how your project also grows. Collect everything you need to make it work: do research, gather materials, visualize your goal. At the full moon, look at what you have—see what is revealed in the full light of the moon. Often there is a realization, insight, or new understanding of what you are doing. Acknowledge the fullness of the light. This is also a time to present your project to others, if appropriate. Then as the moon wanes, use, teach, disseminate, give away, release, analyze, criticize, edit your project. Continue to follow the cycle of the moon, and as the light wanes, watch the darkness grow; realize that as you act on your project, you are increasing your inner knowledge and understanding with the growing darkside of the moon. At the new moon phase, when no light shines, you have taken all of your energy back into yourself; now release and let go of all previous expectations and activities and await the emergence of your new focus from deep within. This may be a new phase of what you have been working on, or something entirely different.

THE MINOR ARCANA AS YEAR CARDS

While the minor arcana are not individually described here, they are indicators of the gifts and challenges (lessons and opportunities) you will have in the corresponding year. Lay out the minor arcana cards that correspond to a memorable year in your past. Look at how these cards might express the situations that brought your most powerful learning experiences that year. (For instance, in a Fool Year (22) all the minor Four's will be significant.)

Year   Why Memorable?

———   ——————————————————————————————————————

Year Card   Principle of Its Constellation

——————————————   ——————————————————————————

Minor Arcana   Specific Situations from That Year
  Cards   as Described by the Card
——— of Wands   ——————————————————————————
——— of Cups   ——————————————————————————
——— of Swords   ——————————————————————————
——— of Pentacles   ——————————————————————————

Describe the major lessons and the abilities developed.

Continue this exercise with other significant years. Don't try to "predict" how they might function in the current or coming years unless you understand how the minor cards have worked in the past.

While the next chapter suggests some of the lessons and opportunities of the different Year Cards, nothing substitutes for your own observation of what actually happened to you in past years, and for dialoguing directly with the images on the cards, which should be done at least once a year with your current Year Card.

NOTES

1. Barbara Hand Clow, "An Interview with José Argüelles," *Welcome to Planet Earth*, Vol. 6, No. 10 (1987), p. 31 ff.

CHAPTER FOURTEEN

INTERPRETING YOUR YEAR CARDS

The following interpretations of the major arcana cards* as Year Cards suggest lessons to be learned in each year (see Chapter Thirteen, with its *Year Card Chart*). They are intended to be suggestive rather than authoritative. Don't use them as a substitute for dialoguing with the cards yourself, as described in Chapter Three. In other words, try to discover directly what they have to tell you. The various symbols on your current Year Card are psychic (and sometimes literal) tools you can use, but you must ask the figure(s) on the card what the symbols are for and how to use them. When you dialogue with your Year Card (preferably addressing one or more figures on the card in turn), the best way to begin the dialogue is with a question. For instance, the key question in this case is: "What do I need to learn from you this year?" Remember to do this with an air of spontaneous nonchalance, beginning playfully and saying whatever comes to mind. Your pen should be in constant motion. Your first dialogue should be no more than ten to fifteen minutes.

*The cards illustrated here are from a generic Marseilles-style deck. I've reversed its traditional 8–11 sequence for the sake of consistency throughout the book. Refer to Appendix A for further discussion.

Date these dialogues and keep them in your Tarot Notebook, along with written observations about previous years and the correlations of the cards to the events of each year. You may also want to use the margins of this book to note (next to the description of each card) your age and the year(s) during which it is your personal Year Card.

YOUR MAGICIAN YEAR

Forget it! No one in our era can experience The Magician as a Personality, Hidden Factor/Teacher, or Year Card. Since January 1, 998 the number 1 has not appeared by itself, and it won't again until we get dates adding up to 10,000, beginning on December 31, 9,957 A.D.

YOUR HIGH PRIESTESS YEAR

The High Priestess will only appear once in anyone's life as a Year Card, and for many people not at all. There will be no more High Priestess Years after January 1, 1998 until December 31, 9958 A.D.—which will add up to 10,001 = 2. If you were born with a four-digit Base Number (the sum of your birthdate—see the previous chapter) greater than 2000, you will not experience the High Priestess at all. This does not mean you cannot develop her qualities. If the work has been done well by those who came before, then you will have more opportunity to access her wisdom than previously. Look to your Justice (11) Year (Strength Year if you use it as 11) to see how you are using her energy in your life.

Look at your High Priestess Year if you have one. It is part of a two-year cycle of the feminine, as it is followed by an Empress Year. Women are very important to your learning. Often there is an increased interest in the psychic, metaphysical, or dream worlds. It is a year of learning to trust in yourself and of being independent and self-sufficient. Many people are drawn to the women's spirituality movement (new to this generation of feminists).

As a woman, you may find that people come to you for advice and understanding —a confidante or lover to many but belonging to none. As a man, you might find yourself inspired by a woman in your work or personal life, a muse to your creativity. As a projection of your anima, she awakens in you the feminine principle.

Take your vacation and holidays at seaside or watery places—for healing and meditation and to bring yourself back into balance with nature. Be aware of the cycles of the moon and how they affect you. This is a year in which you must trust to your instincts and inner knowledge to guide you to the lessons you need to learn. Sometimes you come face to face with your deepest fears and hopes, and especially, dreams. (Chapter Thirteen has further commentary on The High Priestess.)

YOUR EMPRESS YEAR

The Empress first appears following the High Priestess Year, extending the feminine cycle into a second year and projecting the High Priestess self-sufficiency out into the world. The Empress uses the intuitive knowledge of The High Priestess, expressing it through her creative imagination. The Empress will later appear in one subsequent cycle without The High Priestess, after which The Hanged Man will take her place in the cycle. During your Empress Year, you can be very creative, even prolific, with your mind a rich field of ideas. Your response to everything is more sensual, intensifying your awareness of color, form, and style.

You're more disposed to relate to others in an Empress Year. Other people will be attracted to you as well, sensing your openness to them and responding to your hospitality. Because of your heightened sense of harmony and beauty, you will want to be surrounded by beautiful things, especially in your home and on your body. You may change your clothing style or otherwise modify your appearance. Watch your weight as well as your pocketbook, for The Empress's sense of luxury can extend into overindulgence.

This is a good year to reconnect with Mother Earth: get out into the country or work in a garden as much as possible. Maternal issues are prominent: relations with your mother, or your own desire to mother. You can be very fertile as well as creative, so if this applies, you may be ripe for becoming pregnant; be extra careful if you don't want to. If a man, you are just as fertile with ideas and ripe for a relationship. You can develop the gracious, hospitable, and sensitive-to-emotions side of yourself—if you dare. The capability to nurture and care for the growth, health, and well-being of others is heightened at this time.

YOUR EMPEROR YEAR

The Emperor Year is the first year of a two-year cycle of learning to establish your own authority. It represents fathers and patriarchy—deciding "who gives the orders around here." Father-issues therefore stand out: being a father, dealing with your own father, accessing your "father-within," or relating to a projected father-figure. The Emperor tries hard to establish rules of order, creating stability in his environment. In such a year you will either be doing this yourself or reacting to orders coming from outside yourself. In the latter case you may be rebelling against what you see as an imposition on your freedom by the dictates of others.

When The Emperor follows The Empress Year, which is a year of abundant creativity, you then take your work from the private sphere and seek a way to go public. You focus on getting recognition or approval for your work and finding ways to establish yourself in the marketplace. You initiate projects that will hopefully make your name. You pioneer new things. You go forth to conquer the world.

Your lessons focus on establishing authority for making your own rules, or learning how to live with the rules of others. You become assertive, and even forceful if necessary, in presenting your ideas. There can be confrontations with the "state" or with the law. You need to know your domain so that you can work efficiently within it. You risk becoming so dictatorial that you stifle those around you. Overdependent on linear reasoning, your thinking can become "square." Leadership and management roles this year may advance you to positions of responsibility and prestige.

YOUR HIEROPHANT YEAR

The Hierophant Year is the second in the power and authority cycle. People often go back to school, complete a course of study, or receive on-the-job training or perhaps counseling. If you are a teacher, trainer, or counselor yourself, this can be an important year to establish yourself in the field or to develop your professional skills. As the minor arcana Five's indicate (they are all problematic), you learn best this year through adversity or when faced with problems to solve. So this may be a year of stress, threatening the stability you tried to establish in The Emperor Year. You may respond by rigidly adhering to tradition, also indicated by its correspondence to Taurus. You can take advantage of this year by learning to listen to your own inner counsel. Taurus is ruled by Venus (The Empress), and the Moon (The High Priestess) is "exalted"—meaning that it is a good time to rely on inner knowledge.

Educational or corrective institutions, religious organizations, and corporations can assume the role of authority figures in this year, and the rebellion you may feel is more generic than personal, although it may be represented by a single person. Or you could become the spokesperson or "rep" for such an organization. You are confronted by all your indoctrinated "shoulds" and "oughts," which you will try to either uphold or oppose. Examine your values and beliefs to determine which ones still apply to your life: which ones limit and which ones produce growth? You can often tell when a Hierophant situation is activated because your emotions get involved. Trace those emotional reactions back to the old teachings that generated them; then assess them for their current appropriateness. In a Hierophant Year there is usually someone you look up to as an authority, perhaps a guru or spiritual leader, or maybe just someone you go to for advice. You probably find people turning to you for assistance since you represent access to some kind of knowledge at this time. Even in passing down traditional teachings, listen carefully to what you say. Are you speaking from your heart in accord with your inner wisdom, or are you routinely transmitting dogma? Use your ability to find your own answers.

YOUR LOVERS YEAR

In a Lovers Year the focus is on relationships. People initiate them and end them, or occasionally will not be in any relationship at all because they are unwilling to accept less than what they really want and need. It may also refer to relationships with your family, co-workers or friends. As a card related to Gemini and ruled by Mercury, one of your lessons is to learn to communicate openly and honestly, with nothing concealed. You expect this from others, as well as yourself, in a Lovers Year.

The greatest lesson is: What do you want and need in relationships? The people with whom you seriously relate reflect your own self-image, and so in a Lovers Year look at how others view and treat you to learn how you feel about yourself.

This is also a year to begin turning to yourself for much of the support and encouragement you need. You do this by realizing that you can establish communication with an inner voice (often perceived as being of the opposite sex) that has a direct line to your highest Self. You learn to withdraw your expectations and projections from the people around you. This year you begin to blend and balance the masculine and feminine energies within yourself.

An old title for this card is "The Two Paths," reminding us that a Lovers Year is a year of choices and often involves a major turning point in your ten-year cycle. Your relationships then will have a major influence on your choices and decisions, and may possibly be the cause of them. Remember that forthright communications are the hallmark of the year and essential in making all decisions.

YOUR CHARIOT YEAR

In the Chariot Year you act and move ahead on the decisions made in the Lovers Year. (For instance, you may decide to end a relationship in a Lovers Year, but may not do so until The Chariot Year.) The Chariot Year focuses on your goals, so you harness your energies to move forward. As a 7, signifying initiation, it is a year in which to master abilities. You have to prove your expertise by handling difficult situations, often with conflicting aspects. You need to work on self-control and self-discipline. If you give free rein to your instincts and emotions (represented by the sphinxes), they may tear you apart. This can be experienced as some kind of breakdown (losing your temper or worse) or an accident (sometimes literally acted out in your automobile/chariot).

You act as a warrior in a Chariot Year. The moons on the shoulders of the charioteer signal a need to serve and protect others, or to champion a cause. Like the knights of old searching for the Grail, when you are goal-oriented and have a definite direction in which to move, your Chariot Year has the most meaning. You are developing assertion and creating an identity in the world. If you drive too hard, you could become belligerent and egotistical, running roughshod over everyone else.

To help you assert yourself in the world, you put on some sort of suitable armor, uniform, or persona of appearance. For instance, an expensive suit promotes you as a successful business person, while a special uniform or set of tools inspires confidence in your mastery. Such devices also cloak your sensitive feelings and insecurities.

People often travel or relocate in a Chariot Year, yet as a card relating to Cancer, your sense of roots is necessary for you to feel secure in a possibly turbulent year. Occasionally you become so attached to home or protected by armor that you "turn to stone" and become an immovable object. As the Moon rules Cancer, being near water can help you to relax those touchy emotions and calm your jangled nerves.

YOUR STRENGTH YEAR

In your Strength Year the central questions are: Is my heart in what I am doing? Is it what I truly desire? After a year of suppressing your feelings in order to get ahead, you find your essential emotions re-emerging. In fact, you will need them if you are to continue in your chosen direction. Without renewed passion, you may not endure the challenges and could be forced to redirect your efforts. It's time to look at your instinctual nature and deal with any fears you have around it.

As a card relating to Leo, this year you experience a "lust" (as Crowley calls this card) for creativity and self-expression. Like the sap rising in spring, you feel a lust for life and a desire to demonstrate your affections, to take the risk of declaring what you love. It can be a year of sensual and sexual exploration. Hopefully you will direct this passion into meaningful projects, and not waste it or allow it to become a destructive force. In ritual magic this is called raising a "cone of power," which when released is directed toward a specific purpose, or else its energy can wreak havoc. So look carefully at what you are doing, because you are metaphorically "playing with fire." And like fire, your emotions can be a great civilizing force or a great destructive one, depending on how you use and direct them. Embrace what you feel to be ugly or beastly in yourself, because through such acceptance you build strength of character.

The Strength Year may challenge you to use all your fortitude in order to persevere through situations of great difficulty, such as career, health, or family problems. You must balance your own needs with the needs of those you love. You may be tested in your ability to handle something heart-rending, to stick with it no matter how hard it gets. By being courageous, you build inner strength as you plumb the depths of your heart. Strength is the beating pulse of the heart that says, "One step at a time, I continue in the direction my heart calls.'' From those things you love, which often conflict with each other, you discover what you really want.

YOUR HERMIT YEAR

In a Hermit Year you become isolated and are alone, usually right from the beginning of the year. You try to get together with friends, but they are busy, have moved, or are involved in other things. But then you find that you like having more time to yourself. There are things you need to reflect on and things to complete, and you need time alone to do this. In a 9 Year (last of the prime numbers) you need to finish any projects or any other loose ends from the last several years, so that you will be unencumbered and can begin new things in the following year. Tie them up and send them out of your life, or else they'll become part of the baggage hanging you up in a Hanged Man Year.

Your Hermit Year is a year of introspection: you look back at where you've been and forward to where you're going. Acknowledge your accomplishments and see what you have mastered in this last cycle. You are standing on the peak of some kind of achievement: what is it? It is time to reconnect with your long-term goals. The Hermit has actually captured the star from The Star card and is using that vision to light the way. What is the light that illuminates your path?

You may find a teacher or guide to help you in a Hermit Year. Such a person usually seems older and wiser and represents a role model to emulate. Or you can be such a guide to someone else, remembering that with The Hermit energy you teach by example, not by what you say. From your withdrawn position, you gain a broad perspective and compassionate humanitarianism that could benefit many people within your circle.

After the energy expenditure of the Strength Year, you may feel the need of some well-deserved rest. So let any wounds heal and reconnect with your sense of self. As a card corresponding to Virgo, you work hard and selflessly to prepare for the future. Remember that prudence can become overcautiousness, persistence can become obstinacy, and wisdom can become sanctimoniousness.

YOUR WHEEL OF FORTUNE YEAR

The beginning of a Wheel of Fortune Year is usually unmistakable. After a year of solitude and inner focus, you find yourself out in the limelight. You're in the middle of a social whirl, or spinning like a top.

With The Wheel of Fortune Year as your Year Card, you have come to another turning point. From your past experience, you bring seeds for a new direction, but also burdens and obligations. The wheel is the equilibrium of contrary forces, irreversibly set in motion. You probably move or change jobs this year, or make some other turnaround in your life. After the introspection of The Hermit Year, you find yourself being more social again and expanding your horizons. New opportunities and choices present themselves, and you'll see options you never noticed before.

Depending on what projects you completed last year, and how well, you begin to see the results in this year. You receive recognition for your accomplishments and appear in public or are thrust out beyond your usual niche in some way. You may find yourself flying high and wide, literally or figuratively.

It's an excellent time for educational pursuits, communicating or publishing your ideas, and initiating new projects—although these seeding actions might not bear fruit for some time yet. Now's the time, though, to set goals, acknowledge dreams, and make long-range plans, visualizing the whole before becoming embroiled in the details. This is also a year in which things literally turn up, often the results of processes begun long ago. For example, friends not seen in a decade may pop up, perhaps to make you aware of the effects of your actions over that time, with all its growth and changes.

All in all, this is a fortunate year, in which experience gained as the wheel turns now helps you focus on your new direction.

YOUR JUSTICE YEAR

The Justice Year heralds a new beginning, with decisions to be made after assessing the pros and cons of various proposals. It is also a year of adjustment. You need to assimilate the changes that occurred during the Wheel of Fortune Year.

In a Justice Year you could be involved in legal matters (the scales of justice) or handling financial affairs (the scales of business). You might consider a partnership of some kind, whether in business or your personal life. Contracts and documents are therefore important and should be examined carefully. For instance, getting married in a Justice Year has special significance as a contract, so it's a good idea to write your marital agreements down.

In our society you were trained (especially if a woman) to compromise first—to assess what the other person probably wants, and then figure out how far you can go along with that, *before you even know clearly what you want.* Sit down by yourself and make notes about what *you* would want if you could have anything, no holds barred: your fantasy situation, perfection without compromise. Then negotiate. If everyone involved does this, it opens the way to mutual trust. In any case, the challenge is to be true to yourself, to see clearly what things you can give up without resentment and what you cannot let go of. Justice is a symbol for inner judgments relating to personal guilt and sin. Anything you get involved in that is not fair to you will become untenable in the following year.

Therefore, this is a year to accept responsibility for yourself, to assess the effects of your actions and judgments, and to make adjustments as necessary. You need to evaluate the changes that have been happening in order to determine what you want to keep in your life and what no longer truly or fairly expresses who you are. You need to judge how you spend your time and energies and whether you are getting fairly recompensed for your efforts. If you are self-employed, adjustments in what you charge or how you do things may be necessary.

YOUR HANGED MAN YEAR

In a Hanged Man Year you will have to release things from your past. Sometimes, when this involves the loss of someone you are attached to, it feels like a betrayal. The painful or wounding experiences of such a year, however, do serve the purpose of inward spiritual growth. You let go of old patterns so that new ones can form in accordance with your new commitments. Sacrifices are made in Hanged Man Years, in which you put someone else's needs first or sacrifice one thing for the sake of another.

It can be a year in which you feel confused or thwarted, with your activities suspended. You may devote yourself selflessly to some task, or you may have to deal with an "impossible situation" requiring you to trust unquestioningly in some force beyond you. The Hanged Man is a symbol of mystical isolation as a ritual of purification. Thus the sacrifice of your self-interest in dedication to a cause will bring understanding of the deeper meaning of your acts.

If you find yourself in situations in which you feel powerless and unable to act, you may turn to fantasy, alcohol, drugs, or workaholism—anything to escape. A completely different perspective can help; don't expend energy negating a problem; instead put your focus and energy on its opposite. It can mean a reversal of everything you formerly stood for. Humility is essential, as you discover in your Hanged Man Year that there are many things you cannot control. Nevertheless, you can experience the spirit of divinity flowing through you, releasing you from limitations in your imagination, art, or devotion to the task.

YOUR DEATH YEAR

It is rare that in your Death Year an actual death will occur, for it signifies transformation rather than termination—a time to shed old skin for new growth. Following a Hanged Man Year in which you faced whatever was hanging you up, now you are liberated, often resulting in a new surge of energy. You cut through stagnation to get to the things that work for you. By trimming off the dead branches and dying aspects of your life, you allow all the lifeforce to flow into the healthy parts so that they can spring forth with new energy. Whatever is destroyed this year makes way for new life.

While you may experience feelings of being dismembered, you will find yourself getting down to the bare-bones scaffolding of your life or of a creative project. Once you've gotten rid of all that's unnecessary, what's left is something you can really trust and believe in. With nothing to block them any longer, your creative energies are set free to explore new possibilities.

So the Death Year is actually a year of great vigor, liberated from inadequate forms. Since Scorpio is the corresponding sign, you have the drive to plunge deeply into investigating hidden things, to do research, or to be involved in some underworld schemes. You might court danger, enjoying the thrill of living close to the edge. Having the ability to merge totally with something else means that your experience will be deeply transformative. Your sexual experiences likewise can be ones in which you lose your sense of self in merging with the other—what in Elizabethan times was known as the "little death." You are passionately aware of life and love, but can also become jealous and possessive; if so, beware—for what you try to possess may be wrenched away even more painfully. The question you need to ask yourself in a Death Year is: "What needs to be cleared away so that new growth can surge forth unhampered?"

YOUR TEMPERANCE YEAR

Your Temperance Year is one in which you creatively combine things in new and different ways. You have the inner endurance to slowly wear away all obstacles with patience and grace. You find resources and assistance you didn't know were available before: some from friends and co-workers, but mostly from within.

You can go traveling, or redistribute your energy or possessions. It is a year for rejuvenation of your higher mind—for philosophy, communications, or healing. You are interested in new forms for old things and how to revive stale ideas. You may even work on some kind of restoration or conservation project.

You build bridges and heal breaches, perhaps through networking or acting as a mediator. You want to make things work again. You seek spiritual guidance but you want practical results.

If the Death Year was painful and disintegrating, then in the Temperance Year take time to restore yourself, balancing your energies and building your new self. Being near water, taking time alone to commune with your inner self, and finding a compassionate friend will all be of great help. If you have been through this before, you can now serve as a compassionate friend and healer to another.

YOUR DEVIL YEAR

In your Devil Year you want to develop the resources you discovered in the Temperance Year. You established lines of communication and networks last year and now you want to use them to build grand projects. Any doubts now cause you to create elaborate schemes that promise success. Ambition makes you work hard, perhaps compulsively, to keep ahead of the competition. You are possessed by your desires, embattled by crises, and have little time for anything else.

You may feel blocked and angered by the "big boys" like government, the military, big business, and even organized religion, whose corruption and dishonesty you have become sensitive to. If so, you want to break taboos, cheat on your taxes, or become involved in disruptive action. Guilt over such thoughts will build up frustration and apprehension until you see evil and pandemonium everywhere, leading to personal pessimism and distrust of everyone, even yourself.

On the other hand, the Devil Year is a time for learning to play with your own power. You can stir up excitement devilishly with imaginative and daring escapades. You defy conventions and throw open Pandora's box, this time not to release demons but the gifts that her name ("all gifts") implies. Using mirth and imagination, your potential here is to free yourself and others from all forms of enslavement.

YOUR TOWER YEAR

Your Tower Year is one of revolution, with the shattering of unnecessary forms and structures. It presents an opportunity to dissolve barriers between yourself and others and to discover what is really important to you.

The extent of change this year depends on what happened last year. If you built a tower of achievement by using your power over others, this will be a year of violent testing. Even if your achievement was modest, expect tremors in your life. Organizations fall, belief structures crumble, and repressed forces are likely to release suddenly, as indicated by the correspondence of this card to the planet Mars. Falsehoods will be revealed. You either break through old forms with new insights consciously, or nature may do it for you through accidents, natural disasters, or other people's actions. You may lose or change jobs, relationships, or living arrangements. Your physical appearance is affected: you have surgery, an accident, burn up with fever (and burn out impurities), or lose weight.

Recognize this need to regroup and reform, and take action to bring it about consciously. Release energy blockages by becoming aware of them and acknowledging the feelings they engender. When you lose your temper, get stressed out, or behave badly or inappropriately, you have located blocked and repressed energy. When released consciously, this energy can power you through previously insurmountable problems.

You may have become rigid and no longer able to grow; now is the time to liberate yourself. The question of the year is how to break open your blockages without guilt and without releasing destructive energies. First accept that action is necessary. Draw upon intuitive hunches, enlightened ideas or "improbable" solutions; act on them as new possibilities for future development.

This is an excellent year to make breaks with the past. Literally and figuratively, clean up your house and your act. Break some old habits and start some new ones. Let go of preconceptions about how things are going in your life and make room for a fresh new future.

YOUR STAR YEAR

Your Star Year is usually a time of reflection and hope. You are completely exposed, as all falsehoods and false ambitions were stripped away last year. You rejoice in your freedom and effortlessly grow toward new aspirations, using abilities previously untapped. You may feel overwhelmed by potentialities and unknown frontiers, yet aware that all answers lie within you.

Another possibility for a Star Year is that you awaken from your previous year's shake-up to emerge as some sort of luminary: you are in a state of grace, admired by others, a fixture in the firmament.

The Star Year offers you the opportunity to begin to see the pattern of your destiny, to recognize the images that most influence your life, and to acknowledge the light that guides you. By unrestrainedly giving yourself up to fate and your protective stars, you will be guided on your journey.

In a Star Year, corresponding to Aquarius, you have aspirations for humankind: you perceive the grand patterns and connecting links between particular groups and the needs of the people. You may identify with altruistic causes in which you channel your energies through good works and humanitarian projects, claiming nothing for yourself. You are then noticed for your grace and inner illumination. Ask yourself: What are my hopes and what must I do to achieve them?

YOUR MOON YEAR

Your Moon Year can be one of disillusionment with the ideals you worked for last year. This is actually a test to see if they can last through the hounding of others and your fears that your dreams aren't substantial enough. Your sensitivity to the mass consciousness of the public is very strong in these last two years, deeply affecting your individual identity, so you are confused about which are your own values and feelings and which are from the collective unconscious, being worked out on a world level that you instinctively experience.

This can be a year of psychic and intuitive awakening, as indicated by the corresponding sign Pisces. Your dreams may be vivid and your imagination working overtime, so at times you may not be sure what is illusion and what is real.

The Moon is a card of karmic relationships, so you are engaging issues that affect other lifetimes, past and future. You are struggling to accept and understand who you've been and why. Events this year have unforeseeable aspects and consequences. You feel penned in by circumstances, misunderstood by friends, out of touch with current events. But it is probably your own imagination playing tricks on you, as your reasoning powers are eclipsed. Symbolic interpretations of situations work much better in such a confusing year.

You may want to explore occult and hidden things that allow you to work with, rather than against, the energy of a Moon Year. You can use your active imagination to great effect by visualizing and affirming whatever you want to create. Working with those who are incapacitated or institutionalized also uses this energy beneficially.

YOUR SUN YEAR

As a Year Card, The Sun represents success. It augurs the birth of a new project conceived in the dreams and imagination of the previous year. You radiate good will, and people love to bask in the light of your enthusiasm and happiness. You arrive at new realizations, and situations that were cloudy last year become clear. Secrets may be revealed. You can be receptive again, relieved of the fears you have been carrying. Reconciliations with others are possible now. If you have kept faith with your dreams, now you will reap the rewards.

It's a good year either to have children or to be with them, for this is a more playful time than usual. Your conceptualizations bear fruit as you discover how much can be achieved through affirmative thinking. Ride your instincts with confidence and you'll find they won't let you down. Be warm-hearted and generous and expect to see some good results next year.

It's also a good time to take a gamble, but in the spirit of play, as again the effects will appear next year, when the wisdom of your actions will be judged. The Sun is the source of riches both temporal and spiritual. Therefore, be prosperity-conscious and let each day bring more wisdom and understanding. It is a year of luck; many opportunities will present themselves, so be ready to respond.

YOUR JUDGEMENT YEAR

In a Judgement Year, corresponding to Pluto, you come face to face with your own mortality, whether through a personal experience, the death of someone you know, or the ending of something. The results of this are liberating, although the process is slow and it may take you years to recognize it. A full-scale restructuring of some aspect of your life is likely to take place. You are unexpectedly freed from a limitation or obstacle. You could choose a whole new vocation because you hear a calling.

During this year there are concerns with your family structure and transformations of your emotionally based relationships: spouse, family, community. If you awaken to a new level of awareness, or experience a spiritual rebirth, you announce your new knowledge (glad tidings) to others in the hopes of awakening them also.

You realize a sense of personal power. You may be in a position to judge others or their projects. It is important at this time to avoid using this power for personal aggrandizement, and instead apply it unselfishly for the good of others or society. But as the cross on the banner shows, it's your choice. You may also find yourself and your past actions judged: you may be stripped bare and confronted with your motives.

YOUR WORLD YEAR

Your World Year indicates the completion of major projects, being at the end of a cycle, and giving birth to yourself. It can be a very successful year, witnessing the culmination of some larger process. You may find yourself working within a narrow or even confined sphere, although possibly on tasks of wide applicability. You make the most of every opportunity, using whatever is at hand in original ways.

You experience a strong connection with Mother Earth and are concerned and involved in issues of world import. You need to establish firm contact with your own nature, which becomes a foundation in the outer world for your projects. Orienting yourself to your surroundings will be important to you, so that you know "where in the world you are," with control over your life and freedom from dependency. Your success in getting your bearings will have a major impact on the following year of The Fool.

Since The World card symbolizes the concept of creative cosmic synthesis, you need to integrate your physical self with your spirit self. Dancing, as pictured on this card, is symbolic of the creation of the universe and suggests a symbolic way to do this. The hermaphroditic qualities of the dancer indicate that you might do things that draw on a full range of human characteristics or work in a different gender-related field.

YOUR FOOL YEAR

In your Fool Year, a year of loco-motion, you are very likely to make a major move, travel in a carefree manner, or at least take unusual or unexpected trips. You take risks and do things that seem quite out of character. Travel gives you the opportunity to experiment with new personas and to forget your responsibilities for awhile. You live in the present, following every momentary whim. The future seems far away and the past is forgotten.

In caring only for the moment, you may do some foolish things from a long-term perspective, but you can't think about that now. You are heedless of order, admit you know nothing, wear mismatched clothes, and upset standards of conduct. You may annoy people because you mimic their folly, refuse to falsify, and parody their values. This makes you The Fool, and it's clear you don't fit in with the norm.

Yet you are also divinely inspired. You follow your instincts and frequently turn up in the right place at the right time. Your naiveté and innocence enables you to see things from a fresh perspective and discover exciting possibilities where others with jaded senses perceive nothing. You will succeed in doing things that others, far too prudent, won't even attempt.

Your haphazard attitudes can create problems for you next year in what is most likely your Hierophant Year. When you overturn traditions and espouse anarchy, you stir up a lot of trouble. On the other hand, your belief in the basic joy and spontaneity of life is exalting. You are an original being, representing a wonderful truth: the world is full of possibilities if you will only step off the beaten track.

CHAPTER FIFTEEN

YOUR NAME CARDS

THE SIGNIFICANCE OF YOUR NAME

From earliest antiquity in most cultures, the name of a person was synonymous with their soul. This is a reflection of a long-ago golden age when magic, religion, and reality were all one. Name-giving was an important rite. In some cultures newborns had to be named before they could be suckled. In matriarchal societies, children were usually named by their mothers—the source of the food of life. In other societies the child was named by a shaman or tribal elder who used divination to discover the name already known to Spirit that expressed that child's purpose and character. In most magical systems, to name a thing, or to know its name, was to gain power over it. Thus one's real name, that is, one's soul-name, was often a secret known only within the immediate family.

Names have always been profound psychological expressions of one's true self, and even in written form, one's name is a hieroglyph of spiritual power. Consider the secret Hebrew name of God, the Tetragrammaton, symbolized by the initials YHVH, which was forbidden to be pronounced. Even in Christian times the concept of name has been equated with character and destiny, so that children are often named after saints whose qualities the parents wish them to reflect. Today, people are more likely to name a child after a movie star, sports hero, or character from a book, but again with the hope that a little of their personal magic will rub off on the child. Therefore, historically and symbolically, your name is a vehicle of your power and your personal magic. "A good name is better than precious ointment" (Ecclesiastes 7:1).

THE NAME CARDS

Therefore, in addition to Birth Cards determined by your birthdate, you have a set of major arcana cards called Name Cards that are determined by your birth name. There are Name Cards for each letter of your name, literally spelling it out in images, and other Name Cards derived by the numerological addition and reduction of those letters. By means of the tarot you can discover the hidden significance of why you were given your particular name and what it tells you about your character and your soul's destiny. Again, as with the Birth Cards, you will find this information most valuable once you have used the system on yourself and friends. Then you will begin to recognize your own trends and patterns. All such Lifetime Cards are tools for understanding and therefore should be used as intuitive indicators, not as absolutes.

*If at any point you become confused by the card nomenclature, refer to the *Summary of Card Names Chart* at the front of the book for clarification.

Your Lifetime Cards, which consist primarily of Birth Cards and Name Cards,* are like personal readings that apply to you your whole life long. Should you ever change your name, you are choosing to modify or redefine your personal direction. You can consider anniversary dates (or spiritual rebirth dates, etc.) as the beginning of a new phase of your life or a dedication to a chosen purpose, but you can never get rid of your actual birthdate and your ''official'' birth name. Granted, there will always be people with unusual birth circumstances: I have met people with two birthdates, not knowing which is right, and I've known children who were not named until more than a year after they were born—their birth certificates simply say, ''Baby Girl Jones'' or ''Baby Boy Williams.'' In such cases you must work with whatever feels right to you or accept all the possibilities as aspects of yourself.

NUMERICAL EQUIVALENTS

There are two major methods of determining numerical equivalents for the letters of your name.

The first is the standard English system in which the 26 letters are numbered consecutively from 1 to 9 and then begin with 1 again. ''A'' equals 1, as does the 10th letter ''J'' and the 19th letter ''S'':

A B C D E F G H I J K L M N O P Q R S T U V W X Y Z
1 2 3 4 5 6 7 8 9 1 2 3 4 5 6 7 8 9 1 2 3 4 5 6 7 8

The second system is a Kabbalistic one in which an attempt is made to match the English alphabet with the Hebrew alphabet of only 22 letters. Since each Hebrew letter *is also a number*, once you are sure of the corresponding letter from English to Hebrew, you know the number. However, none of the various systems for transliterating the English alphabet into Hebrew is precise, indicated by the wide disagreement found among authorities. The Hebrew letter *Heh*, for instance, stands for our ''h'' and sometimes our ''e,'' while *Cheth* is ''ch'' in some systems and ''h'' in others. *Teth* is usually ''t'' and *Tav* is ''th,'' but in some lists they are switched, and *Tav* is also occasionally ''x.'' *Tzaddi* is especially difficult, as it is usually designated as a ''tz'' sound such as that found in ''czar'' (spelled ''cz'' to make it even more difficult). You can see the problems!

Linguists have determined that babies, before they are a year old, recognize and have learned to form all the basic sounds of the language or languages spoken to them daily. After the age of ten, it is difficult if not impossible for a person to learn another language without an accent. As with the Gregorian calendar, we have all been imprinted with particular cultural conventions that frame our perceptions of reality.[1] It makes little sense for most of us to spell an English name with Hebrew letters that we are completely unfamiliar with.*

*The Hebrew alphabet can be used most effectively for determining the cards of your ''magical self'' when working in a Kabbalistically based magical system: See Appendix C for a variety of possible correspondences.

To create a symbolic representation of my essential self through the medium of the tarot cards, I chose to use the numbers of the 22 major arcana as the numeric base. I matched them with the English alphabet in the order I learned as a child, imprinted as deeply in my unconscious as in my conscious mind, just as I teach it to my child in the traditional ABC song.

CHART 12
**ALPHABET
KEY NUMBERS
CHART**

A	B	C	D	E	F	G	H	I
1	2	3	4	5	6	7	8	9
J	K	L	M	N	O	P	Q	R
10	11	12	13	14	15	16	17	18
S	T	U	V	W	X	Y	Z	
19	20	21	22	23/5	24/6	25/7	26/8	
				Fire	Earth	Water	Air	

In the above chart, each letter directly corresponds to the number below it and the major arcana card corresponding to that number. Thus, A = 1 = The Magician; L = 12 = The Hanged Man, etc. The numbers in this chart are called "Key Numbers" and are the numbers used in all calculations. Any two-digit Key Number can be reduced down to its "Root Number," which is always a single-digit number between 1 and 9. The Root Number is the number used in standard numerology calculations, whereas in this book you always work with the numbers 1 through 22.

You'll notice that in English there are four more letters than there are major arcana tarot cards. Thus, the letters W, X, Y, and Z correspond to the numbers 23, 24, 25, and 26, *but for our purposes here are automatically reduced to their Root Number and card*; that is, 23 = 5, 24 = 6, 25 = 7, and 26 = 8. The reduced numbers are the ones you should use in all calculations involving the final four letters. They also represent the four elements that correspond to the four tarot suits: W = Fire; X = Earth; Y = Water; and Z = Air.

YOUR BASIC NAME CARDS

Now let's use the preceding chart to find some of your personal Name Cards. Place all the vowels above your name and all the consonants below. Add them separately as shown and reduce the sums to a number that is 22 or less. (Do this in the space provided in *Your Personal Cards Chart*.)

For example:

1 + 7 +		1 +		5 + 9 + 5 +			5 + 5	= 38 = 11	*Vowels*
M A R Y		K A T H E R I N E				G R E E R			
13 + 18		+ 11 + 20 + 8 + 18 + 14			+ 7 + 18 +		18	= 145 = 10	*Consonants*

SUM OF VOWELS PLUS CONSONANTS = 183

1 + 8 + 3 = 12

(Note: Always add whole numbers together *before* reducing!)

Adding the vowels together and reducing to a major arcana number of 22 or below gives you your DESIRES AND INNER MOTIVATION CARD. *In my case (see above), this is the 11th trump: Justice, which is in the Constellation of the High Priestess.*

Adding the consonants together and then reducing that sum gives you your OUTER PERSONA CARD. *In my case, this is the 10th trump card: The Wheel of Fortune in the Constellation of The Magician.*

Your DESTINY CARD comes from adding together all the numbers in your name and then reducing them to 22 or below. *In my example, I have the 12th trump card: The Hanged Man in the Constellation of The Empress.*

YOUR PERSONAL BLUEPRINT

Let's look at this entire concept more closely. According to Hermetic and metaphysical philosophy, the individual soul chooses a life to be born into for the particular lessons and challenges it will find there. Usually it is a life that will offer the greatest opportunity for soul-development through a framework of experience offered by a particular historical time; the national, ethnic, and cultural belief structures, and the genetic contributions of the physical parents. As Jane Roberts' spiritual mentor, Seth, says, "Unconsciously, then, you have within you what you might think of as a set of blueprints for the particular kind of physical reality you want to materialize. You are the architect."[2] Your Name Cards can therefore help you realize the particular qualities and individual characteristics that are innately yours.

Your job is to use the talents you have to the best of your ability—knowing, as Seth puts it, "that in them [your talents] lies your own individual fulfillment."[3] This is your destiny! Your Birth Cards and Name Cards are pointers or indicators of the talents, abilities, and characteristics that you can maximize by creatively facing the challenges that are your lessons in daily life. Your job is to actualize your *name* to the best of your ability. Free will means that you can choose to do this or not. If you don't, then your name becomes all those things you are "fated" with. This reminds me of a study I read about in which it was found that people with extremely unusual names tend to stand out, either as unusually individualistic, creative, and successful or as lonely, disturbed, and maladjusted.

Charles Garfield's work on "peak performers" in business and industry indicates that these people value achievement in their work and the full development of their human faculties. Garfield says, "they have what used to be called *character*: an inner strength that comes from an existential decision to excel,"[4] and they have a need for challenges through which to develop that excellence. Any of us can become peak performers if we accept the challenge of using our talents to their fullest extent.

In this regard the individual letters of your name represent basic beliefs or assumptions that are natural to you and which form your character. *For instance, in my name the letter M = 13 = Death and indicates that I experience life deeply by transcending the barriers between things. My pattern is to continuously regenerate by eliminating or cutting off forms that no longer serve their purpose. Since M is the initial letter of one of my names, this becomes a leading or primary characteristic.*

Even more important than the totals of your name are the patterns made by all the individual cards in your name. Also, since each card is in a Tarot Constellation, those constellations that appear most often, as well as those not represented at all, are indicators of major personality characteristics.

CHART 13
YOUR PERSONAL
CARDS CHART

Using your name as it appears *on your birth certificate* (that is, your full, original name), change each letter into its corresponding number as given on the *Alphabet Key Numbers Chart*. Later you can determine the numbers of any other name you currently use.

Write your name in the space provided below. Above your name, write the numbers corresponding to the vowels: A, E, I, O, U, and Y (if it is used as a vowel). Below your name, write the numbers corresponding to the consonants. Total the individual vowel and consonant numbers before reducing.

Vowels: = _____

Full name: _____

Consonants: = _____

SUM OF VOWELS PLUS CONSONANTS = _____
(Using the vowel and consonant totals before reduction)

My DESIRES & INNER
     MOTIVATION CARD (vowels) = _____ _____
                                       #   Major arcana card

     Root Number   _____
     Constellation of _____
     Principle of   _____ .

The Desires and Inner Motivation Card indicates what inspires your actions and what drives your urges. It represents the spiritual and karmic forces at work, wanting to be expressed. It shows how you feel, and your inner strength.

My OUTER PERSONA CARD (consonants) = _____ _____
                                        #   Major arcana card

     Root Number   _____
     Constellation of _____
     Principle of   _____ .

The Outer Persona Card indicates your surface qualities and public identity, how you present yourself, and how you are experienced by others. It suggests your physical expression and how you manifest your inner drives in the outer world.

Although there are several cards that I call "Destiny Cards" (explained later in this chapter), for the time being simply add together the vowels and consonants to obtain:

My DESTINY CARD (total vowels & consonants) = _____ _____
                                        #   Major arcana card

     Root Number   _____
     Constellation of _____
     Principle of   _____ .

The Destiny Card shows why you were born, what you were named to do, and the kinds of experiences necessary to accomplish your task.

MARY   KATHERINE   GREER

Waite-Smith

"SPELLING" YOUR NAME

1) Laying Out Your Cards

A = Magician (1)
B = Priestess (2)
C = Empress (3)
D = Emperor (4)
E = Hierophant (5)
F = Lovers (6)
G = Chariot (7)
H = Strength (8)
I = Hermit (9)
J = Fortune (10)
K = Justice (11)
L = Hanged Man (12)
M = Death (13)
N = Temperance (14)
O = Devil (15)
P = Tower (16)
Q = Star (17)
R = Moon (18)
S = Sun (19)
T = Judgement (20)
U = World (21)
V = Fool (22)
W = Hierophant (5)
X = Lovers (6)
Y = Chariot (7)
Z = Strength (8)

(Note: The cards illustrating the remainder of this chapter are from the Hanson-Roberts deck.)'

Lay out the major arcana cards that "spell" your entire name, using the list of letters and cards in the margin. Because there will probably be repetitions of several letters, hence repeated cards, you will need one of the following: the major arcana from several decks, photocopies of the repeated cards, or pieces of paper (cut to size) on which you write the names of the repeated cards. Counting how many times the most frequent letter comes up will tell you how many different decks are necessary.

Place the vowel cards slightly higher than the consonant cards so that you can clearly see which is which. If using multiple decks, arrange the cards from your decks in any combination that appeals to you. Try several variations. Refer to the illustration as an example of how to lay out your cards.

2) The Vowel Cards

Examine the vowels in your name. Try to get a sense of their energies. Remember that the vowels are your basic desires and inner motivations. They tend to propel you and give you the drive to accomplish things. They show what is likely to bring out your inner strengths. The first vowel in your name is especially important—your most characteristic energy expression.

Short interpretations of the vowels are provided below, including their source in the Hebrew alphabet. These descriptions are provided primarily to give impetus to your own interpretations.

At the end of each entry are various names from mythology that begin with that letter. Because these mythic names are seldom used for individuals and immediately evoke certain characteristics to anyone familiar with their stories, they often demonstrate the archetypal energies of the letter. Look up some of these figures in the mythology section of your library or in the *New Larousse Encyclopedia of Mythology*. For instance, notice how many of the "I" names make long journeys or searches, especially into the underworld. You will discover other such "coincidences" that will help you understand these letters.

Vowels are either long or short in sound. A long vowel sounds like the letter itself. The short vowel can have a variety of other sounds. Check the pronouncing section of any dictionary for examples of long and short vowel sounds. The long vowels tend to be more active, assertive, and projective in their qualities, while the short vowels are more inner, receptive, and self-possessed.

A (Derived from *Aleph.*) THE MAGICIAN is communicative, skillful, and full of new ideas. He is multitalented but can become scattered. His task is to remain focused. This card gives you a focused will, high aspirations, and a pioneering spirit. It is impulsive, begins things and creates activity, but requires others to follow through. It can be selfish and egotistical. The Magician knows what he wants. *(Adam, Agni, Amaterasu, Amon, Anahita, Anubis, Aphrodite, Apollo, Athena, Astarte, Ashera, Avalokitesvara.)*

E (Derived from *Heh.*) THE HIEROPHANT is confident, authoritative, and silent when he wants to be. Especially with several "E's," you tend to be active, adventurous and curious, changeable but opinionated. Learning is a great motivator for you. Perception is a strong quality as you seek significance and meaning. Sensuality and spirituality are major forces in your life. This letter's individual power is lost when it is silent at the end of a word, but it then helps to make the preceding vowel more active. In this context, the Hierophant either helps to support all that has gone before it, or can become dogmatic and rigid. *(Ea, El, Elijah, Enlil, Epona, Erinyes, Eros, Europa, Eurynome, Eurydice, Eve.)*

I (Derived from *Yod.*) THE HERMIT is careful, prudent, and patient, with a desire to complete things. You are stimulated by the intellect and seek wisdom but approach things critically. You search for perfection. You need peace and time to reflect. People with many "I's" can have natural healing qualities. You find value in the inner meaning of things, with love as your prime motivator. You can be overly sensitive and tend to pessimism, irritability, and quarrelsomeness. *(Icarus, Ida, Imams, Imhotep, Inanna, Indra, Io, Iris, Ishtar, Isis, Israel, Isvara, Izanagi and Izanami.)*

O (Derived from *Ayin.*) THE DEVIL is earthly, powerful, ambitious, and experiences things wholistically. It concentrates, absorbs, and draws things to itself, with a natural drive to organize and an ability to understand and visualize whole systems. You will finish what you start, rarely acknowledging defeat. You can be stubborn and tenacious, melancholy and brooding, and sensitive to criticism, in which case you withdraw into yourself. Many "O's" will slow a person down through trying to take in everything. You are then cautious and obstinate. Eliminating the superfluous will help free up an "O" person. *(Obatala, Oceanus, Odin, Odysseus, Oedipus, O-Kuni-Nushi, Olympia, Omphale, Orion, Orpheus, Oshun, Osiris.)*

U (Derived from *Vav.*) THE WORLD is sensitive, nurturing, and desires to protect and contain. It resists outer influences, fears ridicule, and is conservative; it maintains personal dignity and exclusiveness and can appear aloof and clannish. It feels free to express itself creatively only under conditions with sharply defined boundaries and limitations, yet likes to travel. You "U's" are very responsible to those who need your protection or assistance and fear being scattered. You are intuitive and likely to be a good judge of character. *(Uazit, Uma, Uni, Unkulunkulu, Uraeus, Urania, Uranus, Ur-Nammu, Uzza, Uzume.)*

Y (Derived from *Yod*.) THE CHARIOT is intuitive and introspective with a talent for penetrating mysteries. It is emotional, irresponsible, yet assertive and challenging. It can harness the imagination to work toward goals, but hates any bondage, desiring above all else freedom of movement. "Y's" require mental, spiritual, and physical fulfillment and the freedom to pursue it. They develop the patience to work toward long-term goals. They need to be careful of losing their temper or getting "carried away" with things. *(Yahweh, Yama, Yarilo, Yemaya, Yggdrasil, Yseult, Yuki-Onne.)*

3) Your Personal Rhythm

Can you feel the rhythms that the vowels create in your name—the energy pulses or beats? Notice when and where they repeat and what it does to the structure of your name.

Each of your names has its own beat and rhythm. According to numerologist Martita Tracy, "You are an instrument. Your physical experience and conditions of your life are the results of the harmonies or discords played by you—or upon you—by your personal name."[5] Initially, let's take just your first name and learn how to beat its rhythm out with your hands. Let your left hand beat the consonants and use your right hand for the vowels, clapping your hands against your knee. Emphasize the first letter of your name as the downbeat. You can use marks similar to those used for scanning poetry to mark the beat like this:

$$\acute{W} \hat{I} \acute{L} \acute{L} \hat{I} \hat{A} \acute{M}$$

Write out your full name here with the vowels and consonants marked as beats:

Beat out the rhythm for one name at a time. Finally, when you can do all the beats easily, put them together so that you can beat out your whole name as one long personal rhythm, repeating it in cyclic pulses of energy. Do this until it becomes automatic and you don't have to think about it. Sway to the rhythm. Feel it deep within you as a pattern you were given at birth. Feel yourself moving through the years with this pattern. Stay with it for awhile. Once you can feel this rhythm within yourself, try any other names you have used, such as nicknames. Get a feel for how the rhythm is different. What has changed?

4) Musical Correspondences

There are several systems of correlating the major arcana with musical notes. The *Musical Correspondence Chart* below uses the system developed by Paul Foster Case, as derived from the Order of the Golden Dawn.[6] Use any of these systems or one of your own devising, and play your name on a musical instrument. Using the name spaces provided below, mark the corresponding musical notes below the letters of your name. If you play the tune it will probably not be melodious, but allow yourself to experiment and play around until you find something that sounds like you. Don't be afraid to create your own system. One way would be to choose a tune that fits your name and then develop the correspondences from that.

A —Magician	E	N —Temperance	G#
B —High Priestess	G#	O —Devil	A
C —Empress	F#	P —Tower	C
D —Emperor	C	Q —Star	A#
E —Hierophant	C#	R —Moon	B
F —Lovers	D	S —Sun	D
G —Chariot	D#	T —Judgement	C
H —Strength	E	U —World	A
I —Hermit	F	V —Fool	E
J —Wheel/Fortune	A#	W —Hierophant	C#
K —Justice	F#	X —Lovers	D
L —Hanged Man	G#	Y —Chariot	D#
M —Death	G	Z —Strength	E

CHART 14
MUSICAL CORRESPONDENCE CHART

My name: _____

My notes: _____

5) Leading Letters

Look at the first letter of your first name. This is what you lead with. If it begins with a vowel, you've already examined it while looking at your drives and motivations. Leading with a vowel means you lead with your energy and emotions. It might give you the ability to act quickly, but usually without thinking first. *For instance, the name Elizabeth starts with an E. With The Hierophant as the associated trump, it means something like this: "You confidently and authoritatively express your opinions, yet your curiosity motivates you to seek experience with new things."* With a consonant first, you will "characteristically" react with the qualities of that letter.

6) The Consonants

Notice how consonants in general give a certain quality or "air" to the name. There are many more consonants than vowels. They are more personal and lend nuance to your basic drives. They define you more clearly. Their function linguistically is to differentiate between sounds. They create rhymes. Note especially the first consonant in each of your names. By changing it you radically alter the name; for instance: Ted, Ned, Fred, Jed, Red.

Keep in mind that the meanings given here for each letter are merely my own personal suggestions. Let the cards themselves, particularly in combination with each other, suggest their meanings to you in your own name. By looking at the cards themselves laid out in *your* name, you will begin to see how they integrate and flow together.

B (Derived from *Beth*.) THE HIGH PRIESTESS is receptive to the subtle currents of emotion around her. She is an intuitive, sensitive dreamer, yet ordered and wise. She is self-sufficient, independent, and secretive. Good at diplomacy and mediation, she builds and constructs forms and combines what already exists in novel ways. *(Baal, Baba Yaga, Bacchus, Balder, Baphomet,*

Bast, Bel, Bellerophon, Blodeuwedd, Bona Dea, Brahma, Bran the Blessed, Brigit, Buddha.)

C (Derived from *Gimel.*) THE EMPRESS is concerned with the creative, imaginative, and aesthetic aspects of anything. This card/letter is sociable, cooperative, loving, gracious, and noble of bearing. *(Cain, Cassandra, Castor, Cerberus, Ceres, Cernunnos, Cerridwen, Chango, Chalchiuhtlicue, Chiron, Circe, Coyote, Cybele.)*

D (Derived from *Daleth.*) THE EMPEROR is efficient, orderly, practical, and conservative, with a keen, discerning mind. This card/letter is purposeful—jumping at opportunities and tenacious with possessions. Self-expression is difficult, so it needs encouragement. *(Daedalus, Daevas, Dagda, Dainichi, Dakini, Danu, Demeter, Devi, Diana, Dionysus, Domovoi, Dumuzi, Durga.)*

F (Derived from either *Peh* or *Vav.*) THE LOVERS card is very aware of life's choices and is sometimes weighed down by the responsibility, struggling with dilemmas. It suggests a need for companionship. When inspired and in harmonious surroundings, it works to actualize dreams, but disharmony and strife bring anxiety. *(Fates, Faunus, Firanak, Flora, Fortuna, Frey, Freyja, Frigg, Fudo-Myoo, Fujiyama, the Furies.)*

G (Derived from *Gimel.*) THE CHARIOT knows the value of leadership and goals. This card/letter is assertive, determined, and active. It is concerned with controlling the emotions, suggesting meditation or exercise for focus. You will find it hard to work with others, preferring to nurture and care for them, as you struggle and see opposition in other people's points of view. *(Gaea, Gandharvas, Ganesha, Ganga, Garuda, Gawain, Geb, Genii, Gilgamesh, Gorgons, Graces, Guinevere, Gwydion.)*

H (Derived from *Heh.*) STRENGTH uses its talents to aid others, the community, the nation. It is broadminded and tolerant, courageous and fearless, with innate spiritual power. It means you work from the heart. *(Hades, Hanuman, Hapi, Harmonia, Hathor, Hecate, Hel, Hephaestus, Hera, Hercules, Hermes, Hestia, Horus, Hoshang, Huitzilopochtli, Hygieia.)*

J (Derived from *Yod.*) THE WHEEL OF FORTUNE is a leader who moves easily with change. It suggests that you have good friends but can be overly influenced. It is enthusiastic, benevolent, and loves new ideas and things, being naturally inventive and original itself. You strive to improve and expand on things. *(Jadapati, Jade, Janus, Jason, Jehovah, Jesus, Jemshid, Jocasta, Jove, Joy, Juno, Jupiter.)*

K (Derived from *Kaph.*) JUSTICE is concerned with truth and honesty. This card/letter points to a decisive executive ability, is analytical, and depends on reason. It makes adjustments easily and seeks to maintain a balance. It means you can be articulate or literary, using words to good advantage. It is firm and unyielding when justice is offended. *(Ka, Kadi, Kali, Kami, Kannon, Kashiwa-no-kami, Keres, Kherpera, Khepri, Kore, Krishna, Kuan-yin.)*

L (Derived from *Lamed.*) THE HANGED MAN sacrifices himself for his dreams. This card/letter has a love of justice but leans toward irony, pessimism, and worry. It indicates that you find happiness in service to others. It often needs a stimulus or push to get going. *(Lada, Lagash, Lakshmi, Laomedon, Lancelot, Lao-tzu, Leda, Leto, Libera, Lilith, Llew, Loa, Loki, Loo-Wit, Lucifer, Lug, Luna.)*

M (Derived from *Mem.*) DEATH efficiently brings about physical change and effectively eliminates past issues and concerns. Bitterness and sorrow are associated with this card/letter, but it is also concerned with regeneration and reconstruction. It makes you a capable and intuitive leader or executive. This letter goes with great depth of feeling but has difficulty taking things lightly. It is sensual. *(Ma, Maat, Macha, Maia, Maitreya, Mama Quilla, Marduk, Mars, Medea, Medusa, Mercury, Metis, Midas, Minerva, Minotaur, Mithra, Mohammed, the Muses.)*

N (Derived from *Nun.*) TEMPERANCE is outgoing, adaptable, and versatile. It can be nervous and restless and overconscious of details. It likes travel and exercise. You react to others with compassion but have strong personal values. *(Nammu, Narcissus, Neith, Nemesis, Nephthys, Neptune, Nereus, Nergal, Ningirsu, Ninigi, Ninlil, Niobe, Norns, Nuada, Nun, Nut.)*

P (Derived from *Peh.*) THE TOWER is power-oriented. This card/letter suggests tremendous willpower and moral courage but quickness to anger. It is concerned with reform combined with great power of expression and can make you either a philosopher or a revolutionary. It focuses only on its own sense of power and place. *(Pachamama, Pallas, Pan, Pandora, Parsival, Parvati, Pegasus, Persephone, Perseus, Phaedra, Pluto, Poseidon, Prometheus, Prajapati, Psyche, Ptah, Pygmalion.)*

Q (Derived from *Qoph.*) THE STAR is inspiring, hopeful, and cheerful. It is proud-spirited and calmly powerful, therefore often followed by others. It is also insatiably curious. You use your intellect well and can work on a vision that will not manifest until a distant future. At its worst, the letter suggests unscrupulousness and dogmatism. *(Qadesh, Qamaits, Qebhsnuf, Quetzalcoatl.)*

R (Derived from *Resh.*) THE MOON inspires confidence through its intuitive understanding. This card/letter has a keen sense of discrimination and deep stores of knowledge. It bears hardship well and quietly, or has some problem or sorrow not revealed to others. It follows its own sense of timing. It makes you magnetic and generous, and perhaps draws you to the occult. *(Ra, Radha, Rama, Ravana, Rhadamanthys, Rhea, Rhiannon, Romulus and Remus, Rudra.)*

S (Derived from *Samekh.*) THE SUN has a powerful will, yet is benevolent, outgoing, and optimistic. It is self-regenerating, inspiring, and independent, while loving social contact. This card/letter may manifest in your desire to appear wise and all-knowing and to be known as a peacemaker. You are an original and independent thinker, but sometimes lack sincerity and frankness. *(Samson,*

Satan, Saturn, Savitri, Sekhmet, Selene, Seth, Shakti, Shamash, Shango, Sheki-nah, Sin, Shiva, Siddhartha, Skalds, Solomon, Soma, Sphinx, Sybil.)

T   (Derived from *Teth* or *Tav.*) JUDGEMENT has a "call" or purpose, often with some spiritual dimension. It is domestic and a peacemaker but concerned first with self-mastery. People with this card/letter are concerned with raising mass consciousness. They can be critical and love to investigate anything they question. They love a challenge. *(Tammuz, Tanet, Tara, Tartarus, Tefnut, Tethys, Tezcatlipoca, Themis, Theseus, Thetis, Thor, Thoth, Tiamat, Tirawa, Tlaloc.)*

V   (Derived from *Vav.*) THE FOOL has the mark of the master. People with this card/letter are very individualistic, take risks, and are inveterate vagabonds (even if only in their heads). They can become scattered because pulled to the new and unusual, or depressed from attempting to cut themselves off from sensation. They need to be appreciated. *(Valkyries, Vanir, Varuna, Venus, Vesta, Victoria, Vidar, Vishnu, Volcanal, Vulcan.)*

W   (Derived from *Vav.*) THE HIEROPHANT in his fiery, consonantal phase is proud-spirited, versatile, and clever. People with this card/letter are good diagnosticians and determined and tenacious in their loves and desires. They like to give advice or counsel and are good learners. They feel comfortable with things that are "ordered" and follow laws or rules. *(Wakan-Tanka, Walpurga, Wen Ch'ang, Woden.)*

X   (Derived from *Tav*—as cross.) This letter represents THE LOVERS in its earthly form. The card is concerned with success in business and worldly matters, crafts, and artistic endeavors. It is quite aware of the burdens of responsibility, but at the crossroads of life is willing to take the hard and difficult path if sure of a reward. You choose friends who will profit you. *(Xerxes, Xipe Totec, Xiuhtecuhtli, Xochiquetzal.)*

Y   (Derived from *Yod.*) This letter represents THE CHARIOT in its watery and consonantal form. It is psychic and prophetic, with a talent for penetrating mysteries, assertive and determined when its idealism is aroused. It can be mediumistic and channel energies. *(See the vowel listing for Y for mythic names.)*

Z   (Derived from *Zayin.*) This is STRENGTH in its airy form. These people are extremists. They have self-confidence, push, and the energy to go for what they want. They magnify and exaggerate situations and seek to organize and control others, or else they become very restless. They can be very successful promoting and developing the creative ideas of others. *(Zagreus, Zarathustra, Zend-Avesta, Zenobia, Zephyrus, Zeus.)*

7) The Name Patterns

Divide each of your names into syllables. Look at any diphthongs or blended sounds; overlap these cards to indicate that they don't stand alone. (A good dictionary will provide the pronunciation and syllable division of most names.)

Combine the meanings of the cards in these groups. *As an example, my middle name is Katherine, which I pronounce "Kath'-er-in." The first syllable is "Kath," containing a "th" blend, and is emphasized. In the second syllable the "e" is barely heard, sliding into the "r." And the final "e" in the last syllable is silent. The "th" blend of Judgement (T) and Strength (H) is suggestive of my calling to be useful to others. The leading letter/card of Justice (K) emphasizes honesty and articulateness, while the connective vowel-card, The Magician (A), stresses my drive to be focused in order to communicate. Thus the first syllable clearly harmonizes with my work as teacher and author. In the second syllable, the almost silent Hierophant (E) points to my need to learn intuitively—Moon (R). The remaining Hermit (I) and Temperance (N), with a silent Hierophant (E), point to a restless energy that insists on perfection and attention to detail in learning, as well as compassionate concern for the well-being of others.*

YOUR NAME SPREAD

Take the cards for each one of your names and arrange them in any pattern that feels balanced or right to you. Don't worry about correct order—just create a picture with the cards that seems to express your name. Study each name. Your destiny is to fulfill your overall personality characteristics—to actualize your name. Although this gives you your basic Name Spread, there is much more you can discover about yourself from your name.

ADDING IT ALL UP

Most of us are given three names at birth: a first or personal name, a middle name, and a last or family name. The following processes will give you some idea of how each of these names affects you individually. But many of you will not have the "usual" English and American name structure. For instance, I have a cousin who was given only a first and last name. Finally in college she legally added a middle initial (but no name) in order to end the hassle of having application forms returned or rejected for leaving an item blank. Adapt the following ideas in any way that seems appropriate for your situation, especially if your name follows some other naming tradition or is unique.

Your Personal Name

Your first name is also called your "given name." It is usually very personal. Until this century, only one's family and friends used it. It was a sign of intimacy and trust to permit someone to address you by your first name. Today we are more casual and openly friendly, so this is probably how you usually identify yourself. (A little later I'll discuss nicknames and other names you assume for yourself.) Your first name is the "I" or thinking self and deals with what you are most conscious of in yourself. It is also most closely aligned with your peers in your generation. The popularity of certain first names comes and goes in the form of fads, societal mores, styles, and even events. You may have an uncommon first name for your generation that was quite ordinary in another, or vice-versa. For instance, I've never known anyone near my age named Jason, yet now I know at least six boys all born since 1972 with that name. Many children born during the 1960's and 70's were given names that reflected their generation's preoccupation with nature, cultural heritage, or mythology. Thus, first names are generally indicative of historical eras.

Your Middle Name

Your middle name may represent a variety of things. It is usually your hidden self, in that most people don't know you by that name, so it can indicate undeveloped potential. If it is your mother's maiden name, it has a genetic and hereditary function, referring to ethnic roots that may not otherwise be apparent. If it is also a ''given'' name, it may be from the family roots, like being named after great-aunt Arabella, or perhaps it reflects some of your parent's farther-out fantasies. Ask yourself (or your parents) why you were given this name. You must judge for yourself the significance of this position in your name, but in general it indicates subtle inheritances, things you don't know about yourself, or personal aspects with which you may not outwardly identify (unless you use your middle name as your personal name). It also acts as a connecting link between your personal self and your social/cultural self.

Your Family Name

Your last name (on your birth certificate) is likely to be your father's last name, although that is not necessarily the case. It could be your mother's last name, a combination of mother's and father's last names, or a completely original name given just to you (the rarest of all). I call it your family name, because even if you took it for yourself it tends to categorize you in some social or cultural framework. Your last name represents your most formal self and usually comes from your cultural and hereditary background. It is the ''we''-thinking self, which you identify with some group of which you are a part, from nuclear family to national or ethnic kinship.

YOUR INDIVIDUAL-NAME CARDS

The cards that spell your name and the cards that represent the numerical total of each name should be examined with the following keywords in mind:

PERSONAL/FIRST-NAME CARD	MIDDLE-NAME CARD	FAMILY/LAST-NAME CARD
Conscious sense of self	Hidden self	Formal self
Personal & generational	Genetic & hereditary	Social & cultural
''I''-thinking self	Undeveloped potential	''We''-thinking self

Use the chart that comes after these instructions (*Name Cards & Life Potential Card Chart*) to add up each of your names individually and thus determine the tarot card that sums up each.

First-Name Card

First, add all the vowels in your first name and write the total on the chart where indicated. Do the same for the consonants, writing the total in the space provided. Add these two together (from your first name only) to find Sum 1 and then reduce to a number that is 22 or below. This indicates the tarot card that expresses your personal self, called your FIRST-NAME CARD. Write this on the chart.

Middle-Name Card

Do the same with your middle name to find the card that expresses your underlying self, called your MIDDLE-NAME CARD.

Last-Name Card

Then do the same with your family name to determine the card that expresses your social/cultural self, called your LAST-NAME CARD.

Theme Chord

The three cards you have just identified are like individual musical notes that express the essence of each of your three names. Together they strike a chord, a combination that is your three names in unison. I call this three-card combination your THEME CHORD. It "sounds" the dominant chord in the "theme-song" of your life. (These three cards may or may not have a constellation in common.) The way to reflect upon your Theme Chord is as a three-card tarot spread, using the keywords on the previous page as the three position meanings.

| Conscious | Hidden | Social |
| Self | Self | Self |

YOUR DESTINY CARDS

When you add up the numbers in your name, you may notice that there are a variety of ways to do it, and each way will give you slightly different sums. For instance, if you sum up your first, middle, and last names *separately*, reduce the numbers to tarot cards between 1 and 22, and then add these totals, you might arrive at an answer of 21 (The World); yet by adding up all the letters in your entire name *before* reducing them, you would get a 12 (Hanged Man). Both 21 and 12 reduce to the Root Number 3 and so are in the Constellation of The Empress, representing the principle of Love and Creative Imagination.

*This is not the same as the Destiny Card referred to in *Tarot for Your Self*, which is a minor arcana card concept of Muriel Hasbrouck in *The Pursuit of Destiny*, recently republished as *Tarot and Astrology* (New York: Inner Traditions/Destingy, 1987). As used here, the Destiny Cards are major arcana cards with standard numerological correspondences.

So there are three different ways of adding the numbers in your name to reach a grand total, resulting in your DESTINY CARD(S),* individually known as your THEME NOTE CARD, your RHYTHM CARD, and your MELODY CARD. *These cards are always from the same constellation and add up to the same Root Number.* They are variations on your basic destiny theme (as noted by your name).

Theme Note Card

Add together the reduced sums of your first, middle, and last names as indicated on the chart. Reduce them in turn to a tarot card number (22 or less). This is your Theme Note Card, the single "note" that expresses the sum of your Theme Chord (the three cards derived from your first, middle, and last names). By referring to the *Musical Correspondence Chart* earlier in this chapter, you can actually sound out your Theme Note as well as your Theme Chord.

Rhythm Card

Earlier in this chapter you added up all the vowels in your entire name to give you your Desires & Inner Motivation Card, and you added all the consonants in your name to find your Outer Persona Card (refer to *Your Personal Cards Chart*). Simply add the number of these two cards together (reduce the sum to 22 or below, if necessary). Since your vowels and consonants represent the inner beat of your name, I call this card your Rhythm Card. It sums up your personal beat and shows the way in which you manifest the tempo of energy flow in your life.

Melody Card

Add all the individual numbers in your entire name together before you reduce (in the chart, take the total of Sum 1 + Sum 2 + Sum 3, then reduce). This process requires you to listen to each card's unique tone, played one after another as your personal melody. I call this your Melody Card. The sum is its essence.

Hidden Factor Name Card

Since your Theme Note Card, your Rhythm Card, and your Melody Card are derived from the various ways in which you can sum up your name (you are adding the same numbers, only reducing the totals at different places), they will all add up to the same Root Number and are therefore in the same Tarot Constellation. *This constellation is the final expression or summing up of your personal destiny as described by your name.* Any card in your constellation that does not appear as Theme Note, Rhythm, or Melody Card acts like the (Birth) Hidden Factor Card did in your birthdate calculations. This is your HIDDEN FACTOR NAME CARD(S).

CHART 15
NAME CARDS
& LIFE
POTENTIAL
CARD CHART

	Unreduced Totals	Reduced to 22

FIRST NAME
Vowels Nos:
Letters: _____
Consonant Nos: =   _____
                    =   _____   or below
Sum 1 =   _____   = _____ : _____
                                        FIRST-NAME
                                           CARD

MIDDLE NAME
Vowels Nos: =   _____
Letters: _____
Consonant Nos: =   _____
Sum 2 =   _____   = _____ : _____
                                        MIDDLE-NAME
                                           CARD

LAST NAME
Vowels Nos: =   _____
Letters: _____
Consonant Nos: =   _____
Sum 3 =   _____   = _____ : _____
                                        LAST-NAME
                                           CARD

THEME NOTE CARD
(Reduced sum of above cards)
                          ===== : _____
                                   THEME NOTE
                                      CARD

MELODY CARD   ===== = _____ : _____
(Sum 1 + Sum 2 + Sum 3)   MELODY CARD

from
*Your
Personal
Cards
Chart*
{
**DESIRES & INNER
MOTIVATION CARD**
(Reduced sum of all vowels)   _____ : _____

OUTER PERSONA CARD
(Reduced sum of all consonants)   _____ : _____

RHYTHM CARD
(Reduced sum of above two cards)   ===== : _____
                                           RHYTHM CARD

My Theme Note Card, Melody Card, and Rhythm Card (my DESTINY CARDS) are all in the:

Constellation of _____
Principle of _____

The following card(s) of this constellation did not appear as
Destiny Cards and therefore are (NAME) HIDDEN FACTORS: _____

LIFE POTENTIAL CARD:

4-digit sum of birth day, month and year _____ (Base Number)
Plus unreduced total of Sum 1 + Sum 2 + Sum 3 _____
Reduce total to 22 or below _____ = _____

MY LIFE POTENTIAL CARD is: _____

LIFE POTENTIAL CARD

This is the card that sums up both your name and birthdate. It shows your greatest potential and the highest that you may achieve. It is always read in its most spiritual and idealistic manner to represent the ultimate goal that you may achieve by marshalling all your forces to fulfill your destiny according to your soul purpose. Take the four-digit total of the month, day, and year of your birth (don't reduce), and add to it the total of all the unreduced letters of your name (Sum 1 + Sum 2 + Sum 3). Finally, reduce this number to between 1 and 22. This is your LIFE POTENTIAL CARD.

CHART 16
NAME CARDS
CHECKLIST

Desires & Inner Motivation Card = Reduced sum of full-name vowel numbers
Outer Persona Card = Reduced sum of full-name consonant numbers
First-Name Card = Reduced sum of all first-name numbers
Middle-Name Card = Reduced sum of all middle-name numbers
Last-Name Card = Reduced sum of all last-name numbers
Theme Note Card = Reduced sum of the previous three cards
Rhythm Card = Reduced sum of the first two cards above
Melody Card = Reduced sum of all full-name numbers
                 (Sum 1 + Sum 2 + Sum 3)
Destiny Card = Any of the three previous cards (same Root Number)
Hidden Factor Name Card = Any remaining card(s) of same Root Number as
                 the above card
Life Potential Card = Reduced sum of full-name numbers plus birthdate Base
                 Number

Note: ''Reduced sum'' means any number from 22 to 1, which is then equated with the major arcana card of that number.

COUNTING CONSTELLATIONS

CHART 17
CONSTELLATION
COUNT CHART

1	2	3
4	5	6
7	8	9

This figure is sometimes called a ''magic square'' because the two opposing numbers in any line crossing the center (vertical, horizontal, or diagonal) always add up to 10. The numbers themselves correspond to the nine Tarot Constellations, and we will use the square to determine which constellations are emphasized in your name.

First you need to find the Root Number of each letter in your full name: Write the letters of your name in the spaces below, with the corresponding Key Numbers (1 to 22, corresponding to the tarot cards), then reduce each of the numbers to its Root Number (1 to 9).

For example:

Letters:	*M*	*A*	*R*	*Y*	*K*	*A*	*T*	*H*	*E*	*R*	*I*	*N*	*E*	*E*	*G*	*R*	*E*	*E*	*R*
Key Numbers:	*13*	*1*	*18*	*7*	*11*	*1*	*20*	*8*	*5*	*18*	*9*	*14*	*5*		*7*	*18*	*5*	*5*	*18*
Root Numbers:	*4*	*1*	*9*	*7*	*2*	*1*	*2*	*8*	*5*	*9*	*9*	*5*	*5*		*7*	*9*	*5*	*5*	*9*

MY NAME:
Letters: __ __ __ __ __ __ __ __ __ __ __ __ __ __ __ __ __
Key Numbers: __ __ __ __ __ __ __ __ __ __ __ __ __ __ __ __ __
Root Numbers: __ __ __ __ __ __ __ __ __ __ __ __ __ __ __ __ __

Now, for each letter of your name, place a mark in the square (dot, check, line, etc.) somewhere within the box of its Root Number. Then do the same for each of the cards found in Charts 15 and 16 (there are at least nine of these).

Which constellations are the most strongly represented (probably with 5 or more marks for the average name)?

What are their core principles?

Tarot Constellations	Principles

Which constellations and principles are not represented in your name at all?

Any constellations that are missing indicate characteristics or qualities that you lack. Unless these are compensated for by your Birth Cards, you will probably find yourself strongly drawn to people in this constellation (or constellations). These are qualities that you have to consciously work at developing, because they are not part of your natural expression. Nevertheless, they are strong motivators because you see them outside of yourself and are probably fascinated by them. This may give you some insight to as to why you are irresistably attracted to certain people.

TAKING OTHER NAMES

At long last we get around to looking at any other names you may have: nicknames, married names, spiritual names, professional names or aliases, or other name changes. You can never totally change the basic underlying rhythm of your birth name, which is why you've spent so much time getting to know it here. Other names, though, represent the ways in which you have chosen to modify or change or add to your destiny. They are very important. When you take a new name there is a corresponding change in your outer life. Often when you take on the name of a husband or partner, or create a new one for the two of you, the new name will indicate what you are taking on in that relationship.

The nicknames that other people call you indicate your particular characteristics to which they respond. These represent the part of you that they align with, and probably those that they need from you. You represent to them what they call you. They will also bring out those traits in you.

Although you might want to check out a name change with numerology or the tarot cards before you finalize it, I do not believe that there are any "bad" or "wrong" names, or that because your Birth Card is one number your Destiny Card *should* add up to a certain number in order to be in harmony with it. Many people have made growth-producing challenges out of difficult and inharmonious number patterns, developing great strength, compassion, and personal abilities out of so-called adversity. Every name has its own potential; the harmony comes from maximizing the lessons contained therein.

When you take on a new name, you can inaugurate it with a ritual. This ritual should be your own, but basically you might want to include some of the following:

Acknowledge and thank the name you are putting aside for all you have learned from it. Perhaps begin with your old name laid out in cards and then change it card for card, noting the cards you need to add and those you must take away. Rearrange them to form the new name.

Go over the new name with all the ideas from this chapter, getting to know it and its beat, rhythms, and melody. Acknowledge aloud the qualities and personal characteristics that you have chosen to bring into your life through this name. Call them to you as you call out your name.

If you are hesitant or ambivalent about taking this name, such as a married name or alias, include affirmative statements that will help you get the most from your experience with this name. Your intuitive feelings of ambivalence might show up in comparing your birth name with the new one, especially if you now have to take on many qualities that were lacking or weak in your original name. Look to see the kinds of lessons you are most likely to face so that you will recognize them when they occur.

YOUR MAGIC MIRROR AND LIFE MANDALA

Take all the cards that make up your name and lay them on the floor in any pattern that feels right to you, so that it forms a mandala or complete picture. (This is your basic Name Spread, but now you can work with it magically.) Put a small mirror in the center and look at yourself so that you can see only your eyes in the mirror, while the cards around it become your "face." Breathe deeply, evenly, and rhythmically. Become aware of your strengths and weaknesses, what you possess, and what you lack. Remember that your name carries a magical rhythm and melody that can be heard on the other planes of existence. Realize that if you fight against that rhythm and song it will limp along, stifled and crippled. Reclaim your personal energy! Feel it within yourself. Beat out the sound of your name. Move with it, creating a dance of vitality and joy. Rise and spontaneously improvise your own individual movements. Dance your name; dance your destiny. Realize that the dance doesn't stop, it is only that you are not always aware of it. Learn to dance your dance consciously. This is a beginning.

If you are taking a new name, make a magic mirror for it and look at yourself in your mirror. In your imagination step bravely through this magic mirror and into your personally chosen destiny.

You may wish to photocopy, photograph, draw, or collage the image you have created with your cards. Add pictures from magazines and postcards. Use an actual mirror or some other symbolic image as the center. Hang it on your wall.

NOTES

1. For information about how language and cultural conventions of time structure our world view, see *Language, Thought, and Reality* by linguist Benjamin Whorf.

2. Jane Roberts, *The Nature of Personal Reality: A Seth Book* (New York: Bantam, 1978), p. 413.

3. Ibid., p. 444.

4. Norman Boucher, "In Search of Peak Performance," *New Age Journal*, February 1986.

5. Martita Tracy, *Stellar Numerology* (Mokelumne Hill, CA: Health Research), p. 1.

6. Paul Foster Case, *Highlights of Tarot* (Los Angeles, CA: Builders of the Adytum, 1970), pp. 46–47.

CHAPTER SIXTEEN

THE PEOPLE CARDS: MIRRORS OF PERSONALITY

In *Tarot for Your Self* I presented a chapter on the People Cards and thought I had said everything about them, but of course I had only scratched the surface. Since then I've been intrigued by the tarot decks that are presenting these cards in unusual and exciting ways. This chapter is based on a talk and slide show I presented at The Fifth International Tarot Symposium.

The number of new tarot decks being designed and published each year seems to be increasing steadily; certainly there have been dozens of noteworthy decks in just the last few years. One of the major features of many of these decks is that they are taking the people out of the medieval court environment and finding new contexts for our experience of them. In the process they are also changing what they call these Court Cards. Some of the new names are: Family Cards, People Cards, Tribal Figures, Royalty Cards, and even the Three Faces of the Great Goddess.

THE ROLES YOU PLAY

Whatever these cards are called, they primarily represent the roles, masks, or subpersonalities we wear as our "identities" in life.

There are many ways to determine the roles you play and the varied aspects of yourself. One that may hold some surprises for you is to go through your closet and look at the clothes you have. Who are the different characters within yourself who wear these costumes? There is perhaps your business-suited downtown self, your casual weekend traveler persona, and your Saturday night special. Then there's the hiker, backpacker, skier, swimmer, boater, cyclist, or biker. And what about those sensual nightclothes, or that outfit stuck in the back that your mother bought you, or your equally buried hippy togs waiting for a revival, and are the paint-spattered jeans those of an artist or a housepainter? Obviously there are a lot of "you's" around.

Another place to look for your roles is on your bookshelf, with its old and new interests, its hobby and activity guides, and your fantasies of what you'd like to do and be. And don't forget to look around the rooms of your house, or even in the corners of your own room.

So let's take a look at all the facets of yourself, which are like the facets on a cut crystal, reflecting different aspects under different lights.

In the space below make a list of six or seven of the roles you play or masks you wear in your life right now. (If you did the similar exercise in my first book, you'll find it useful to do it again, as your responses may differ, based on changing perceptions of yourself.)

1.
2.
3.
4.
5.
6.
7.

Now separate all the People Cards from your deck and look through them, keeping their elemental qualities in mind.

DEVELOPMENTAL STAGES

These cards represent stages in your psychological development and in the development of your skills, as well as personality types. Since most books discuss the latter, I will focus on the developmental stages. (Waite-Smith illustrations.)

The Pages

The Pages (or Princesses, or Daughters) are the least developed but most open and willing to take risks. As a Page you are an eager learner trying things out, an apprentice using and carrying knowledge whose significance you don't yet fully understand. Pages have many of the qualities of the Strength card. They are related to the element Earth.

PAGE of WANDS.   PAGE of CUPS.   PAGE of SWORDS.   PAGE of PENTACLES.

The Knights

The Knights (or Princes, or Sons) have reached the stage of thinking they know something. As a Knight you are exploring what you can do with your new skills; you are actively using and further honing them. You are rebelling and discovering things for yourself, learning from experience. Knights are related to The Chariot card. They are usually related to the element Fire, while some make them Air. You must determine this by what corresponds to your deck.

The Queens

While the Queens and Kings are equally skilled, the Queens have fully developed talents that are personal and interpersonal and they focus on understanding the deeper underlying meanings of things. As a Queen of Cups or Pentacles you are caring, nurturing, and comforting. As a Queen of Wands or Swords you are directing, teaching, observing, and implementing. Queens accomplish things. They give advice. Queens are most like The Empress. They are related to the element Water.

The Kings

The Kings demonstrate their talents, which are outer and public. They seem confident of their expertise and secure in their positions. As a King you administer, judge, take charge, and handle your outer affairs competently. You establish procedures and build empires. Kings show where you have developed mastery, but also where you can be inflexible, and where you think you have nothing more to learn. Kings are much like The Emperor. They are usually related to the element Air, but may be considered Fire by some.

Developmental Role Exercises

Quickly and without thinking too carefully about it, look through these cards and pick one card for each role that you play. Be spontaneous rather than analytical. If possible, do not use a card more than once. Write their names in your list of roles above, next to the roles they represent for you.

After you have chosen your cards, answer the following questions: Have you used all the suits? If any suits are missing, which are they and what qualities do they represent? Where in your life are you able to manifest these missing qualities?

Which suit predominates? What does this say to you about conditions in which you are most comfortable? Do that suit and its related element also appear in other symbol systems (your astrological chart, dominant Jungian functions, etc.)?

Is there any figure (King, Queen, Knight, Page) that you did not choose or don't feel comfortable with? At which developmental level is it? Is it masculine or feminine? Older or younger than you feel yourself to be? What qualities does this missing figure(s) represent that you haven't listed among your roles?

Which figure did you use most often? At which developmental level is it? What does this indicate about your own perception of your self-mastery?

With all 16 People Cards spread before you, look at the Kings. Acknowledge some area of your life in which you have developed mastery and can demonstrate it to others. In this you are kingly. Pick one of the Kings to represent this in yourself. Also, state your expertise:

Look at the Queens. Acknowledge some area of your life in which you have developed mastery and can nurture that in yourself or another. In this you are queenly. Pick one of the Queens to represent this in yourself. Also state your expertise:

Look at the Knights. Acknowledge an area of your life in which you are actively using a skill, or putting energy into an area of interest or inquiry (quest). In this you are knightly. Pick one of the Knights to represent this in yourself. Also, state your skill or interest:

Look at the Pages (Princesses). Acknowledge an area of your life in which you are taking a risk, learning something new, or acquiring some information through your senses. In this you are like a youthful Page. Pick one of the Pages to represent this in yourself. Also, state your information or learning:

For instance, as a mother I feel I am the Queen of Cups to my daughter. When writing books and presentations I become the Queen of Swords. I am the King of Wands when expounding passionately on my favorite topic—the tarot. To my mother I will always be her Page of Cups learning to grow up, and in my determination to create a stable financial base I am the Knight of Pentacles, and so on.

Now, just to take this a bit further: List three or four of the major people in your life. Do it right now.

1.
2.
3.
4.

Next to each person write the Court Card that you most associate with each of them *as they relate to you.*

Take a moment to look at what you've written and realize that each of these people have their own masks and roles just as you do. Try to imagine which Court Card each of these people *would have picked for themselves.* How are your impressions of them different from how they would probably see themselves? When you get the opportunity, ask these people to actually pick the card they feel most describes them and find out why.

FROM THE COURTS TO THE PEOPLE

The People Cards are difficult yet intriguing. Most tarot students and even longtime tarot readers have more trouble with these than any of the other cards. The traditional Court Cards depicting figures from a medieval court are about as foreign to my personal experience as one can get. Of course I can envision my father and mother in the roles of king and queen, and I've known a few knights in shining armor in my time. And my daughter occasionally looks as sweet and winsome as the Page of Wands.

But for the most part, I've wondered when the Knight of Pentacles appears if he's someone at work, an old boyfriend, someone I haven't met yet, or any of a half-dozen Earth-sign people I know.

In creating their decks, many tarot artists simply follow traditional royalty designations. Yet the court environment is irrelevant in our society. It lacks the richness of personal symbology, as revealed by the awkwardness of Court Cards in readings. Luckily many of the contemporary tarot designers have been intrigued by this family of figures and are reconceptualizing them according to our contemporary settings, mythological symbologies, and current psychological understandings of human nature. They are revolutionizing our fixed conceptions of the Court Card roles and creating different models for us to reflect on.

Even if you use a deck with the traditional Court Cards, your appreciation of them can be deepened by the work these tarot artists have done.

For instance, Magda and J. A. Gonzales in their NATIVE AMERICAN TAROT use instead of Court Cards the Tribal Figures of *Matriarch, Chief, Warrior,* and *Maiden.* Their deck features symbolism from at least 18 North American Indian tribes. They have also varied the symbolism of the suits while keeping to the basic elemental meanings. For Fire they use the sacred pipe, for Water they have clay containers and woven baskets called vessels, for Air they feature blades, and for Earth they have medicine shields.

Matriarchs are older women respected for their skills and wisdom. They represent ''spiritual power within.'' Chiefs are older men who have earned their title and its responsibilities through the wise use of their power. They represent ''potential intellectual power.'' Warriors are young men still proving themselves. They represent ''active power manifesting on the material plane.'' And Maidens are young women who must prove their worth. They represent ''power which flows from the emotions.''

Vicki Noble and Karen Vogel, in creating the MOTHERPEACE TAROT, were among the first to radically change their Court Cards as well as the shape of their cards. Their People Cards are named: *Shaman, Priestess, Son,* and *Daughter.*

Shamans represent power and experience. They have developed mastery and control over the qualities of their suit. Priestesses work from the heart. They receive and channel the energies and forces indicated by the suit and are concerned with the sacredness of life. Sons have a light, playful quality. They use words and analysis and are focused and goal-oriented. They represent the ego. Daughters are young and enthusiastic, representing the child within us all. They experience things through their senses and use wholistic thinking.

Jim Wanless and Ken Knutson's VOYAGER TAROT features the figures of *Sage, Child, Woman,* and *Man* in order to point out two great dualities: masculine and feminine, youth and age. These cards form what Wanless calls a family of images that work on both the inner and outer levels. Internally, they represent levels of self-mastery. When externalized, they are teachers or models of success or difficulties. The suits are: Crystals for Air, Worlds for Earth, Wands for Fire, and Cups for Water.

Sage   Woman   Man   Child

Wands   Crystals   Worlds   Cups

The Sage represents wisdom, know-how, and the expertise that comes from experience. The Child represents new growth and learning, exploration and spontaneity, openness and curiosity. The Woman or Mother card stands for our receptive, feeling qualities. She is introspective and self-aware, sensitive, nurturing, and people-oriented. The Man or Father card is the revolutionary. He is external-directed, action- and goal-oriented. He seeks change and desires to transform things.

An even more recent deck is called DAUGHTERS OF THE MOON, originally conceptualized by Ffiona Morgan and Shekinah Mountainwater, and drawn by a variety of women who worked to make this a beautiful and compelling black-and-white deck, awaiting your contribution of color. This is a feminist deck with minimal male imagery, in which the "female archetype" cards express the triple aspect of the Goddess, and the Waxing, Full, and Waning phases of the Moon. They are the *Maiden, Mother,* and *Crone.* So all the People Cards are female in this deck and each represents a Goddess from a different culture.

Maidens are developing and discovering the knowledge of their suit. They are daring, enthusiastic, and take risks. We learn from them how to be spontaneous and grow. Mothers are the care-givers and midwives. They sustain and nourish. They express the developed skills and fullness of the suit. Crones express the reclaiming of our inner wisdom. They represent authority and are secure in their knowledge. They release outgrown modes, thoughts, and forms. They know the secrets that the Maiden embodies.

There are many other decks that express, through cross-cultural symbolism, our developmental processes and inner psychic states. You might wonder how to resolve the differences between a Queen, Priestess, Crone, and Woman, for instance; yet they can all broaden our understanding of the essence of the Feminine.

Each deck contains its individual symbolism that can guide you through your inner landscapes. Therefore it is important to find a deck that expresses the values with which you feel most in accord. To some extent, each deck (because the pictures themselves are so evocative) must be interpreted within its own symbology.

For instance, let's compare the People Cards of the Crowley-Harris Thoth deck with those of the Waite-Smith deck:

The Waite-Smith deck follows the traditional Court Card designations. But Crowley (the conceptualizer) and Harris (the artist) chose to follow and further develop some changes made by McGregor Mathers for use in the Order of the Golden Dawn. Thus their primary couple is the Knight (still called King by Mathers) and the Queen, with their son and daughter, the Prince and Princess. The reason for this switch changes the meanings of these cards and needs to be told, as it has from time immemorial, in the form of a fairy tale.

Once upon a time, communities were so isolated they became genetically inbred, lessening vigor and fertility. Because the rulers were often seen as gods, their health and well-being symbolized that of the land and the entire community. As a king became old and infertile, or was injured (like the Fisher King in the Grail legends), the land would dry up and become a wasteland, or the king

CHART 18
COMPARISON CHART OF THE PEOPLE CARD FIGURES

Waite/Smith Marseilles Standard	KING	QUEEN	KNIGHT	PAGE
Thoth	KNIGHT	QUEEN	PRINCE	PRINCESS
Golden Dawn	KING	QUEEN	PRINCE	PRINCESS
Papus	KING	QUEEN	CAVALIER	VALET
Knapp/Hall	KING	QUEEN	WARRIOR	SERVANT
Xultun Maya	LORD	LADY	WARRIOR	SERVANT
Voyager	SAGE	WOMAN	MAN	CHILD
Native American	CHIEF	MATRIARCH	WARRIOR	MAIDEN
Motherpeace	SHAMAN	PRIESTESS	SON	DAUGHTER
Amazon	COMPANION	QUEEN	AMAZON	CHILD
Daughters of the Moon		CRONE	MOTHER	MAIDEN
Kabbalistic	*YOD*	*HEH*	*VAV*	*HEH*
Elements	AIR(FIRE)	WATER	FIRE(AIR)	EARTH

would be unable to vanquish a ravaging monster. And so it came to pass that new blood (and genes) were needed to revivify the royal lineage passed through the queens. When a strange knight rode into town, he faced a test to determine his strength and wisdom. He was required to vanquish a dragon or a sphinx, solve a riddle, or kill the old king. If he succeeded, he was given the hand of the queen in marriage. The son of their union was the prince-in-training to be king. He was required to be a diplomat and a leader but not to possess the fieriness of spirit necessary to the knight. The princess was their daughter but also represented the young fertile state of woman, and the queen mother represented the royal lineage.

Thus we do have to read the characters in the two decks differently—Crowley's Knight is more powerful and masterful than Waite's Knight, taking on many of the qualities of Waite's King, yet retaining the vitality and adventuresomeness of Waite's Knight. And Crowley's Princess brings out the feminine potential rather than the childlike aspects of Waite's Page card.

In both these decks and most others, the People Cards can be seen as steps or stages in our growth and development. They illustrate the different kinds of mastery that we must bring into balance within ourselves to be full, rounded individuals. They are our inner family, as well as the people we know. And as we are always sliding up and down the scale of so-called "maturity," we can appear in any of these forms.

For example, when you offer your advice to someone, based on your wide experience, you speak with kingly authority. But at 55, when you take up the guitar for the first time, you approach it like a Page, with the innocence of a child, and risk appearing naive or even silly. Luckily, we are usually able to switch roles when appropriate. And in a tarot reading we have the opportunity to see just which persona we are displaying to determine how appropriate it is to the particular situation we are involved in.

A NUMERICAL ANALYSIS OF THE PEOPLE CARDS

The tarot cards were given to us as a model of our process of coming to *know ourselves*. So in trying to understand the People Cards I turned to numbers, since numbers form the inner structure of the tarot. There are no individual numbers associated with the People Cards, but there are 16 of them! I thought that perhaps this could yield the significance I was looking for.

So let's look at the 16th major arcana card to see what it can tell us about the purpose and significance of the People Cards.

The 16th trump (or triumph) is of course The Tower, which is also known as The House of God, Tower of Destruction, or The Great Liberator.

This is the card that liberates us from the structures and forms that inhibit us from perceiving our true self. In it, the lightning-bolt of Truth destroys all false boundaries and beliefs. And the structures, boundaries, and beliefs that are destroyed in this card are, of course, the roles that each of us play in our daily life. These roles are the masks we hide behind. They are the fences and walls we build to keep us from the realization of who we really are. These roles and personality structures become fences behind which we isolate ourselves from one another. They form our "identity," or that which makes us different from others. These enclosing walls protect us from the unknown; thus we nest down in a structure of false security, false because these personality structures—the ones you've listed earlier on these pages—are not who you really are. You are not the walls around you, but rather the multiform spirit that resides within.

Thus The Tower expresses the fact that the People Cards are the roles we play, the masks we hide behind, and the towering forms we've crystallized into, which must ultimately be destroyed if we are to awaken to who we really are. The Tower stresses the impermanence of worldly position and rank and the false sense of importance and pride of achievement in which we cloak ourselves. We are truly *liberated* when we have no more roles to play; our infinite possibilities are no longer limited.

Now if we numerically add 1 + 6, we get 7, and perhaps the seventh trump card can tell us something more about the essential nature of these 16 People Cards.

Seven is the number of The Chariot, also known as Victory or Mastery. The vehicle pictured on the card represents our own personal temple from which our power flows into our daily experience. The Holy Order of Mans, in their work on tarot, *Jewels of the Wise*, explain how we have built vehicles or enclosures to imprison our inner subconscious Self. These are the enclosures within which we cultivate who we are and develop our various masteries in our daily life.[1]

The lunar masks on the charioteer's shoulders and the duality and mixed characteristics of the sphinxes show that we wear the masks to pose our own riddle to the question, "Who am I?" The zodiacal belt suggests that we wear these masks of personality as long as we are bound by time and space.

Our individual vehicle is the enclosure in which we cultivate ourselves. The People Cards are therefore the ways in which we gain mastery and perfect ourselves. They are the developmental steps we take to discover our own identity. The People Cards show us how to develop control over our physical environment, how to harness our personal resources towards our purpose, and how to use our skills and abilities to move us instinctively through the challenges presented in the minor arcana Number Cards.

The People Cards picture us on our journey of personal development. As the *Bhagavad-Gita* says: "The Self is the rider in the chariot of the body, of which the senses are horses and the mind the reins."

And thus we see how we develop and perfect our personality structure, and then go through a process of breaking down all that is false in that structure, only to slowly build it up again, and then find that that too is *not* who we really are, until we have burned away all the forms that keep us from mirroring Truth and Perfection. Then we too can see our reflection in the Holy Grail as pictured in the Crowley/Harris Chariot card.

THE MAGICIAN.

THE LOVERS.

Finally, I looked at the 16 People Cards again, and at the number 16, and I realized that it was made up of two other numbers: the 1 and the 6. Translated into major arcana cards, these are The Magician and The Lovers.

This seems appropriate because I have found that in interpreting the People Cards they work in two ways: the first relates to the number 1 and the second relates to the number 6.

1) As The Magician indicates, these cards always represent some aspect of you; that is, the person the reading is about: old Numero Uno, "Number One," Me, I.

2) As The Lovers shows, the People Cards also refer to someone you are in relationship with. In The Lovers card a mirroring is taking place between the inner and outer self. According to Paul Foster Case, the conscious mind looks to the subconscious mind, which is focused on the Higher Self for guidance. We can look at the people we draw into our lives as mirrors of our own inner processes—sometimes our shadowy negative self-images, and other times those highest qualities we are blind to in ourselves. So when the People Cards appear in a spread, you need to read them from both points of view: as an aspect of yourself, and in the role of others teaching you about yourself.

And, of course, 1 + 6 add up to 7, and so we are back to The Chariot: we develop self-mastery through our interactions with others, by seeing the different aspects of ourselves reflected in some way by everyone we come in contact with.

THE PEOPLE CARD READING

This is a simple two-card reading, yet I've found it to be helpful in understanding the changing dynamics of an ongoing relationship, or to gain a quick insight into why certain people come briefly into your life. You can also discover things about yourself that you were never consciously aware of before. Use it for all kinds of relationships: family, friends, co-workers, teachers, lovers, and between different parts of yourself. It can be expanded for more information, as I'll describe later.

Using only the 16 People Cards, you will choose one card to tell you what qualities you are learning from a particular person at this time. And a second card to tell you what qualities they are learning from you at this time. These images will probably correspond to how these people currently appear to you and how you appear to them. If there is a disparity between the qualities the cards describe and your perception of yourself, you can ask why you are unaware of these qualities.

Although you can do this reading by yourself, you will have more insight as to how it works if you first try it with a friend. Each of you randomly pick a card representing what you are learning from the other. Then tell your partner what you are learning from them, based on the card you drew. You may be very surprised by what they see in you. They might perceive you as having qualities you've never seen in yourself. Once you have experienced this with a friend, you will be better prepared to understand what such a reading can mean when you do it alone.

Selecting the Cards

Shuffle your 16 People Cards, then spread them in a fan, face down.

1) With your left hand, pick a card to represent the qualities you are learning from the other person. Place this card to the left.

2) With your right hand, pick a card to represent the qualities they are learning from you. Place this card to the right of the first card.

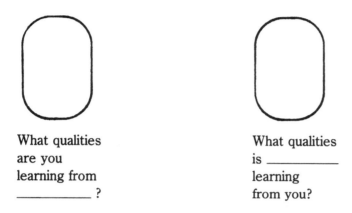

What qualities
are you
learning from
_____ ?

What qualities
is _____
learning
from you?

Expanding the Reading

If you want more information, then by drawing three additional cards for each of the above cards, you can determine the kind of situation in which you will find your learning opportunity.

Shuffle the remainder of the deck together (leaving out *all* the People Cards). Cut the deck into two stacks, cutting from the right to the left. Turn over the top three cards from the left stack and place them under the People Card representing what you are learning. Turn over the top three cards from the right stack and place them under the People Card representing what your friend is learning from you. Blend the meanings of the three cards until they seem to describe a recognizable situation or interplay in your relationship. You might find that they will show the developmental stages of your interaction and learning: 1) How it was, 2) The current situation, 3) Its potential.

Doing this exercise together is even more enlightening than doing it by yourself, as you can discuss what you feel you have to give and receive from each other and how you go about doing so.

NOTE

1. The Holy Order of Mans, *Jewels of the Wise* (San Francisco: Holy Order of Mans, 1974), pp. 73–79.

THE 8–11 CONTROVERSY

In writing this book one of my greatest dilemmas has been deciding what to do with the Strength and Justice cards. Since my first (and only) deck for many years was the Waite-Smith deck, and my early studies all supported that order, I hold a personal allegiance to Strength as card number 8 (VIII) in the sequence and Justice as number 11 (XI). This is different from what I call the "French School" decks (see Appendix B for a description of the "schools" of tarot), epitomized by the Marseilles Tarot, in which Justice is number 8 (VIII) and Strength is number 11 (XI). This numbering sequence first appeared in 1557 on the Catelin Geofroy pack of Lyon, France. But it was not until the 1700's that the numbering stabilized and the images known as the Marseilles type appeared.[1] However, many variations in sequence exist historically, and tarot scholars and deck creators continue to suggest alternative orders.

The oldest numerical listing of the tarot cards is found in the *Sermones de Ludo Cum Aliis*, a late 15th-century discourse against gambling. The cards are listed in the following order:

1	The Magician or Juggler	12	The Hanged Man
2	The Empress	13	Death
3	The Emperor	14	The Devil
4	The Popess	15	The Arrow or Tower
5	The Pope	16	The Star
6	Temperance	17	The Moon
7	Love	18	The Sun
8	The Triumphal Car	19	The Angel or Judgement
9	Strength or Fortitude	20	Justice
10	The Wheel	21	The World
11	The Hunchback or Hermit	0	The Fool[2]

There is a 16th-century uncut sheet of cards from the Rosenwald Collection of the National Gallery of Art, Washington, D.C., in which both Strength (shown as a woman holding a pillar) and Justice are numbered 8![3] And Florentine Minchiate decks often place the four cardinal virtues (Temperance, Fortitude, Justice, and Prudence [the Hermit]) together between The Chariot and The Wheel.

Since I have chosen to use numerological systems in this and my previous book, the numbers of the cards became vital. Many new tarot deck creators have returned to the Marseilles numbering because they feel it is more "traditional," although the Marseilles system is hardly the oldest one. *In this book, I chose to follow the Waite-Smith numbering, which makes Strength 8 and Justice 11.*

It was Christine Payne-Towler, a tarot teacher and Hermetic scholar in Portland, Oregon, who suggested to me that the change was made in an attempt to disguise the "true path" from casual seekers. She thinks it may have been part of Waite's subterfuge, of the sort that deliberately waylays those seekers with insufficient knowledge, or those who have not been initiated into an occult order. Thus, she gives her allegiance to the French school.

Originally, the departure from the Marseilles order, common for some 200 years, seems to have been made by MacGregor Mathers, head of The Order of the Golden Dawn (OGD), a Rosicrucian group of ceremonial magicians in England at the end of the 19th century who used the tarot extensively as a key to their levels of Initiation. In one of Mathers's notebooks, Strength is found on the path of the Tree of Life corresponding to the Hebrew letter *Teth*, which should belong to the 8th major arcana card, yet it still retains the number 11. Justice is on the path corresponding to the Hebrew letter *Lamed*, the 11th major arcana card, yet is numbered 8.[4] (Perhaps because all available decks were numbered so?) Aleister Crowley in his deck did exactly the same thing, and in *The Book of Thoth* he sometimes calls Strength 8 and sometimes 11.

However, A. E. Waite was the first person in modern times to actually change the numbers on a published deck. But since he had been a member of the OGD too, it must have been in keeping with their traditions. As a translator of a tarot book by the French occultist Eliphas Levi, he was making a clear statement of his own allegiance, rather than trying to plant a false trail away from a 200-year tradition. Paul Foster Case, an initiate of the OGD and founder of Builders of the Adytum (which still publishes his outstanding tarot correspondence course), follows Waite on the numbering of the cards.

Waite himself makes only the following statement about his change: "For reasons which satisfy myself, this card [Strength] has been interchanged with that of Justice, which is usually numbered eight. As the variation carries nothing with it which will signify to the reader, there is no cause for explanation."[5]

Eliphas Levi, with the publication of his *Ritual and Dogma of High Magic* in 1855, was the first person to make a connection between the tarot cards and the 22 letters of the Hebrew alphabet, each of which also stands for a number. He began with The Magician as *Aleph*, since both represent the number 1. On the other hand, MacGregor Mathers, perhaps as early as 1893, maintained that

The Fool (0) came first as *Aleph* and then the other cards followed in sequence. This was done (according to both Crowley and Waite) because in mathematics the decimal scale begins with zero, so that the schema resulted in the analogy of 0 = 1.[6] (For a comparison of how the major tarot theorists have linked the Hebrew letters to the signs and planets of the zodiac and the tarot cards, see Appendix C.) In one of the central Kabbalist books called the *Sepher Yetzirah* (believed to be from somewhere between the 3rd and 6th centuries A.D.), the letters of the Hebrew alphabet are specifically linked to the signs of the zodiac. Most tarot theoreticians honor that link, but they vary greatly in assigning the letters (and thus the signs of the zodiac) to the cards.

The probable reason for Mathers to have changed the order is this: although Mathers said that The Fool (0) equaled *Aleph* (which has a numerical value of 1), and that The Magician (1) equaled *Beth* (which has a numerical value of 2, and thus seems out of alignment), there is a definite logic to the way the letters and the signs of the zodiac fit the images on the cards—except for Strength and Justice. Card 8 was assigned (since the cards follow in order) to the letter *Teth* (meaning "to twist"), which the *Sepher Yetzirah* said was Leo. Card 11 was assigned to the letter *Lamed* (meaning a whip or lash used for correction), equated with Libra—so shouldn't it go with the figure of Justice holding the scales? Anyone with any knowledge of astrology could immediately see that something was wrong with the order of the Marseilles cards.[7]

Angeles Arrien has said that the two cards were actually once one card that had two sides, back to back. They may have represented two aspects of the operation of a single power. This is supported by the Rosenwald Collection of tarot cards from the 16th century in which *both* Strength and Justice are numbered 8. I would like to suggest that the single power found in both these cards is LAW. Strength represents "natural law," in which a being is required to live and act in accord with its nature. A lion should not be punished for killing a lamb in order to eat, for its nature is to do so. But if it wanders village streets, it would be out of harmony with the laws of its nature and probably diseased. Justice, then, represents the attempts of a culture to codify those natural laws, creating a standard against which our actions can be weighed objectively. It is when society's laws are not in accord with natural law that we have injustice—when we force a being to do something that is not in its nature, or not to do something that is.

Since MacGregor Mathers and the Order of the Golden Dawn appear to have had no intention of producing a deck of tarot cards for the public, I find it hard to believe that Mathers would attempt to distort the order of the deck for his own followers. Rather, I believe he determined his ordering of the deck as a part of the hidden knowledge explained in Initiation, believing it to reveal the correct significance of the cards that had been hidden up to that time. In a manuscript originally circulated only among members of the OGD, Mathers places Strength (which he calls "Courage, Strength, Fortitude") following The Chariot and says it is "power not arrested, as in the act of Judgment, but passing on to further action. . . ." Justice, which follows The Wheel of Fortune, he calls "Eternal Justice and Balance; Strength and Force, but arrested, as in the act of Judgment."[8]

The hidden meaning revealed by switching the two cards might very well have something to do with the fact that the French esoteric schools did not admit women to their ranks, nor did the Masons (whose rites were very influential on all esoteric schools). The esoteric traditions throughout most of the 19th century tended to equate Nature, woman, the physical body, and the Devil with separation from God. It was thus necessary to reject these in order to do "the Great Work" of achieving union with Spirit. The Order of the Golden Dawn was therefore radical for its time, since women could be full participants at all stages of the Order. This necessitated a rethinking of the capabilities of women and their importance in occult and mystical work. They became, for the OGD, necessary partners in balancing the forces that would eventually be brought into union, giving birth to a new consciousness of unity with Spirit.[9] Thus the reordering of the cards could have been a sign of Initiation into a new esoteric order requiring a new interpretation of the cards, and perhaps a rectification of a teaching that had lost its balance. In fact, there are strong indications that Moina Bergson (sister of French philosopher Henri Bergson, wife of Mac-Gregor Mathers, and a talented artist in her own right) "received much of the early teaching of the Inner Order of *Roseae Rubeae* and *Aureae Crucis* [the inner levels of the OGD] . . . clairaudiently."[10] Perhaps she—like Pamela Colman Smith, Frieda Harris (artist of the Thoth deck), and Mrs. Yeats (who "channeled" the work that was published as OGD member William Butler Yeats' book *A Vision*)—was more responsible than has been previously thought for the metaphysical revolution that took place just before the turn of the last century.[11]

When Strength follows The Chariot, we see a comparison of two forms of power and victory. The Chariot requires physical force that is used to dominate nature through exerting power over the elements. Strength demonstrates the value of the soul and the body working in unison and perfect trust to achieve power within. In this way the Strength figure becomes the female Magician, which is demonstrated when the cards are placed in three rows of seven cards each so that the eighth card appears directly below The Magician. The Hermit, which then follows Strength, represents the androgyne—composed of the masculine and feminine energies unified in one being. Justice following the turn of the karmic Wheel of Fortune and preceding The Hanged Man and Death is clearly a sensible order, indicating that a judgment must be made before the punishment or sacrifice is determined and carried out.

One way you yourself might be able to come to terms with this core tarot dilemma is to consider which cards when added together yield 8 and 11. Lay out your tarot cards and pair them together as indicated; now make your own decision about which card best epitomizes these combinations:

8 =	11 =
7 + 1 (Chariot + Magician)	10 + 1 (Wheel + Magician)
6 + 2 (Lovers + High Priestess)	9 + 2 (Hermit + High Priestess)
5 + 3 (Hierophant + Empress)	8 + 3 (? + Empress)
4 + 4 (Emperor + Emperor)	7 + 4 (Chariot + Emperor)
	6 + 5 (Lovers + Hierophant)

You might also ask yourself which card is the octave of The Magician; that is, which card returns to the same point but at a new level?

And which card belongs in the very center of the series of 21 cards (not counting The Fool)? What does that card, as the pivot or meeting point for all the cards that come before and after, represent?

Or take the major arcana (leaving The Fool aside), shuffle them, and lay them out in three rows with seven cards horizontally in each row. Now begin rearranging them in whatever order makes sense to you at the moment. All the cards adjacent to each other should show some kind of relationship (a similarity, contrast, or development). When you have completed your arrangement, you will have created your own order. I believe that the variations in tarot order reflect variations in world view. Some are extremely personal while others serve humanity in general, thus standing the test of time until a radical revisioning requires radical changes.

NOTES

1. See: Stuart Kaplan, *The Encyclopedia of Tarot*, Vols. 1 and 2, and Michael Dummett, *The Game of Tarot*, for specific references and a scholarly discussion on this topic.

2. See: Stuart Kaplan, *The Encyclopedia of Tarot*, Vol. 2 (New York: U.S. Games, 1986), pp. 182–196, for a full discussion of sequence and titles of major arcana cards with charts comparing the variations among 26 decks from the late 1500's to 1909.

3. Ibid., p. 186.

4. From a photograph of a diagram of paths and grades from S. L. MacGregor Mathers' notebook, in Kathleen Raine's *Yeats, the Tarot and the Golden Dawn* (Dublin: The Dolmen Press, 1976), p. 17.

5. A. E. Waite, *The Pictorial Guide to the Tarot* (New York: Causeway Books, n.d.) p. 100.

6. Aleister Crowley, *The Book of Thoth* (Berkeley: Kashmarin Press, 1969), p. 39, and A. E. Waite, "Introduction" to *The Book of Formation (Sepher Yetzirah)* by Rabbi Akiba, trans. by Knut Stenring (New York: KTAV Publishing House, 1970 [originally 1923]), p. 12.

7. To further complicate things: According to the French school, Justice is the eighth Hebrew letter, *Cheth* (a fence or enclosure), and astrologically relates to Cancer. Strength is the eleventh letter, *Kaph* (the palm or fist), and equates to the planet Mars (see Appendix C), which might fit with those rare cards that picture Samson toppling a column, or a man beating a lion.

8. From *Book "T"—The Tarot*, signed "S.M.R.D." (MacGregor Mathers' identifying motto in the OGD). This manuscript is now available in Robert Wang's *An Introduction to The Golden Dawn Tarot*, and also as Volume 9 of *The Complete Golden Dawn System of Magic*, by Israel Regardie.

9. Most members of the OGD *did not* interpret this as requiring sexual magic of a physical nature, as most of their "work" was done on the inner planes.

10. Raine, p. 5.

11. I can't pass up this opportunity to mention a few more women who were vitally important to the workings of the OGD: actress Florence Farr, philanthropist Annie Horniman, Irish revolutionary Maud Gonne, and occult author Dion Fortune.

THE "SCHOOLS" OF TAROT

When you go to choose your tarot deck, you will discover that as many as 50 different decks might be available at a good metaphysical bookstore. How do you even begin to know what deck to select from among so many? The availability of all these decks is a major indicator of how interest in tarot has grown over the last 20 years (only the Marseilles and Rider-Waite-Smith decks were generally available before 1970).

When you look over the available decks, at least three major groupings can be discerned, which also refer to three quite different developmental trends in tarot. I call these: 1) the French School (including Italian and Spanish decks); 2) The English School (including the majority of American decks); and 3) the Feminist Circle (which either follow the English School or create their own context). In the following chart I have compared and contrasted the major characteristics of each of these. Determine what you most want in a deck from this comparison chart, then look through those decks at a store for the artwork and style that appeals to you. Remember that tarot cards are visual tools, so the images should speak to you.

An asterisk (*) in the table indicates decks that have pictures on the minor arcana and are usually available at metaphysical and New Age bookstores. Thus they are relatively easy to begin using without extensive knowledge of Tarot. Several excellent decks are self-published by their creators and therefore harder to find.

A double asterisk (**) indicates those feminist tarot decks that are most likely to be available at women's bookstores (or ask them to order these decks for you). Most of these are self-published in limited runs and therefore more expensive, but buying them supports these special endeavors.

The decks without asterisks are excellent decks, but often speak to a more limited or specialized audience, or are difficult to find.

These descriptions do not include decks produced after 1987.

FRENCH SCHOOL (FRENCH/ITALIAN/ SPANISH DECKS)	ENGLISH SCHOOL (ENGLISH/AMERICAN DECKS)	FEMINIST CIRCLE
Major and minor arcana are two very different decks. The majors are primarily for spiritual and developmental guidance; the minors for fortune-telling.	Major, minor, and court cards are seen as three modes and are all present in a spread that can be for spiritual questions, fortune telling, or psychological and clarifying purposes.	Major and minor arcana are often considered to be five elemental suits, including "aether." Usually used for psychological and spiritual guidance from your higher self. Fortune-telling is rare.
Illustrations are late medieval to 18th century (Napoleonic) or neo-Egyptian. Early styles often from colored woodcuts. Some interesting new decks have appeared since 1980.	Illustrations are turn-of-the-century, nouveau, cubist, illustrator, futuristic fantasy, or collage. Usually in color, employing all mediums. First deck of this style published in 1910, the remainder after 1970.	These decks have appeared since 1982. Often round and black & white so that you can color them yourself. Usually self-published. Symbolism is cross-racial, of all ages, sizes, and shapes, but rarely pictures men, and then can be negative. Use references to worldwide myths of the Great Goddess or scenes from women's lives or dreams.
Majors are illustrated with little variation in essential symbols. Major card numbers follow a system from the 17th century. The Fool is usually placed at the end or before The World. 8 is Justice, 11 is Strength.	Majors have many symbolic differences from the French tradition, yet are immediately recognizable. Majors are numbered as French except that The Fool often leads, or links beginning and end, 8 is often Strength, and 11 Justice; otherwise the French order is used—you must look.	Major cards are sometimes radically reconceptualized. Goddesses from world myths are often pictured. There can be more or less than 22 cards, and these are often not numbered. If numbered, 8 is usually Justice because it is more "traditional."
Minors have no pictures except for the suit markings of the same number as the card number. Their use is often separated from that of the major arcana and is primarily for fortune-telling.	Minors have pictures or symbols that can be used to tell a story. Most decks follow the illustrations created by Pamela Colman Smith. Number symbolism and development important to interpretation.	Minor cards are always illustrated, the elements are depicted, but number symbolism is not always used to determine meaning. An attempt is made to balance the number of positive and negative cards in a suit. All cards are considered important for a reading.
Court cards are from a medieval court or Napoleonic figures. They represent people you know determined by age, sex, and hair color.	Court cards often medieval but recently have more variety and new names as they become "people cards." Zodiac sign, appearance, and level of maturity determine their characteristics. More emphasis on aspects of self.	The medieval court cards completely disappear as new possibilities for personal relationships and characteristics are portrayed. The number of cards may change. Some are specific people from history or myth. Levels of development, astrological sign, and image determine referent.

FRENCH SCHOOL (continued)	ENGLISH SCHOOL (continued)	FEMINIST CIRCLE (continued)
Correlation of elements and suits varies a great deal. Wands often Earth, Swords often Fire, Pentacles are then Air, Cups are Water.	Elements to suits usually standard: Wands/Rods = Fire, Cups = Water, Swords = Air, Pentacles/Discs = Earth. Some new suit markers are appearing but closely relate to above.	Although some of these decks create completely new suit markers, they correspond to the elements and are easily recognizable as such.
Correlation with Hebrew letters and paths on the Tree of Life usually begins with The Magician = *Aleph* = 1, Strength = *Kaph*, Justice = *Cheth*.	When correlated with the Hebrew alphabet and Tree of Life, The Fool = *Aleph*, Strength = *Teth*, Justice = *Lamed*.	There is no deliberate attempt to correlate with Hebrew alphabet or Tree of Life, as these are felt to be "patriarchal" systems.
While the original artist is usually unknown, women were often employed to apply color to the woodcut prints.	The art for the majority of these decks was by women, while the conceptualizer was often a man. Many new decks have male artists.	These decks are conceptualized and created by women (though some men find them powerful guides). Often many artists will work together to create a deck.
Examples include these decks: Visconti-Sforza, Swiss IJJ, Tarot Classic, Marseilles, Rolla Nordic, Gran Tarot Esoterico, Basque Mythical, Cagliostro's, Papus, Balbi, Enoil Gavat, Church of Light, Egyptian, Oswald Wirth, Zigeuner/Wegmuller, Tavaglione, Angel, Spanish, Knapp/Hall, Ukiyoe, Maddonni, Dali. (I can recommend the major arcana of all of the above decks as useful and evocative.)	Examples with pictures on the minors after Pamela Colman Smith's Rider-Waite* deck: Aquarian*, Morgan-Greer*, Hanson-Roberts*, Fez Moroccan*, Sacred Rose*, Xultun (Maya)*, Native American*, Fantasy Showcase, Hurley's New Tarot, Ravenswood Eastern, Tarot of the Cat-People, Pendragon.†	Examples include such decks as: Motherpeace*, Daughters of the Moon**, Thea's**, Amazon**, A Poet's,† Barbara Walker (traditional structure).*

The following are Order of the Golden Dawn-inspired decks with little or no imagery on the minors, but with valuable major arcana. They cross over with the French-School decks in that Strength is usually 11.

Crowley-Harris Thoth*, Neuzeit (New Age) Tarot*, B.O.T.A., Golden Dawn, Hermetic, Tree of Life, Angelic,† Gareth Knight, Tarot of the Witches, Yeager Tarot of Meditation, The Prediction Tarot.

The following are Major Arcana Decks only:
Millennium Tarot,† Ansata Tarot, Tarot of Initiation,† B.O.T.A. large size,† Epiphany 22 Keys.†

The following new decks maintain tradition, yet are creating their own frameworks. The first two have pictures on the minors: Voyager*, Mythic*, Elksinger's,† New Tarot for the Aquarian Age.

*Decks with pictures on the minor arcana, usually available at metaphysical and New Age bookstores.
**Feminist decks, usually available at women's bookstores.
†Self-published decks that must be special-ordered, or try Magickal Childe, 35 W. 19th St., N.Y., NY 10011, or Bodhi Tree Bookstore, 8585 Melrose Ave., Los Angeles, CA 90069.

CORRESPONDENCES
AMONG THE HEBREW LETTERS,
ZODIAC SIGNS AND PLANETS,
AND TAROT CARDS

CORRESPONDENCES AMONG THE HEBREW LETTERS, ZODIAC SIGNS AND PLANETS, AND TAROT CARDS.

Letter	Shape	No. Equiv.	Meaning of Shape	English Equiv.	Levi/Papus/Wirth Cagliostro (1856)	Golden Dawn (189?) Case/B.O.T.A./Waite	Crowley (1945) Thoth Deck	Stenring (1923) Book of Formation
Aleph	א	1	Ox, Cow, Bull	A	△ Juggler	△ ♅ Fool	♅ Fool	△ Juggler
Beth	ב	2	House, Courtyard	B	☽ High Priestess	☿ Magician	☿ Magus	⊙ Sun
Gimel	ג	3	Camel (transport)	G	♀ Empress	☽ High Priestess	☽ Priestess	☽ Moon
Daleth	ד	4	Doorway (to open)	D	♃ Emperor	♀ Empress	♀ Empress	♂ Chariot
Heh	ה	5	Window (to see)	H,E	♈ Pope	♈ Emperor	♒ Star	♈ Empress
Vav	ו	6	Nail (to build)	U,V,W	♉ Lovers	♉ Hierophant	♉ Hierophant	♉ Emperor
Zayin	ז	7	Sword (to cut)	Z	♊ Chariot	♊ Lovers	♊ Lovers	♊ High Priestess
Cheth	ח	8	Fence (to enclose)	Ch	♋ Justice	♋ Chariot	♋ Chariot	♋ Strength
Teth	ט	9	Serpent (to twist)	T	♌ Hermit	♌ Strength	♌ Lust	♌ Temperance
Yod	י	10	Hand (to jot)	I,J,Y	♍ Wheel of Fortune	♍ Hermit	♍ Hermit	♍ Lovers
Kaph	כ	20	Palm (to grasp)	C,K,Kh	♏ Strength	♃ Wheel of Fortune	♃ Fortune	☿ Death
Lamed	ל	30	Goad (to chastize)	L	♎ Hanged Man	♎ Justice	♎ Adjustment	♎ Justice
Mem	מ	40	Sea, Womb	M	▽ Death	▽ ♆ Hanged Man	♆ Hanged Man	▽ World
Nun	נ	50	Fish (to move)	N	♐ Temperance	♏ Death	♏ Death	♏ Wheel of Fortune
Samekh	ס	60	Peg (to support)	S,X	♑ Devil	♐ Temperance	♐ Art	♐ Tower
Ayin	ע	70	Eye (to part)	O	☿ Tower	♑ Devil	♑ Devil	♑ Fool
Peh	פ	80	Mouth (to feed)	P,Ph,F	♒ Star	♂ Tower	♂ Tower	♃ Pope
Tzaddi	צ	90	Scythe (to harvest)	Tz	♓ Moon	♒ Star	♈ Emperor	♒ Hermit
Qoph	ק	100	Back of Head, Knot	Q	♄ Sun	♓ Moon	♓ Moon	♓ Judgement
Resh	ר	200	Face (to reason)	R	△ Judgement	⊙ Sun	⊙ Sun	♀ Star
Shin	ש	300	Teeth (to harp)	Sh	⊙ Fool	△ ♇ Judgement	♇ Aeon	△ Devil
Tav	ת	400	Sign (to mark)	T,Th,X	⊙ World	♄ World	♄ Universe	♄ Hanged Man

CORRESPONDENCES (continued)

Letter	Baldi (1961) Italian/Spanish	Maritxu Guler (1976) Gran Tarot Esoterico	Dali (1984) Spanish	Egipcios Kier Argentinian (1979)	C.C. Zain (1936) Sacred Tarot	Corinne Heline (1969) The Bible & the Tarot
Aleph	El Mago ☉	El Consultante ☉	El Mago	El Mago Creador ☉	Magus ☿	Magus
Beth	La Sacerdotisa ☽	La Consultante ☽	La Sacerdotisa ☽	La Sacerdotisa ☽	Veiled Isis ♍	High Priestess
Gimel	La Emperatriz ☿	La Emperatriz ♂	La Emperatriz ♀	La Emperatriz ♀	Isis Unveiled ♎	Empress
Daleth	El Emperador ♃	El Emperador ☉	El Emperador ♃	El Emperador ♅	Sovereign ♏	Emperor
Heh	El Sumo Sacerdote ♑	El Maestro ♑	El Sumo Sacerdote ♈	El Jerarca ♃	Hierophant ♃	High Priest ♈
Vav	Los Enamorados ♍	Los Dos Caminos ♑	Los Enamorados	La Indecision ♂	Two Paths ♀	Two Ways ♉
Zayin	El Carro ♊	El Carro de Hermes ♊	El Carro	El Triunfo ♌	Conqueror ♆	Chariot ♊
Cheth	Justicia ♎	La Justicia ♋	Justicia ♋	La Justicia ♐	Balance ♄	Balance ♋
Teth	El Ermitano ♆	El Anciano ♌	El Ermitano	El Eremita ♎	Sage ♂	Sage/Teacher ♌
Yod	Rueda d/Fortuna ♑	Rueda d/Fortuna ♍	Rueda d/Fortuna ♍	La Retribucion ♆	Wheel ♃	Wheel ♍
Kaph	Fuerza ♌	La Fortaleza ♀	Fuerza	La Persuasion ♌	Enchantress ♀	Strength
Lamed	El Colgado ♓	La Picota ♎	El Colgado	El Apostolado ♈	Martyr ♈	Hanged Man ♎
Mem	(Death) ♄	Morte	La Muerte	La Inmortalidad ♅	Reaper ♈	Reaper
Nun	Templanza	La Templanza ♏	Templanza	La Temperancia ♄	Alchemist ♑	Angel ♏
Samekh	El Diablo ♂	Aker ♐	El Diablo	La Pasion ♒	Black Magician ♒	Typhon ♐
Ayin	La Torre ♈	La Torre ♑	La Torre	La Fragilidad ♈	Lightning ♂	Lightning Struck ♑
Peh	La Estrella ♀	El Astro ♀	La Estrella	La Esperanza ♀	Star ♎	Star
Tzaddi	La Luna ♋	Luna ♒	La Luna	El Crepusculo ♋	Moon ♊	Moon ♓
Qoph	El Sol ♅	El Sol ♓	El Sol	La Inspiracion ♐	Sun ♌	Sun ♒
Resh	El Juicio ♒	El Ciclo ♄	El Juicio	La Resurreccion ♑	Sarcophagus ☽	Rebirth
Shin	El Loco ♏	El Loco	El Loco	La Transmutacion ♒	Adept ☉	World
Tav	El Mundo ♀	El Mundo ♃	El Mundo	El Regreso ♓	Materialist ♀	Fool

SELECTED BIBLIOGRAPHY

Balin, Peter. *The Flight of the Feathered Serpent*. Venice, CA: Wisdom Garden Books, 1978.

Case, Paul Foster. *The Tarot: A Key to the Wisdom of the Ages*. Richmond, VA: Macoy Publishing Co., 1947.

Cowie, Norma. *Exploring the Patterns of the Tarot*. White Rock, B.C., Canada V4B 4Z7: NC Publishing, P.O. Box 51, 1987.

Crowley, Aleister. *The Book of Thoth: An Interpretation of the Tarot*. New York: Samuel Weiser, 1974.

Dummett, Michael. *The Game of Tarot from Ferrara to Salt Lake City*. London: Gerald Duckworth and Co., 1980.

Fairfield, Gail. *Choice Centered Tarot*. No. Hollywood, CA: Newcastle Publishing Co., 1985.

Greene, Liz. *The Astrology of Fate*. New York: Samuel Weiser, 1984.

Greer, Mary K. *Tarot for Your Self: A Workbook for Personal Transformation*. No. Hollywood, CA: Newcastle Publishing Co., 1984.

Hasbrouck, Muriel. *Tarot and Astrology* (formerly *Pursuit of Destiny*). New York: Inner Traditions/Destiny, 1987.

Harding, M. Esther. *Psychic Energy: Its Source and Its Transformation*. Princeton, N.J.: Princeton University Press, 1963.

Heline, Corinne. *The Bible and the Tarot*. La Canada, CA: New Age Press, 1969.

Kaplan, Stuart. *The Encyclopedia of Tarot, Vol. 1*. New York: U.S. Games Systems, 1978.

————. *The Encyclopedia of Tarot, Vol. 2*. New York: U.S. Games Systems, 1986.

Knight, Gareth. *The Treasure House of Images*. Rochester, VT: Destiny Books, 1986.

Moakley, Gertrude. *The Tarot Cards: Painted by Bonifacio Bembo for the Visconti-Sforza Family: An Iconographic and Historical Study*. New York: New York Public Library, 1966.

Morgan, Ffiona. *Daughters of the Moon Tarot*. Willits, CA 95490: Daughters of the Moon, P.O. Box 888, 1984.

Nichols, Sallie, *Jung and Tarot: An Archetypal Journey*. New York: Samuel Weiser, 1980.

Noble, Vicki. *Motherpeace: A Way to the Goddess Through Myth, Art and Tarot*. San Francisco: Harper and Row, 1983.

———— and Jonathan Tenney. *The Motherpeace Tarot Playbook: Astrology and the Motherpeace Cards*. Berkeley, CA: Wingbow Press, 1986.

O'Neill, Robert V. *Tarot Symbolism*. Lima, Ohio 45802: Fairway Press, 1986.

Pollack, Rachel. *Seventy-Eight Degrees of Wisdom: A Book of Tarot, Part 1: The Major Arcana*, 1980, and *Part 2: The Minor Arcana and Readings*, 1983. Wellingborough: Aquarian Press Ltd.

Pollack, Rachel. *Tarot: The Open Labyrinth*. Wellingborough: Aquarian Press Ltd., 1986.

Raine, Kathleen. *Yeats, the Tarot and the Golden Dawn*. Dublin: The Dolmen Press, 1976.

Roberts, Jane. *The Nature of Personal Reality: A Seth Book*. New York: Prentice-Hall, 1974.

Roberts, Richard and Joseph Campbell. *Tarot Revelations*. San Francisco: Richard Roberts, 1979.

Shavick, Nancy. *The Tarot: A Guide to Reading Your Own Cards*. Hampton, N.J. 08827: Prima Materia Books, P.O. Box 338, 1984.

Stenring, Knut, trans. *The Book of Formation (Sepher Yetzirah) by Rabbi Akiba Ben Joseph*. New York: KTAV Publishing House, 1970.

Von Franz, Marie-Louise. *On Divination and Synchronicity: The Psychology of Meaningful Chance*. Toronto: Inner City Books, 1980.

Waite, Arthur Edward. *The Pictorial Key to the Tarot*. New York: Causeway Books, n.d.

Wanless, James. *New Age Tarot: Guide to the Thoth Deck*. Carmel, CA 93921: Merrill-West Publishing, P.O. Box 1227, 1987.

Tarot Resource

Tools And Rites Of Transformation (T.A.R.O.T.)
P.O. Box 31123, San Francisco CA 94131
Offers consultations, classes, workshops, and lectures by **Mary K. Greer**. She is available to lead workshops in both the U.S.A. and abroad. Books, decks, and tarot materials by mail order.

CRITICAL RAVES FOR MARY K. GREER'S *TAROT FOR YOUR SELF*

"Undoubtedly the best book on Tarot that has appeared in 25 years—possibly forever."
SHE TOTEM

"The most thorough tarot book that I have ever read."
BEEF
(Quarterly of Art, Music and Culture)

"Exceptional."
PSYCHIC GUIDE MAGAZINE

"A book not meant to be read in the traditional sense. It is meant to be experienced."
NEW REALITIES MAGAZINE

"Tarot is carefully probed, explained, and unfolded in this amazing workbook."
MAGICAL BLEND MAGAZINE

"One of the most holistic and in-depth books on the tarot I've seen."
HARVEST

"A very different book and very powerful. I can't do this book justice. This book is positive and powerful."
THESMOPHORIA

"Thoroughness seems to be the watermark of this book."
THE WISE WOMAN

"Lots of new ideas to work with and ways of using the tarot for thinking, meditation, reading, and as a general study."
PEGASUS

"Absolutely lovely, a wonderful idea. I'm very impressed and think it's just what has been needed."
VICKI NOBLE,
co-creator of *Motherpeace Tarot*

"A delight and a treasure. A MUST for every Tarot student and professional. I wish I'd written it!"
GAIL FAIRFIELD,
author of *Choice-Centered Tarot*

"Your book is wonderful and I plan on using it in my teaching."
FFIONA MORGAN,
creator of *Daughters of the Moon Tarot*

"One of the best Tarot self-teach books I have seen."
RUTH WEST, creator of *Thea Tarot*

"So useful, playful, thorough, and exactly what I've wanted."
GINA COVINA,
author of *City of Hermits*

"I'm writing to say how much I like TAROT FOR YOUR SELF!"
DIANE WAKOSKI, Poet